Becoming an Existential–Humanistic Therapist: Narratives from the Journey

Edited by
Julia Falk
Louis Hoffman

Colorado Springs, CO
www.universityprofessorspress.com

Copyright © 2022

Becoming an Existential–Humanistic Therapist: Narratives from the Journey
Edited by Julia Falk and Louis Hoffman

All rights reserved. No portion of this book may be reproduced by any process or technique without the express written consent of the publisher.

Published in 2022, University Professors Press.

Hardcover ISBN: 978-1-955737-05-0
Paperback ISBN: 978-1-955737-06-7
ebook ISBN: 978-1-955737-07-4

    University Professors Press
    Colorado Springs, CO
    www.universityprofessorspress.com

Cover Design by Laura Ross
Cover Art by Ted Mallory

Becoming an Existential-Humanistic Therapist: Narratives from the Journey is a fascinating and unique book. It presents a vision one rarely encounters, a collective autobiography of the many paths taken as these therapists sought a calling centered within the Existential–Humanistic tradition. The editors chose a stunning array of individuals to tell their stories and the ways in which their mentors and patients helped shape their practices and lives: Men and women, young and old, various religions and ethnicities, varieties of sexuality, all benefiting from a method that at its best fosters an expansive and creative attitude toward self and life.

Robert H. Abzug
author of *Psyche and Soul in America:*
The Spiritual Odyssey of Rollo May

One can study the "how-to's" of becoming an existential-humanistic therapist for years, but our paths are ultimately lit by encounters with others—and with ourselves—along our journeys. The stories in this book are more than professional narratives. They are stories of experiencing pain and learning to overcome—of reaching for light, touching it, and learning to wield it for others. They are stories that touch the depths of the soul. This book is a must-read for both aspiring and seasoned existential-humanistic therapists.

Sarah Kamens, PhD
Editor, *Journal of Humanistic Psychology*
Assistant Professor of Psychology, State University of New York College at Old Westbury

Becoming an Existential-Humanistic Therapist presents a diverse group of travelers on the journey to becoming psychotherapists. They find disappointment in the limitations of mainstream psychotherapies that promise quick fixes for human suffering. They seek to understand human experience without pathologizing it. The professional is personal along these roads less traveled as we see personal and professional lives unfolding along parallel paths.

Kevin Keenan, PhD
Core Faculty, Michigan School of Psychology
Co-Editor, *Humanistic Psychotherapies:*
Handbook of Research and Practice

Becoming an Existential-Humanistic Therapist is a collection of narratives containing vulnerable discomfort, honest reflections, and ways of being, which stands to demystify the term existential into its more authentic form of seeing humanity and how choices from within one's struggle form these stories of existence—both personally and professionally. These varied voices and perspectives stand to strengthen the understanding of existential therapy through the breadth and depth of their sharing.

Michael Moats, PsyD
Author, *Sunrise Through the Darkness* (with Will Jimeno)
Psychologist in Private Practice

Dedication

For Charlotte Howorth, humanistic teacher and therapist, who has led me and so many others on a journey through inner and interrelational space.
~ Julia

For the mentors and colleagues who most influenced my early journey to becoming an existential–humanistic therapist: H. Newton Malony, Robert Murney, Brad Powers, A. J. Whitmire, Brittany Garrett-Bowser, Anne Elise Parkhurst, Myrtle Heery, James F. T. Bugental, and Emory Cowan.
~ Louis

Table of Contents

Acknowledgments		i
Introduction *by Louis Hoffman & Julia Falk*		iii
Chapter 1	Existential–Humanistic Psychology: Connecting to Values *HeeSun Park*	1
Chapter 2	Kirk Schneider's Path to Existential-Humanistic Psychology *Kirk J. Schneider & Andrew M. Bland*	25
Chapter 3	My Existential Journey *Lisa Xochitl Vallejos*	44
Chapter 4	Middle Europe: Journey and Madrash *Ed Mendelowitz*	54
Chapter 5	Becoming an Existential–Humanistic Therapist *Katerina Zymnis*	77
Chapter 6	An Existentialist for Eternity *Mark Yang*	100
Chapter 7	Looking Over My Shoulder *Myrtle Heery*	116
Chapter 8	Fifty Years of Evolution: Becoming an Existential Therapist on the Journey to Becoming My Authentic Self *Nathaniel Granger, Jr.*	130
Chapter 9	Standing on the Shoulders of Giants: Becoming an Existential–Humanistic Therapist *Orah T. Krug*	154

Chapter 10	My Journey to Existential Psychology: A Dialogue with Colleagues at the Zhi Mian Institute *Xuefu Wang*	176
Chapter 11	It Began in My Father's Library: On Becoming an Existential Therapist *Kathleen Galvin*	195
Chapter 12	The Making of a Counterculture Therapist *Shawn Ari Rubin*	219
Chapter 13	Concluding Thoughts *Julia Falk & Louis Hoffman*	236
Appendix A	Activities for Students Considering Becoming an Existential–Humanistic Therapist *Louis Hoffman & Julia Falk*	248
Appendix B	Guides for Reflection on One's Journey to Becoming an Existential–Humanistic Therapist *Louis Hoffman & Julia Falk*	259

| Index | 261 |
| About the Editors | 269 |

Acknowledgments

First and foremost, we would like to thank the contributors to this volume. It is much different to ask someone to write about themselves, as opposed to writing about an academic or clinical topic. We were very pleased that all these authors—individuals who have made important contributions to the field and to their clients—agreed to share about their own lives in such honest and vulnerable ways.

Julia would like first to thank Louis for the invitation to serve as a co-author on this meaningful project. His openness to my interest in narrative expressions of existential experiences originally set me on this path. I am especially grateful for the blessing of interacting with writers from other nations and cultures, awed by the breadth of their interests and talents. Thanks also to those who have offered opportunities to learn the art of reviewing and reflecting on the work of others: Louis, Paul Wong, Shawn Rubin, and Sarah Kamens. Finally, I am grateful to my husband, Carl, and sons, Fraser and Torrey Langdon, who have always been supportive of my need to reach out and explore the new.

Louis would like to thank Kirk Schneider, Mark Yang, and Ed Mendelowitz. My own reflections on a book of this nature begin with conversations with these close friends and colleagues. I would like to thank my co-author, Julia, who was wonderful to work with on this project. I also would like to acknowledge some of the early influences on my own development as an existential-humanistic therapist, which includes a number of people who do not identify as existential or humanistic: H. Newton Malony, Winston Gooden, Robert Murney, Anne Elise Parkhurst, Bradley Powers, Brittany Garrett-Bowser, Myrtle Heery, and James F. T. Bugental. My colleagues in the Unearthing the Moment Training were my first existential community: Myrtle Heery, James F. T. Bugental, Martha Cravens, Joe LeFevre, Christine Martinez-Suzukawa, Sandra Harner, Gene Kranz, Anita Lafollette, Debra Shepard, and Nirmoha Vargas-Gladen, as well as many others who were not able to continue with the training over time. The Society for Humanistic Psychology became my second existential community, particularly Shawn Rubin, Richard Bargdill, and Brent Dean Robbins. A third existential community that greatly impacted me was a community that developed in China, particularly friendships with Mark Yang and Xuefu Wang; however, there were many others beyond what would be possible to name. Finally, the Rocky Mountain Humanistic Counseling and Psychological Association has become an important new existential community for me in Colorado. I would also like to acknowledge a few other international existential communities, including the World Congress of Existential Therapy, the International Meaning Conference (London and Canada), the Hellenic Association for Existential Psychology (Greece), and the Centre for Existential Practice (Australia). I am thankful for growing connections with these communities. Several other close colleagues not mentioned above, including Nathaniel Granger, Michael Moats, and Lisa Xochitl Vallejos, deserve acknowledgement for always helping to keep me grounded in my existential values and growing as an existential-humanistic therapist. Last and most important, I want to acknowledge my family, Heatherlyn, Lakoda, Lukaya, and Lyon. You are my eternal inspiration and will always occupy a central place in my heart. I love you dearly.

Introduction

Louis Hoffman
Julia Falk

Conversations that I (Louis) had with Ed Mendelowitz, Kirk Schneider, and Mark Yang between 2005 and 2008 prompted years of reflection about how one journeys to becoming an existential-humanistic therapist. In these conversations and reflecting upon what I knew of the stories of other existential-humanistic therapists, such as Rollo May[1] and James F. T. Bugental, a few themes emerged. The theme of the death of significant people in one's early life as well as other confrontations with death stood out. Encounters with important mentors or therapists in early adulthood, and sometimes earlier in life, also were noteworthy. While the connection of these themes made sense, I was surprised by other themes, such as a number of prominent existential-humanistic and humanistic therapists growing up in the rural Midwest of the United States—a place not typically associated with the deep philosophic ponderings of existential psychology and philosophy.

In teaching and training therapists, I noticed other common themes. For example, I had many students tell me that they became disillusioned with psychology after beginning their degree program and were considering dropping out until discovering existential-humanistic therapy. Similarly, many students described finding existential therapy was like finding themselves—it fit who they were not just as a therapist, but as a person.

I encountered other students cautiously interested in existential ideas with some hesitation or fears. They asked questions such as, "What does it mean to be an existential therapist?" and "Who practices existential therapy?" While there also were some questions about what one does as an existential therapist in the therapy room, many of the

---

[1] As we were nearing completion of this volume, Rollo May's biography, which was many years in the writing, was published. This wonderful volume, *Psyche and Soul in America: The Spiritual Odyssey of Rollo* May by Robert H. Abzug, provides an in-depth analysis of May's journey to existential psychology.

questions went deeper to the being-level or identity. There was a recognition that there is something different in this type of therapy. It is not just something that you do with clients—it has to do with, as Carl Rogers (1980) described, developing *a way of being that is healing.*

More than with other more structured and technical approaches, students drawn toward existential-humanistic therapy often want a different type of resource to help them decide if this orientation is the right fit for them. They want to know what it means for them as a person to align with this theoretical orientation and way of being. Undoubtedly, the choice to become an existential-humanistic therapist is more than a career choice. One of the motivations for writing this book is helping students and therapists considering aligning with this approach engage in their own reflections on what this means and whether it is a good fit for them.

When Julia and I first began discussing this book, I was excited to find someone with an interest and expertise in narrative approaches who also shared the interest in existential-humanistic therapy. As we considered who to invite to contribute chapters, we wanted a mixture of therapists, primarily mid-career or more established therapists, along with individuals from different cultural backgrounds. We were pleased that as we began inviting people to contribute chapters, most readily agreed despite their busy schedules. The contributors to this book represent a diverse group of contemporary leaders in the existential-humanistic therapy movement. We hope that their journeys inspire students and other readers considering this approach and validate the journeys of practicing existential-humanistic therapists.

Our Stories

Although not in our initial plan for the book, as we met to discuss the development of *On Becoming an Existential–Humanistic Therapist* it became apparent that the book would not feel as genuine if we did not also share our own stories about being drawn to existential-humanistic psychology. While our stories are not as in-depth, they reflect parallels with the contributors through our own journeys.

Louis Hoffman: My Journey

Not much in my early years suggests the likelihood of becoming a therapist, let alone an existential-humanistic therapist. My mother had been in therapy when I was younger, and I vividly remember thinking that being a therapist was one of the worst imaginable jobs! Growing up in a town of approximately 500 people in rural Iowa, my early childhood revolved around sports. I was a four-sport athlete (football, basketball, baseball, and track) and decent for rural Iowa. In high school, a typical day for me was getting up early to go to the weight room, going to school, going to sports practice after school, rushing home for a quick supper, and then back to the gym to play basketball until bedtime. My identity was being an athlete, and I was good enough to be selected as the homecoming king and receive a college scholarship; however, underneath this identity I was a shy and insecure youth who often felt isolated and alone. I did not feel that I fit in, largely because of the questions I pondered in my time alone. Although I kept them at bay, existential questions were bubbling up inside me.

In retrospect, there were early signs and influences toward becoming an existential-humanistic therapist. The depth psychology of my youth came in the form of music. In high school, I became a fan of Bruce Springsteen and Pink Floyd and consumed all their music that I could find. I remember listening to Bruce Springsteen's "Live: 1975–1985" on cassette until all three cassettes wore out. I loved Springsteen's stories in his music and his personal reflection between songs. Springsteen was honest about life and the human condition, and he did not shy away from the big questions in life—something that later drew me to existential psychology. I listened to his music and reflected on what life meant to me. To this day, I continue to see Springsteen as an existential mentor of sorts. Pink Floyd, too, prompted my reflections on life. I watched their movie "The Wall," 15 or 20 times in high school. Through my "Pink Floyd studies," I learned to reflect upon consciousness and the meaning of suffering—other themes that would later draw me toward existential thought.

Although I did not recognize it in my youth, the big questions pulled at me. Vivid memories of lying on the grass watching the clouds float above while thinking about space are prominent when reflecting on my youth. I wondered how space could be never-ending and then questioned how that was possible. I then imagined an ending to space and questioned what was on the other side of the ending of space. It seemed to me impossible that space was unending but equally impossible that space ended. As I pondered this, my anxiety would grow until verging on a panic attack and my attention was diverted to something else. Yet, this pondering was kept mostly to myself so that others would not think that I was strange.

From rural Iowa, I moved to rural Nebraska to attend Concordia College in the town of Seward. My decision to go there was based on being offered a football scholarship, and for most of my college career I spent more time in the weight room than the library. My major was business, with a focus on accounting because I was good at math and a career assessment from high school suggested it would be a good fit. However, falling asleep in business classes led to me dreading them. I tried switching to a writing major, but this was not offered as an option. I enjoyed my introduction to psychology class with Russell Moulds, and he suggested I consider a career in pastoral counseling, so I gave psychology a try before ending up with a double major in psychology and theology. I had a few good professors—including Moulds, Paul Vasconcellos, and Robert Hennig; however, overall, I was not challenged or inspired in my undergraduate experience. I remained more focused on the weight room and a mobile disc jockey business than my education. Fortunately, my grades were fairly good despite little effort, which allowed me to apply for a doctorate degree. I had developed a strong work ethic—working two or three jobs through much of my undergraduate and graduate education—but did not develop the best study habits until this became necessary in graduate school.

In college, my rebellious nature emerged as part of my identity. Through high school and my early college years, my rebellious side was suppressed through conforming to the conservative religion of my youth. I was not a rebel in the traditional sense but more of a thought rebel. Everything was questioned, especially my faith. A few like-minded friends in college were willing to question with me, and we started an underground newspaper that challenged the theological views of the college. The underground newspaper, which we called "The Sewer" (the official college newspaper was "The Sower"), was an opportunity to explore and nurture this rebellious and questioning aspect of my identity, even though my writing at that time was not as well-developed as the other contributors. With a friend, I also started a Bible study that focused on controversial themes. The recognition that my conservative Christian background was not a comfortable fit was beginning to emerge, even though it would take many years to shed this part of my identity.

In my undergraduate education, Cognitive Behavioral Therapy (CBT) was touted as the only therapy to pursue if you wanted a career in psychology. Humanistic psychology was openly mocked—and misrepresented, though I did not yet realize it—if mentioned at all. As I applied to graduate school, I only applied to programs where I could focus on CBT. Upon discovering Fuller Seminary had a graduate program in psychology, I eagerly applied to Fuller and the University of

Nebraska. These were my top choices and, if I did not get in, I planned to take a year to work on a psychiatric unit at a hospital and reapply the next year. I was not accepted to either program but was offered a waiting list slot at Fuller. A few months later they informed me that someone decided not to attend, and I was accepted.

Moving to the Los Angeles area after never living in a town larger than 6,000 people was daunting. I was terrified of moving to the big city and of graduate school. Not being initially accepted made me wonder about my ability to make it in a doctoral program. For the first time in my life, it was necessary to take my education seriously. That first year, I joined a study group with several other students who became very close friends; I still treasure these friendships today and am certain that they were a big part of what kept me there. I did survive, and I finally became a serious student—a serious student of CBT.

Similar to stories I would hear from my students years later, I became highly disillusioned with psychology while going through my graduate program. My friends were helping me grow personally, and I was learning a lot of facts and skills in graduate school, but it held little interest. Fortunately, H. Newton Malony was my advisor. He was a wonderful, compassionate teacher who encouraged critical thinking. I have fond memories of him walking back and forth across the auditorium stage asking questions that he knew would spark debate. As he continued to pace, he would laugh as the discussions grew more heated. He encouraged us to go more deeply into the issues and not accept easy answers that were given to us. This nurtured the growing rebel in me and kept some spark for psychology alive.

At Fuller we had to pursue a master's degree in theology along with our PhD in psychology. Like my undergraduate days, I pushed the limits on independent studies.[2] This time, I took independent studies reading the systematic theology of the Lutheran Church Missouri Synod—the church I grew up in. As I read through thick 400- to 500-page volumes of systematic theology, I became disillusioned when encroaching on difficult themes that were followed by the author saying something to the effect of, 'We don't know why this is this way, but it is truth and it is sinful to question it." I was not okay with this answer and began contemplating leaving the church of my youth but stayed because of my

---

[2] My undergraduate advisor, Russell Moulds, once asked me, "Can you do anything the way we designed it?" He was joking and remained very supportive of me creating my own path. I am thankful for this, and I believe his openness to my challenging the system was an important part of my personal development.

family, many friends in the church, and the woman I was dating.

Toward the end of my graduate coursework, my roommate told me he was petitioning to take an independent study in existential and interpersonal psychology. Winston Gooden, who was one of my favorite professors, agreed to teach it. I asked to join the class, and this became a turning point for me. While devouring Yalom's *Existential Psychotherapy*, I started to believe again that this was the right career path for me. After completing my coursework, devouring Viktor Frankl, Ernest Becker, and Rollo May was next. With each book, I grew more excited and could not wait for the next book.

When looking for internships, I only searched places with a rural psychology rotation. I wanted to return to the rural Midwest and work with people who had little access to therapy. I was offered an internship at the Forest Institute of Professional Psychology in Springfield, Missouri, which had a rural outreach program. The person running the program at the time had been featured in the American Psychological Association's *Monitor on Psychology*, but he left before I arrived to begin my internship. Brad Powers took over his role and become an important support as I began seeking new directions. Surprisingly, the receptivity to my interest in existential psychology was better than anticipated. Although none of my supervisors at Forest were existential or humanistic, most were psychoanalytic and open to existential approaches. Mark Stocks, Ann Elise Parkhurst, and Robert Murney were wonderful depth psychology supervisors from whom I learned a great deal. Robert Murney became a mentor and close friend who was influential in the development of my identity as an existential therapist. A number of good friends, particularly A. J. Whitmire and Brittany Garrett-Bowser, helped me through a period of deep, transformative self-exploration and reflection. In retrospect, they were more helpful than the first therapist I saw during this time. During this period, I was reading Nietzsche and was drawn, in particular, to the idea of being brutally self-honest. This prompted a painful period of self-reflection that resulted in the loss of several important relationships because of my evolving religious beliefs and worldview. But the supportive friendships and mentoring relationships sustained me through the dark times while concurrently helping me transform this dark period into one of the best periods of my life.

After the loss of a particularly painful long-term relationship, I sought out the support of John Johnson, who was a good friend from graduate school. After sharing that I felt it was my fault that the relationship ended because I questioned too much and had changed,

John compassionately shared with me that all my good friends saw me as someone who questioned. He assured me that I had not changed, that the questioning was part of who I was. This was the final reassurance needed to deeply embrace my questioning nature and, along with it, my rebellious nature. It also allowed me to leave the church I grew up in to find a more compatible spiritual home. This led me to a spiritual home consistent with Schneider's awe-based approach to spirituality.

I stayed at Forest for a postdoc and found a passion for teaching. After co-teaching a course on existential therapy, I was asked to teach it independently and gladly, but nervously, accepted. At this point in my life, I had never met anyone who identified as an existential therapist other than myself. I was terrified to teach something that I only knew through books. The courses seemed to go well, and I decided that two things were certain to be part of my career path and my life: teaching and existential therapy. As long as these two things were part of my life, I was confident I would be happy.

After leaving Forest, I accepted a teaching position in California. In part, I wanted to move to where I could find colleagues with interest in existential psychology so that I could continue my own learning. Unfortunately, the Los Angeles area was not the best place for this. However, I discovered an ad for a course with James Bugental, one of the founders of existential psychology in the United States. I immediately called to see if I could still enroll and, a few weeks later, drove to Petaluma, California to partake in the Unearthing the Moment training. Although Bugental had suffered a stroke that profoundly impacted his memory, he still was involved with some of the teaching along with Myrtle Heery, who would become a mentor and good friend. The Unearthing training was deeply meaningful. I finally found colleagues and mentors in existential psychology. In my experience in the Unearthing training, I recognized the gap between my knowledge of existential-humanistic therapy and my skill as an existential-humanistic therapist. Through the training, my skill began catching up with my knowledge.

Around this time, I began a romantic relationship with a woman, Heatherlyn, who would become my wife. Heatherlyn was also drawn to humanistic and existential therapy. A challenge was that she was from the Bahamas, and early in our dating relationship we felt pressure to decide if this was a serious, long-term relationship because of her visa status. Being in a biracial relationship significantly impacted my development as a therapist in more ways than I can describe. I learned a great deal from Heatherlyn, but I also learned much about life through the challenges we faced as a biracial couple. The depth of love that I felt for Heatherlyn was transforming me. I was teaching about depth in relationships at this time and, while I had some very deep and transforming friendships in graduate school, particularly with Robert Murney and Brittany Garrett-Bower, I had not experienced anything like what I experienced—and continue to experience—with Heatherlyn.

During my time in California, I took additional coursework at the Claremont School of Theology. My religious beliefs were moving in a more progressive direction and Claremont was known as a very progressive school. Although I only took a few courses before moving, they were transformative. The courses were mostly on ethics and multiculturalism. The writings of Karen Baker-Fletcher, a womanist theologian with existential sensitivities, particularly impacted me. In one course, I read Mary Daly's *Beyond God the Father*, which was one of the most important books that I read at this time. Daly questioned whether it was possible to save religion from patriarchy. This question challenged me and helped me take my critical reflection to a deeper level. This questioning of whether religion could be saved from patriarchy and the influence of White culture was something I would carry over to my reflections on psychology. The writings encountered in theology at Claremont were much more progressive multiculturally than what I discovered in psychology.

The short jaunt in California came to an end when I met Emory Cowan, who was a graduate of Saybrook University and, at that time, president of the Colorado School of Professional Psychology (COSPP). At our first meeting at a restaurant in Long Beach, we quickly connected and he invited me to apply for a job at the school. Not much later, I moved to Colorado Springs to join the faculty. At COSPP, I finally had an existential colleague and a work environment that supported my developing scholarship in existential psychology. Heatherlyn and I, now married, developed a clinical and training center, the Center for Growth, that focused on existential psychology. With encouragement from Emory and other colleagues, I started to get involved with the Society for Humanistic Psychology and discovered a much greater network of existential colleagues—particularly Shawn Rubin, Brent Robbins, and Rich Bargdill, who were three other early career psychologists passionate about revitalizing the existential psychology movement. I also started to get to know Kirk Schneider and Tom Greening, who would eventually encourage me to apply for a position at Saybrook University, which was, at that time, still a premiere school in existential-humanistic psychology. While I enjoyed my years at Saybrook, especially the early years, I also missed teaching in a school where there was the chance to help students unfamiliar with existential-humanistic psychology become inspired to pursue this direction with their career.

Beginning during my COSPP years, I had the opportunity to travel to China where I met two people who have remained two of my closest friends and colleagues: Mark Yang and Xuefu Wang. We began developing trainings in existential-humanistic psychology in China. The early days of this work profoundly challenged me. Similar to the influence of Mary Daly, I often wondered if existential-humanistic psychology could be practiced in a culturally sensitive manner in China. At the same time, I had students in the United States point out that most of the presentations at the First Annual Society for Humanistic Psychology Conference were by White males. Shortly after finding my psychological home, I was thrown into a deep questioning of this approach, particularly questioning if it could be culturally sensitive. In China, Mark, Xuefu, and I invited cultural critique and reflected together on the challenges. In the United States, I invited my students to develop and collaborate on cultural critiques. In my marriage, I was learning experientially about the lived experience of cultural differences. This process changed existential-humanistic psychology for me and the way I approached it. However, in the end, a conversation with a new friend and colleague in China, Ren Zhengjia—who pronounced at our first meeting that "psychology is dog shit," in part because of his experience with culturally insensitive Western psychologists who imposed their approaches on Chinese therapists—helped me shift to a place where I believed that existential-humanistic therapy could be practiced in a culturally sensitive manner. Yet, I believe it is vital to continue asking this question.

When I step back from the details of my journey to reflect on the lessons, several stand out. First, I recognize that I began my journey well before I discovered existential psychology in varied existential ponderings, my use of music to explore deeper questions of life, and the gradual acceptance and embrace of the rebellious side of myself. My first connection with existential psychology was through books, which fostered a scholarly understanding that was greater than my ability to practice this approach. The deeper relationships that I developed in graduate school and my early career helped me embrace who I was becoming. Later, becoming part of the existential community in the United States (and more recently an existential world community) helped me thrive. Relationships and experiential learning were critical to advancing my skill as a practitioner into greater alignment with my scholarly understanding of existential psychology.

Through developing a more diverse set of friendships, being in a multiracial and international family, and engaging in multicultural scholarship, I recognized the role of privilege, including a significant amount of White male privilege, that helped me advance my career. This is a journey that will continue the rest of my life. Reflecting upon the impact of privilege on my life has been an important component of my professional development in recent years. My background as an existential-humanistic therapist helped me to stay with and utilize the guilt, including the existential guilt, connected with my privilege. This guilt is a blessing that helps me live more responsibly and authentically. Embracing guilt also emerges from the values I developed facing the world honestly. It motivates me to root my scholarship and practice in cultural humility, and it encourages me to remain committed to continued learning. Part of this cultural humility is to recognize ongoing blind spots and mistakes, which I recognize will always be there. In the last 12 years of my journey of becoming an existential-humanistic therapist, multicultural engagement has been my greatest existential teacher. I feel blessed that many of my closest friendships today are with people from different cultural backgrounds and different countries.

Julia Falk: My Journey

So many of me.

Which filter shall I look through?
Ah...psychology.

All the stories of my early life center around being the oldest child in an Irish Catholic family. I was born in New York in 1952 to parents who were only one generation past the old country. Our family eventually gained three brothers and a sister, in addition to my grandparents, who lived with us. Both my grandparents had left Ireland as young teens—Pa lying about his age (15) to go with his older brother to the Battle of the Somme, and Ma forced by her family at age 15 to emigrate to America on a ship out of Liverpool. I think their anxiety about their situations in the world shaped the temperament of our whole family. My mother was an only child, and my father was raised from babyhood by aunts and uncles during the Great Depression. So our family was insular, without a lot of involved relatives. In addition, we resided in small communities outside New York—first in New Jersey and later in

Becoming an Existential-Humanistic Therapist

Pennsylvania—held and defined by the community of the church. Allow me to share a few self-defining memories that have always represented something important about my developing sense of identity.

I am five or six years old, and I can now ride a two-wheeler bike. I can still remember the exhilaration of whizzing along without training wheels. A neighbor boy has dared me to race him, and we are lined up for a parallel run down the road. Romeo is allowed to ride in the street, but I can only ride on the sidewalk. As I tear down the concrete, I strike a bump and fly over the handlebars, knocking myself out on the pavement. The story is that my little brother ran home shouting, "Mommy, Mommy, Julie's on the sidewalk and she's dead!" Apparently, my dad scooped me up off the ground and carried me home to lie on the kitchen table. The thing I remember next is looking up from the table, my vision gradually clearing. A circle of concerned faces is looking down at me—mom, dad, grandparents… and the parish priest. It wasn't until adulthood that it occurred to me to wonder, "They called the priest and not the doctor?" That was the power and presence of the church in our lives. I will only say that it was not a benign influence because to say more would take a book.

Another of my powerful self-stories takes place in Pennsylvania, at St. Matthew's School in seventh grade. Early in the year, our class felt like a fairly homogeneous mix of young kids without a lot of divisions or internal groups. Then I got a case of pneumonia and had to stay home for three weeks. When I returned to school, the whole world felt changed. While I was gone, some hormonal or social shift had taken place; boys and girls were now paired off and "going steady." I was out of sync and left behind. From there, the kids morphed into cliques of popular girls and guys who were "in" and the homely kids like me who were assuredly "out." It was a painful, visceral experience that I took to heart and carried with me all the way to college. Although I was successful in school and appreciated for other qualities, that wallflower who doesn't quite fit is always with me.

I find that my journey to psychology is rooted in my spiritual history. Although I still had to go to church with my family, by the time I finished high school, I had lost the faith of my childhood. A scholarship enabled me to attend college away from home at Marquette University, where I majored in English. It had the potential to be a great Jesuit education, but I was a confused and unhappy teen in the 1970s, so I really didn't take as much advantage of that as I might have. I didn't experience religious feelings then, but I developed a liking for the intellectual approach of theology along with a liberal social conscience. In that urban environment, though, I also experienced a few assaults that shaped where I would feel safe for decades. Even in my state of depression and groundlessness, my personal values must have been slowly gelling. I knew that I would only be satisfied by a life of service, though I didn't know what that would be.

At the end of my four years at Marquette, I did know that I didn't want to be an English teacher. I went home to Pennsylvania and took a summer job with the National Park Service at Delaware Water Gap, and that was the start of another life. For the next ten years, I worked in several national park areas, mostly as a ranger/naturalist, and I loved it. The people were outdoorsy and had healthy interests (not much sex, drugs, and rock 'n' roll). I felt like I was in service to the environment and the nation, and it suited my strong feminist streak to be doing something unusual for a woman. I met my first husband there, and we traveled from park to park; I felt for the first time like I really belonged. I enrolled in a master's program in geography at Arizona State and came into an ecological view of the planet and my first appreciation of its wonders. And I felt safe in the woods, too, where I grew physically strong from hiking, climbing, and running. The natural world was my temple, and I was often awestruck.

One of the things I enjoyed about all that was training as a park medic, so when we began to think about settling and having a family, I thought that nursing would be a good choice for me. That turned out to be my next life, and the longest in duration. I eventually graduated from the University of Maryland School of Nursing, which was topflight in the discipline. This was my first experience of the humanistic approach. We were grounded in person-centered care, schooled in therapeutic communication, and the whole program was designed around Erickson's developmental stages and Maslow's hierarchy. Nursing and teaching were traditional women's roles back then, and I had some unease about stepping into that sort of identity. However, I found that nursing satisfied my need to care and to serve like nothing that had come before. I worked in many specialties during my 30+ year career and obtained a master's degree in health education and health promotion. Nursing is often a hard and tiring job, plagued by administrative detail and overwork, but there were countless moments of tender mercy between human beings that felt sacred to me. It's quite beyond words.

Most of my nursing career took place in Tennessee in a fundamentalist culture where I certainly was different. I raised two (beloved) sons there, where we were a solitary family who didn't go to church. After 24 years, though, my marriage ended. Rather devastated, I found myself at an Episcopal church the following week, where I was invited to join the choir. As I've moved around in the intervening years, I've alternated between Episcopal and Lutheran choirs, and that has been my spiritual touchstone. I have never rediscovered a dogmatic faith, but I find transcendence in the experience of singing liturgical music. One of the choirs I sing in now specializes in early church music. When we sing for vespers in the large seminary chapel with the light filtering in through the stained glass, it feels like touching the divine.

When I married again almost twenty years ago, I found that I still needed to process the death of my first marriage and the upending of my whole life in a move back north, along with a newly empty nest. My wise, kind therapist suggested that joy happens in the present moment, and she encouraged me to explore mindfulness. And so the next life started.

I began an avid study of mindfulness and Buddhist psychology and was especially drawn to the writing of Jack Kornfield. I noticed that he was a clinical psychologist and had graduated from Saybrook. Mindfulness practices changed everything for me, freeing me from the prison of repetitive thoughts and some of my attachments to old ways of being and thinking. At one of my weeklong silent retreats in Massachusetts (before we went into silence), I met a woman who said she taught Mindfulness-based Stress Reduction (MBSR). I was intrigued because, by that time, I was helping to run meditation sessions at a small local group. I felt that I needed a better foundation for the teaching that I was beginning to do. I applied to the professional training program at the Center for Mindfulness at the University of Massachusetts Medical School, where Jon Kabat-Zinn and his colleagues were still teaching. It took me four years to complete the training, and I've been teaching MBSR in my community for over ten years now. I was nearing retirement age as an ER nurse and saw an opportunity to continue to work with people who are suffering with chronic illness. I was eventually able to get funding through our hospital foundation to teach MBSR in the community, without tuition.

MBSR is a mind/body endeavor and I observed early that illness, pain, depression, and anxiety are intermingled. Through various meditation practices and yoga, I was trying to teach people to experience embodiment and the very important skill of inquiry. I had to hold a steady awareness of my own experience as I related to my participants—sounds like psychology. In my third teaching cycle, years ago now, I happened to draw a group with several members who had suffered complex trauma. We did a relaxing body scan in the first class, and all seemed well. I sent them home to practice the body scan each day. They came back the next week with tales of being very disturbed by the experience in their bodies, some even having blackouts. I was horrified! My prime belief as a nurse was "first do no harm," and I knew I was in over my head. Determined not to damage these people any further, I sought a mentor at the Center for Mindfulness to guide me through the remainder of the eight-week course, and I stepped away from mindfulness readings to learn everything I could about trauma. I read books and took online courses, and we created an experience together that was helpful and not harmful.

I was more and more drawn to learn about working in the area of mental and emotional health. Since I still live in a rural area, I began to look for a doctoral program in psychology that would allow me to work largely online. The Kornfield connection drew my attention to Saybrook University, where I found that my humanistic nursing background was fairly aligned. I didn't think that I would want to undertake establishing a private practice at my age, so I joined the consciousness, spirituality, and integrative health specialization.

It will be evident now that I am not a therapist, so I don't exactly fit into this present group either. To go on with the story, though, I loved the Saybrook experience and the chance to dig into new material and rediscover my academic self. In the first semester, I chanced to run across the series of letters between Carl Rogers and Rollo May in which May (1982) laid out his view of human beings caught in the tension between polarities. There was a lot of agreement between them, but as they fleshed out their differences I was drawn to May's thinking.

Although I am not a therapist, people come to the courses I teach with a degree of suffering that astounded me. I had seen it from a more physical and immediate perspective as a hospital nurse, despite always trying to be holistic in my interactions. Now I was in contact with people for eight weeks, present with them as they touched into death and dying, physical pain, loss of relationships, troubling memories, and profound anxieties. The existential elements that May introduced spoke more to the deep respect I had developed for the range and depth of ordinary people's suffering. I soon changed to a specialization in existential, humanistic, and transpersonal psychology. There I took coursework with Louis Hoffman and Jason Dias, who were always accepting and challenging at the same time.

Prior to my Saybrook experience, I had attempted to quantify the outcomes of my mindfulness teaching at the health system where I taught. With my small class sizes, I could never achieve statistical significance with various assessment tools and measures. However, the greatest frustration was that the results never reflected what my participants were telling me verbally, like "This has changed *every*thing," and "People have been seeing me as my diagnosis for years; MBSR has given me back my identity." Being in an academic environment that was fully welcoming to qualitative research was another opening for me to admit life's complexity into my work. My interest in narrative research deepened. and I stepped into developing a curriculum for life review that could allow people to recognize their most significant life stories—learning from both the stories and sharing their personal meanings in a group.

I had a great deal of experience working with groups, but after graduation I found that I still wanted to hone my skills at working with individuals. I went back to Saybrook and spent most of a year getting certified in integrative coaching. At the same time, I entered a two-year training through the International Focusing Institute to become a focusing practitioner and trainer. I was familiar with focusing through some of my early mindfulness explorations, but this was an incredibly deep and embodied experience. Charlotte Howorth, my principal teacher, delved into the work of Gendlin and others on the focusing process and focusing-oriented therapy. Through hours and hours of practice, we searched out the elements of presence and presence-in-interaction. Cultivating a sustained (or at least intermittent) awareness of felt sense has expanded my experience of nearly everything, incorporating bodily feelings, images, memories, and connections. I'm now enjoying the role of coach for the new class of trainees, which is deepening my own learning. Because it has changed the way I listen, I believe that focusing is my most significant modality, and I can bring it into all my other interactions, including MBSR, coaching clients, and continuing life story work.

When I think now of "being" and "becoming," the threads that have been constant in all my stories help to unify them. The being is the consistent draw toward the spiritual, the perpetual feeling of aloneness and not quite fitting, and always that underlying desire to care and help, and to matter. But the becoming is the restless energy that has moved me from one interest to another, from one life to the next, so that, finally, there is a faith that the journey is, for me, a forever unfolding that will turn out all right.

Embracing the Journey

Becoming an existential-humanistic therapist is different from other approaches to therapy that are focused more on technique and other structured aspects of practice. Becoming an existential-humanistic therapist focuses first on the person of the therapist. Thus, the pathway to becoming an existential-humanistic therapist is more dependent upon the person of the therapist. While each journey to becoming an existential-humanistic practitioner is unique, there are shared experiences and themes that can be identified in these journeys. In his dissertation, Trent Claypool (2010) was the first person to systematically analyze the journey to becoming an existential therapist through interviewing five prominent leaders in the existential-humanistic movement. Building from Claypool's dissertation, HeeSun Park (2020) explored the journey of existential-humanistic therapists with a range of experience (see chapter 1). Both of these dissertations identified themes that were common, such as the role of mentoring relationships and self-growth. This book, in many ways, builds from the Claypool and Park dissertations; however, we focus on sharing the narratives of existential-humanistic therapists in their own words instead of utilizing a research approach.

The first chapter begins by providing an overview of Claypool's and Park's dissertations, written by HeeSun Park. The themes identified in these dissertations can be seen in the narratives that follow. This is not surprising, especially given that some of the leaders in existential-humanistic psychology that were in Claypool's dissertation also contributed chapters to this volume. However, the variances and uniqueness of the paths also can be seen through the narratives that follow. The next 11 chapters are comprised of narratives by various leaders in existential-humanistic psychology. In selecting contributors, we identified 11 individuals who are mid-career or more established therapists from diverse backgrounds. Each of these individuals has, however, made a substantive contribution to existential-humanistic therapy. As there are several branches of existential therapy, we elected to focus specifically on existential-humanistic therapy.

Defining existential-humanistic therapy is not easy. Hoffman (2019) maintained that it is better to understand existential-humanistic therapy as a mosaic in which practitioners tend to align with many, but not necessarily all, of various theoretical and practice principles or values commonly associated with existential-humanistic therapy. After all, it is rather unexistential to have a narrowly defined approach. This would deny the uniqueness of each individual practitioner and the need for cultural variations. Similarly, the individuals we invited to contribute chapters will not agree on what comprises existential-humanistic therapy and they use different labels to identify themselves. Few, if any, would identify as a purist existential-humanistic therapist but this, too, would be somewhat unexistential. Some contributors, such as Mendelowitz, eschew the ideas of labels. Others identify more broadly with the existential label. Xuefu Wang identifies primarily as a *zhi mian* therapist, which is an indigenous Chinese approach to existential therapy that bears the closest resemblance to existential-humanistic psychology of the major branches of existential therapy. Some scholars may question our selection of contributors based upon these factors. However, we believe the contributors represent the diversity within existential-humanistic psychology beautifully.

After the 11 narratives (14 if including Louis, Julia, and HeeSun), we include a chapter reflecting upon the contributor's stories. This is not a formal analysis of themes as would be done in a research approach. In the chapters, we felt it was important to allow each author to utilize their own voice and style as opposed to introducing a more structured approach that decreases individuality and uniqueness. While this means there is less consistency in the approach to the chapters, it increases the authenticity of the voice of each chapter. This also reflects the diversity of ways people come to existential-humanistic therapy and the different ways that they embody it. Our editing choice reflects an attempt to honor the different voices and approaches to the same theme. As existential-humanistic therapists strive to honor the path of their clients, we were intentional about honoring the paths of the authors. For some authors, theory leads the way to frame the stories. For others, the stories lead and the connection to existential themes comes later. Xuefu Wang chose to utilize a discussion forum with some colleagues and students as the basis for his reflections. These unique approaches are relevant to the discussion of being and becoming an existential-humanistic therapist. We see this as another lesson that can be derived from the book. This also led to a context in which the reflection on themes in the final chapter is more informal.

We conclude with two appendices. The first appendix is intended for students who may be considering creating their own path to becoming an existential-humanistic therapist. This appendix provides a number of questions and journal prompts that can be explored to help with one's decision about whether to pursue this path. The second appendix is designed for individuals who identify as existential-humanistic therapists who want to reflect upon their own journey.

Conclusion

This is a very personal book, and not just because we include portions of our own story in this introduction. It is personal because of the nature of being an existential-humanistic therapist, which is rooted in the person. Whether you are an existential-humanistic therapist reflecting upon your own journey or are considering becoming an existential-humanistic therapist, we hope this book enriches your path.

References

Abzug, R. H. (2021). *Psyche and soul in America: The spiritual odyssey of Rollo May.* Oxford University Press.

Claypool, T. R. (2010). *On becoming an existential psychologist: The journeys of contemporary leaders* (Publication No. 3412340) [Doctoral dissertation, University of the Rockies]. Proquest Dissertations and Theses Global.

Hoffman, L. (2019). Introduction to existential-humanistic psychology in a cross-cultural context. In L. Hoffman, M. Yang, F. J. Kaklauskas, Λ. Chan, & M. Mansilla (Eds.), *Existential psychology East–West* (Vol. 1, Rev. & expanded ed., pp. 1–72). University Professors Press.

May, R. (1982). The problem of evil: An open letter to Carl Rogers. *Journal of Humanistic Psychology, 22*, 10–21.

Park, H. (2020). *The journey to become an existential-humanistic therapist.* [Unpublished doctoral dissertation]. Saybrook University.

Rogers, C. R. (1980). *A way of being.* Houghton Mifflin.

Chapter 1

Existential–Humanistic Psychology: Connecting to Values

HeeSun Park

I can trace my path to becoming an existential-humanistic therapist to my early childhood, when I was just four or five years old. I grew up in Korea. Although I had a big family and several siblings to play with, I remember spending many lonely, sad hours sitting in the front yard of my house. The sadness I felt at that young age is still palpable. When I ask myself why I became an existential-humanistic therapist, I particularly recall a time when I was sitting there and explicitly realized that I wanted to become happier and wanted to help others be happier, too.

I have always been drawn to existential themes and have always wondered how to find true happiness despite the pain and hardship that exist in life. As I grew into adulthood, I increasingly embraced the principles of Buddhism, which emphasizes being *present* to circumstances while not being caught up in the chaos and suffering they stimulate. I came to believe that such existential attunement is the most urgent and critical task in life. Convinced of this in my twenties, I wanted to devote my life to this by becoming a Buddhist nun.

Ultimately, I did not choose to live a monastic life. My connection to secular life, my family, and my worldly aspirations were too strong to leave behind. But I didn't abandon my pursuit. It was clear that I deeply wanted to find happiness in the face of existential circumstances, that I wanted to become more mindful, and that I wanted to be able to help others. The existential pain I first felt in childhood led me to leave everything I had in my Korean home—my stable job, family, and friends—to pursue a vocation as a therapist in the United States.

Upon arriving in the United States, I enrolled in a program to study art therapy. I found art therapy to be valuable in many way. It provided an extremely effective approach to help people discover and express their hidden hurts, wishes, conflicts, and traumas through art. Thus, this approach provided a powerful healing experience for me and my clients.

A very valuable component of my work while I completed my graduate program was attending supervisory group meetings with my mentor, Arthur "Art" Robbins. It seemed to me that Art, a retired professor of art therapy, had a deep understanding of how to support aspiring therapists to become attuned and effective. Whenever I was going through personal and professional crises, he was able to establish powerful connections with me. Through these, he helped me grow personally and professionally.

Aside from the specific value of his advice, I was transfixed with how Art was able to connect with me so effectively. When I asked him to teach me how to make such interpersonal connections, he told me that I had to find my own way to deeply connect to people while simultaneously connecting to my own "dark side." From this, I understood that I needed to continually face and explore my own negative emotions and unhealed hurts from the past. But the guidelines he gave turned out to be too abstract for me to apply in my own practice. Although I developed a deeper connection to my own dark side of hidden desires, ambitions, and emotions, I lacked a clear way to transfer the associated insights into my practice.

To continue my education, I enrolled at Saybrook University. It was there that I learned about the "existential approach"—the holistic idea that the ability of therapists to be present with their clients was a means to help those clients connect to their deeper selves, accept existential givens, and discover meaning. This is something that resonated strongly with me. The existential-humanistic approach would allow me to engage the full range of existential awareness—of people, place, death, anxiety, and desire—in a way that would let me connect with and help my clients.

The more I learned about the existential approach, the more confident I became that this was the path that I would choose. However, as much as I read about it, I struggled to establish a clear theory of the approach or how to apply it. It was at this juncture that my dissertation advisor, Louis Hoffman, suggested that I read Trent Claypool's (2010) dissertation, *On Becoming an Existential Psychologist: The Journeys of Contemporary Leaders*.

In his dissertation, Claypool surveyed the professional and personal journeys of five contemporary leaders of existential psychology.

Through these interviews, he was able to identify fundamental themes that informed the careers of these leaders; these themes included significant life events, circumstances, spirituality, existential awareness, and philosophical perspectives. Reading Claypool's study gave me a glimpse into the minds and experience of leading practitioners of existential-humanistic therapy. I found this stimulating; if I could put myself in that mindset, it would greatly improve my ability to understand and perform this work.

Still, there were gaps in Claypool's (2010) research that left me uncertain. By interviewing only leaders in the field, it wasn't clear if the qualities that Claypool discovered were generalizable across practitioners of the discipline. Furthermore, although Claypool studied what factors contributed to the development of these leaders, he didn't enumerate the ways these leaders developed their therapeutic practices. Recognizing my interest in such questions, Dr. Hoffman proposed that I devote my dissertation to expanding Claypool's research. I embraced this challenge.

In my research, like Claypool (2010), I conducted surveys of existential-humanistic therapists, and asked the same questions Claypool used in his study. But instead of interviewing leaders in the field, I reached out to a wider range of therapists, with the aim of getting a more generalized understanding of existential-humanistic therapist development. Beyond this, I also sought to explore details about how existential-humanistic therapy is actually practiced and the journeys undertaken by such therapists in pursuit of their careers.

When I first started my study of the existential-humanistic approach, I learned that it combined the aims of helping others, developing mindfulness, cultivating happiness, and being accepting of existential circumstances. Through Claypool's study of leaders in the field and my subsequent research into commonalities shared by other practitioners, I have gained confidence that it is an approach that suits me, and that can lead to great success when working with clients.

Trent Claypool's (2010) Research:
The Journeys of Contemporary Leaders[1]

Claypool's (2010) research was based on interviews he conducted with

---

[1] This section of the chapter is drawn from Trent Claypool's (2010) dissertation. I would like to thank Dr. Claypool for granting permission to include this summary of his dissertation in this book chapter.

five leaders in the field of existential psychology: Kirk Schneider, Ilene Serlin, Myrtle Heery, Ed Mendelowitz, and Tom Greening. All of them have significantly influenced the development of existential-humanistic psychology in the United States.

Kirk Schneider

Kirk Schneider describes himself as an "existential-integrative psychotherapist" and has been practicing psychotherapy since the 1980s. He also has served as editor-in-chief of the *Journal of Humanistic Psychology*. He has authored a number of notable books on the topics of existential-integrative psychotherapy, existential-humanistic therapy, the paradoxical nature of the human mind, the mystery of being, and many others.

I was especially interested in Claypool's interview with Schneider after having witnessed Schneider's powerful personal presence at a seminar. I regularly engage in meditation and assumed that meditation was the only way to develop such presence. I wondered how much time he spent meditating every day! Therefore, when I saw Schneider after the seminar, I asked him about his meditation practice. He answered with a smile that he does not engage in meditation separate from his daily life. This was extremely surprising to me, and I was eager to learn about how his personal journey produced such a calm and therapeutic presence.

In the following account, Schneider explains what motivated him to develop his capacity to be present:

> My own personal, intensive, existentially oriented therapy was crucial in my blossoming, my growth as an existential psychologist... I do want to highlight that aspect [of the importance of being in therapy], because that not only informed me of psychological theory in a very intimate way, but it freed me, I think it helped to save my life really, freed me to grow up and be able to just expand my ability to be a productive person in the world. What was probably most key was the cultivation of the capacity to be present. That's what I walk away [with] from both of my key therapies, both at six years old and when I was 21 at West Georgia College. They both helped me to stay present to the most horrifying, disjointed places in myself, and, as I was going through extremely disturbing periods of my life, presence was huge. I think behind that, or along with that, was certainly the sense of the caring and support of the therapist in the sense

that they had been through it themselves in some way. They could deeply relate. It wasn't so much about anything they said; it was much more about what they embodied. And a sense of seasoning, that they had been there in their own way and somehow come through, that idea that they were models, they were inspirations. That was really critical, they could hold me and all my stuff no matter where we went, and they presented a sense of freedom to go anywhere. I really recall feeling free to be in any kind of whacko disjointed place with those folks, and I had a sense of safety. (p. 117)

I was fascinated to read this account of how being in personal therapy helped him cultivate the capacity to be present. I was also impressed by how he attributes his ability to be present to continuous effort and not to his given nature.

Ilene Serlin

Ilene Serlin is a psychologist and dance therapist who has written about and taught psychology for many years. She identifies herself as a depth-psychotherapist, influenced heavily by Jungian and existential-humanistic approaches to psychotherapy, and Buddhist spiritual practice. Her work is heavily influenced by her experience in modern dance; she is particularly attuned to psychotherapy that incorporates the entire body, observes details of movement, and emphasizes being in the moment. She has been practicing psychotherapy since the 1970s and has numerous publications including a three-volume set, *Whole Person Healthcare* (2007).

In my early work as an art therapist, my supervisor stressed that dance was a powerful means of artistic expression and could be regarded as a pure form of expressing deeper parts of oneself. He would ask his supervisees to "move like how you feel" or "move like your client." In the course of my work with him, I attended regular movement/dance groups and experienced how movement can, in many cases, allow one to connect more directly to primitive feelings than visual art at times. This experience of the therapeutic value of dance and movement left me keenly interested in learning more about Ilene Serlin's story.

Myrtle Heery

Myrtle Heery is a psychologist in private practice. She is Associate Core Faculty for Master's and PhD programs at Sofia University, Palo Alto,

California, as well as the director for the International Institute for Humanistic Studies. She describes her orientation to psychotherapy as having a foundation in existential, humanistic, and transpersonal therapy. In her early career, she described herself as an adherent to a Rogerian person-centered approach to therapy. However, she recounted how a near-death experience from a car accident transformed her view of therapy and life. As she put it, "Having touched hands with death, I became more of an existential-humanistic therapist" (Claypool, 2010, p. 72).

In addition to her own near-death experience, Heery also shared the impact of the death of her father and how it led her to reflect on meaning and values in her life:

> The one major person I think of is my father when I was 23 and having a very profound experience with him while he was dying. This happened in Georgia in 1970 and I had the profound experience of joy and sorrow as his essence left his body. These paradoxical emotions opened me to a new inner world, but with very little support in Georgia to explore their meaning. It would take my personal journey in psychotherapy in California to explore this loss with many deep questions, opening myself over and over to the pain of loss along with the opportunities of living now. (p. 80)

Claypool's interview with Dr. Heery presented the importance and challenge of being aware of existential givens such as death in order to live more fully.

Ed Mendelowitz

Ed Mendelowitz is a psychologist in private practice, the recipient of the Rollo May Award for "independent and outstanding pursuit of new frontiers in psychology." He is associate editor for *The Humanistic Psychologist*, and is on the board of editors for the *Journal of Humanistic Psychology*. During his interview with Claypool, he shared that he was profoundly influenced by one nineteen-year-old client in particular. This client had multiple personalities, and his work with her led him to find his own presence as well as hers. Mendelowitz described this in his interview:

> It is a kind of miracle that she is still alive. Right from the very beginning I could tell that amid all the obvious mental

disturbance there was an incredible psychological acumen, an uncanny spiritual awareness, just a real integrity in the way she dealt with me. ...I would say she had an enormous influence on me because I learned not to judge, and I also learned, I had to break rules to work with her. By the end of this process, I was so impressed with her own spiritual sensibility, [her] psychological perspicacity, her own ethical standard—and growing up in this hellish situation. I just learned to trust more my own voice because she had developed such a strong voice of her own. (p. 95)

Tom Greening

Tom Greening describes himself as an existential-humanistic, person-centered psychotherapist. At the time of Claypool's study, he had been practicing psychotherapy for 52 years. He was a full-time faculty member at Saybrook University and had served as the editor of the *Journal of Humanistic Psychology* since the 1970s. One of his notable contributions was being part of the Humanistic Psychology Citizen Diplomacy Project in the 1980s. He went to Russia to promote peace between the States and Russia during the Cold War. He authored a number of poems and books, including *Instant Relief: The Encyclopedia of Self-Help* (Greening & Hobson, 1979).

What struck me most about the interview with Greening was his description of his experience while living through the polio epidemic:

> ...but there I am, a kid living in a nice little New Jersey town in summertime. We liked to go to swimming pools and stuff, and then this epidemic strikes and people are getting paralyzed, living in iron lungs, and suddenly the awareness is that you're very vulnerable here. You're in danger. (p. 81)

This account reminded me that there is more to life than what we experience in our day-to-day condition; there is always the chance that sudden change will make us face the frailty and uncertainty of human existence.

Trent Claypool's Analysis

After conducting interviews with these five fascinating individuals, Claypool analyzed the transcripts using the "constant comparative method" from Glaser and Strauss's (1967) grounded theory approach to identify themes. Through this, he discovered six common themes that heavily influenced the journeys of these existential psychologists: significant life events, non-psychological influences, psychological influences, spiritual sensibility, ontological sensibility, and commitment to personal growth.

Significant Life Events
All five of the leaders interviewed by Claypool cited significant life events that shaped their development as existential psychologists. Of these events, what interested me most was their discussion of near-death experiences or the loss of loved ones. These leaders all shared that these traumatic experiences heightened their sense of existential urgency and quest. For example, Myrtle Heery shared how her near-death experience of being in a car accident transformed her perspective:

> It awakened me to being here, and using the time while I'm here turned into a huge urgency... it awakened me to living in the moment. When I began to apply this work to my clients, of being more present and finding meaning in the moment, I got more results. (p. 79)

Similarly, Kirk Schneider shared his experience of losing his older brother at the age of three:

> What happened over that time was I went from a position of abject terror and paralysis, to just beginning to open up to the larger questions about life, because it really, in a most abrupt way, opened me to those larger questions. As to, what's this all about? Of course, why did this happen? How was I involved, if at all? What does this mean for my own life? And, of course, I had a great fear of death myself, a horror of sickness. (p. 80)

These interviews were profound and reminded me of something I had read in a Buddhist book—that living just a single day with an awakened mind is worth more than living for years in darkness. The deeply painful and frightening experiences described by these leaders awakened them to existential truth, and this awakening led to their development of wisdom as existential psychologists.

Non-Psychological Influences
The leaders in Claypool's study also identified "non-psychological

influences" such as philosophy, literature, and art as being important factors in their personal and professional development. As I would have expected, most notable was their connection to philosophy. A good example of this is presented in Claypool's interview with Kirk Schneider, during which Schneider shared his fascination with the existential philosopher and theologian Paul Tillich:

> Tillich has recently become my number one philosophical inspiration. His idea of demonization I think is crucial, not only at the level of societies, but at the level of individual psychopathology or dysfunction. I think he's on to one of the main problems of history, the idea that we run into problems when we mistake a piece of reality for its entirety. That's it right there, that when we exalt or elevate one dimension of reality to the utter neglect of competing realities, we become polarized and truncated in our ability to live a fuller life, and often destructive. You could see these themes vividly in Tillich's *The Dynamics of Faith, The Courage to Be, Ultimate Concern*, and *Systematic Theology*. (p. 87)

In his interview, Ed Mendelowitz also indicates that philosophy heavily influenced his development:

> I have a feeling for mostly Nietzsche and Kierkegaard. I don't read all of these philosophers, but these guys to me, because of the playfulness of their thoughts, they are artists as thinkers. This impresses me. I just have a feeling for this and I return to their work repeatedly. (p. 88)

It is interesting that all five leaders interviewed by Claypool cited literature as an influence—in some cases horror, existentialists, or Greek, German, and American classics—because they reflected existential themes in the stories.

Psychological Influences
A third theme that Claypool derived from his interviews pertains to psychological influences. Most notable to me was the degree to which these leaders were affected by the mentorship that they experienced. The most pertinent example was expressed by Myrtle Heery, who spent 25 years as the mentee of James Bugental:

> [My] relationship with him was huge. He impacted how I did therapy, who I am as a person. [He showed me] the importance of being and being real with myself and the people in front of me. Also, he inspired me more than anyone to teach, and awakened me to the importance of giving back to the profession by teaching other people and giving this way of working with people to many people, not just one client at a time. (p. 91)

Another factor that Claypool groups within psychological influences is the overall existential-humanistic movement that was taking place in the '60s and '70s, together with the struggle and disenchantment with the traditional therapeutic approaches that characterized the practice of psychology at the time.

Spiritual Sensibility

All the leaders interviewed by Claypool cited spiritual sensibility as essential in their journeys to become psychologists. My own spiritual connection led me to find this particularly interesting. In her interview, Ilene Serlin expresses how her sensibility to Buddhism affected her development:

> Then there is Buddhism. It still informs my work a lot. The whole practice of being in the moment, and the emphasis, not so much on the origins of the problem, but on the what are you going to do about it and how you work with it? So, Buddhist psychology in general I think is brilliant, and it informs a lot of what I do today. (p. 103)

In his interview with Claypool, Kirk Schneider recounts the profound importance that being connected to the fundamental mystery of life has had on his personal and professional development.

> This whole cultivation of a sense of awe has been very central to my own thinking and feeling of spirituality that has emerged out of my studies of existential philosophy and psychology, but also my experience of life. I think my growing ability to feel freedom in my life, to explore, to wonder, and to have a wide range of feelings, including anxious and unsettling feelings all contributed. I think all of that, a lot of it coming out of my own personal therapeutic growth, has come together in the last, especially 10 years or so to give me this spiritual sense of life I

> call awe-inspiring, or awe-based. ...It's at that crossroads, and more than that, it's something that one can feel at any time, it's available at any moment, and it's free, free of charge, it's natural, it's something that we tend to grow away from because we become so conditioned to fixed, answer-oriented life. We lose touch with the fundamental mystery of being. I think Viktor Frankl is another great influence. He really set the bar, in terms of how awe is accessible, because he was actually able to experience that in the most depraved circumstances of life, a Nazi death camp. If Viktor Frankl could taste a sense of awe from some light filtered through his barrack in that maelstrom or on a transport train between Bavaria and Auschwitz going between death camps looking through the slats of his train window and noticing the beauty of the Bavarian mountains, then just about anybody could have this experience. To me, it's extremely inspiring, and can speak to the rest of us hopefully it can speak to us in our most depressed and depraved circumstances. (p. 104)

Ed Mendelowitz also discussed the existential nature of his spirituality:

> I like the Zen line that you can't nail a block of wood into empty space. I'm interested in the East where the notion of God isn't that big. Taoism, Buddhism, they're not really talking about God, [they're] talking about the flow of Time and Cosmos. However, once you get that stuff, you learn that we have people who are worshipers of the Tao even here in the West—Emerson and Thoreau and so many of our people in the arts, I think, are in touch with this sort of fluid god. (p. 104)

Taken together, the spiritual beliefs of these leaders support the notion that spiritual sensibility is crucial to the development of an effective psychologist, while at the same time highlighting how unlikely it is that such sensibility can be taught or valued in a traditional psychological education setting.

Ontological Sensibility
At first, the term, "ontological sensibility" (p. 106) came across as too abstract and technical to fully appreciate. But Claypool related that this theme pertained to "deepening one's awareness and experience

through maximal embodiment," and this led me to connect it to *presence*, which is one of the fundamental tenets of existential-humanistic psychology. My own drive to be more mindful in daily life led me to become curious about what leaders in existential psychology had to say in this regard.

In their interviews, the leaders touched on this by relating how their lives were influenced by their connection to the mystery of being, awareness of the paradoxical aspects of life, accepting smallness and greatness at the same time, the experience of living through struggles, and their commitment to living creatively. I was most drawn to Ed Mendelowitz's excerpt about his commitment to living a life of creativity and presence:

> Always there is this idea that we are on our own and that we make our own lives. You are really trying to help a person with an opened up mind, a sort of larger sense of what it's all about, that they can make the best of their finite journey. Implicit somewhere there is courage, the courage to just, Nietzsche says, "be who you are" or become who you are. He's always quoting Pindar, how one becomes what one is—this idea that self creation, again Nietzsche, "is the rarest and most difficult art" and that's our job. (p. 114)

Mendelowitz's idea of making our own lives resonates deeply with me. It reminds me of what Schneider (personal communication) said to challenge my class at his existential-humanistic seminar: "How are you willing to live this moment?"

Together, these perspectives put forth by Mendelowitz and Schneider show the common ground that these leaders share with the fundamental Buddhist idea that one is the owner of one's life, and that one creates one's own happiness and misery, just as wheels leave marks. That is to say, in Buddhism the intention to be wholesome leaves marks that lead to happiness while the intention to be unwholesome leaves marks that lead to misery.

Ilene Serlin's insight into embodiment was also valuable:

> I found in the yoga classes that my world changed after 1 hour. After this I started to ask about the relationship between the body and psychology. After graduating I got involved in the Gestalt Institute because Laura Perls really understood the connection to the body, especially the verbal and the nonverbal. (p. 108)

This sort of embodiment seems to refer to experiencing what emerges in the here and now, not only on the intellectual level but also in a bodily way. It seems to me that this is one of the essential qualities existential-humanistic practitioners must develop in order to sense and mirror what emerges in the practice.

Taken together, what Claypool referred to as ontological sensibility provides a sense of the importance of deepening one's awareness and sensitivity around one's experience in a full, bodily way. This validates my continuous effort to develop these attributes as an individual as well as a therapist.

Commitment to Personal Growth

The final theme that Claypool derived from his interviews pertained to a commitment to personal growth. The leaders all shared that their own experience in personal therapy was particularly integral to their personal and professional journeys. As previously noted, Schneider credited his own growth and capacity for being productive in the world in some part to his experiences with existentially oriented therapy. It was particularly striking that he emphasized how therapy's value was not restricted to any particular situation or problem but to cultivating his capacity to be present.

Aside from cultivating presence, I was also moved by the qualities these leaders presented in terms of their incessant commitment to growth, their striving to live more fully in the present moment, and their humble acknowledgment of the givens of human existence.

Altogether, Claypool's research provided a fascinating sense of the beliefs, motivations, and experiences that shaped the development of leaders in the field of existential psychology. Reading his study left me feeling clearer about the abstract qualities that were manifested in leading practitioners in the field, and the importance of nurturing and exhibiting these qualities in myself as I pursue my own career as an existential-humanistic psychologist.

My Journey to Becoming an Existential-Humanist Therapist[2]

In my own research, it was my aim to ascertain whether the commonalities that characterized the experience of the leaders of existential psychology were more broadly shared by other practitioners, and also to deduce some key characteristics of the

---

[2] This section is drawn from my doctoral dissertation (Park, 2020).

effective application of the approach. To do so, I selected a sample of seven licensed mental health therapists who identify as existential-humanistic practitioners. In order to produce data that was directly comparable to that produced by Claypool's study, I asked these participants the same set of questions Claypool asked regarding experiences and beliefs that relate to their development as existential-humanistic therapists. I also asked my participants to discuss their actual experiences in existential-humanistic training and practice. One significant difference between my work and Claypool's is that I left the identities of my subjects anonymous.

Ultimately, it was validating to learn that the sort of values and experiences elicited through Claypool's study—such as experience, psychological influences, and spirituality—were largely shared by the sample of practitioners I interviewed.

Most interesting, however, was that through these interviews I was able to shed light on how these values and experience directly correlated to existential-humanistic practice. For example, whereas Claypool was able to highlight how a spiritual sensibility was an essential element in the character of leading existential therapists, I was able to elicit insight about spirituality specifically as connected to the existential-humanistic therapeutic approach. I compiled data from my interviews and grouped such insights into six categories, as follows.

The Broad Value of the Existential–Humanistic Approach
All participants shared that the existential-humanistic approach had great value both in their treatment of clients and in their personal lives. When treating clients, participants emphasized that the characteristics of the existential-humanistic approach provided grounding to improve the effectiveness of various therapeutic modalities. This was described by one participant, a 69-year-old woman who had been practicing therapy for twenty years. About seven years ago, she started to take training courses to become an existential-humanistic therapist.

> Very few people are just only E-H practitioners. We're all a little bit eclectic, and we're all bringing in lots of other things. Often that E-H is the grounding. And so that grounding feels appropriate and helpful for anything. ... everybody needs that kind of connection... Everybody is still struggling with all these issues around meaning and how to connect with people and their choices. (Park, 2020, p. 65)

Participant G was a 55-year-old woman who had practiced existential-humanistic therapy for eight years. She discussed how the approach supported the treatment of a wide range of existential, physiological, and sociological conditions such as grief and loss, personality disorders, eating disorders, and family issues. She stressed that in addressing these, the existential themes, the ability to be present, the relationship to their selves, and their relationships with others are fundamental aspects of treatment.

More broadly, participants related how their existential-humanistic perspective offered them more than just a therapeutic approach, but also affected their whole lives. Participant B was a 46-year-old male with 14 years of practice as an existential-humanistic therapist. He shared that his interest in working with clients in an existential-humanistic way was sparked in his early career when he saw that his teenage clients at a group home were not treated in a humanistic way. He illustrated how devoted he became to spreading the essential qualities of the approach to other parts of his life.

> It's a lifestyle, I believe . . . Being a therapist is part of my existence and part of what I do with others. I want to continue to cultivate that, but I also want to cultivate other parts of my life. Being a genuine, authentic person, looking at growing. I see the E-H approach as really kind of a lifestyle . . . I think you're really living . . . it really embodies a lifestyle of commitment. (p. 67)

Participant F was a 62-year-old female with 14 years of practice as an existential-humanistic therapist. Before she became a therapist, she worked for years as a nurse in labor and delivery and neonatal intensive care. As a therapist, she was involved in a regional existential-humanistic organization and participated in their consultation group for years. Currently in private practice, she is deeply connected to the value of poetry and yoga to enhance her awareness. She described how the existential-humanistic approach is in sync with her life, impacting many aspects of her life in a meaningful way.

> After the first four or five years I think I was able to see that I was really, really drawn to this form of therapy. It didn't just relate to my therapy practice. It related very well and in sync with my entire life. The synchronicity with this philosophy, with the way that I choose to live, always trying to grow and learn,

> and be alive and present, and be open to change. There are so many aspects of it that worked for me. They are meaningful for me on a work level, and in my life level. (p. 68)

Personally, I was deeply moved to learn that participants related to the existential-humanistic approach as not just something to utilize in their practice, but a lifestyle that is directly connected to a sense of integrity and who they are. When a therapy approach becomes synced with one's lifestyle, involving the whole being of the person, the synergistic effect for personal and professional growth coming from that connection will be much greater than that of therapists who relate to their therapy approach as a simple choice of work.

Healing Through Presence
The second theme that emerged in my study is how participants value "healing through presence." Cultivation of presence is the most essential part of development as an existential-humanistic therapist, as it becomes the foundation for healing. All participants emphasized the importance of presence for healing to take place in their existential-humanistic practice.

Participant D was a 51-year-old man who had been practicing existential-humanistic therapy for ten years. He used to work in the field of horticulture and then began to develop an interest in therapy, which led him to graduate school to become a therapist. He took part in a training led by Myrtle Heery and also participated in training at the Existential–Humanistic Institute. He worked as a clinician at a day treatment clinic for people with severe mental illness and had a small case load at a private practice. He eloquently explained the process of his own presence mobilizing his patients' capacity to see and accept things, and how he uses this presence to treat individuals with persistent and severe mental illnesses:

> There's something about just learning how to, just the presence, like holding presence, holding space. Kind of holding that non-judgmental space. Just being able to listen to people, because that's sometimes all I can offer people... I ended up spending a number of years working with people with severe and persistent mental illness, which is what I mostly do now... I know for a lot of people that work is a lot about behavioral kind of work. But for me, it was always really learning about just how to hold space and just be present and just focus on the

> relationship. And yeah, being able to kind of look, not just see someone like, well the same with not just seeing someone as being homeless or seeing someone as being mentally ill, but just to actually make a connection with them. What I was able to offer often was just being able to be very patient and present, and actually have a connection with people. And that turns out to be offering a lot for people that are often very isolated and have a lot of difficulty making connections. (p. 69)

This perspective is especially notable considering that some therapists may be quick to focus on pharmacological and psychosocial interventions for patients who present severe mental illnesses. However, as this excerpt describes, there is clearly a place for therapeutic presence in the treatment of any patient.

Participant A explained the following steps she takes to provide fertile ground for healing to take place:

> [A]s you begin to re-establish your relationship in the moment, then these feelings of caring and of engagement and openness begin to come into it more... So if you can really meet the client in a deep space, I would call that the I–thou kind of presence. So presence isn't just one thing, there's different levels. But it has to do with kinds of attention and an openness and feeling and spiritual values, like valuing the client and their experience and caring and you can't just make those things happen, that has to come from who you are. (p. 70)

Considering the value of therapeutic presence, and the fact that developing such a presence—through values of existentialism, spirituality, and mindfulness—falls outside the scope of most traditional therapeutic approaches, it becomes clear that effective therapy calls for the sort of values, experience and methods that comprise the existential-humanistic approach.

Self-Growth

As was observed in Claypool's study, the participants I interviewed all shared that self-growth was very important in their journey to become an existential-humanistic therapist. They also identified their experience of being in personal therapy as an important component in their journeys. Interestingly, the participants I interviewed specifically identified their existential-humanistic training as an important factor in their development.

Self-growth took many forms. Several participants cited existential-humanistic workshops, and the challenges they posed in terms of interacting with people, being present, and getting feedback. They referred to various areas of growth that they pursued, including yoga, poetry, journaling, meditation, and getting in touch with nature. The participants stressed that these areas of growth were holistically related to how they connect with the world. Participant F illustrated this in her description of practicing yoga.

> ... I felt the way I grew significantly was through a practice of yoga. I think by going almost every day for 11 years, at six in the morning, something inside of me lined up different and it was extremely helpful in seeing, not seeing but having more awareness of the bigger world and the bigger cosmos of what part I might be in that, what little ripple I might be ... (p. 77)

Participant D stressed the importance of continued effort toward self-growth.

> ... I have a practice I do almost every morning. This is my personal practice. I either meditate or I journal. I do one or the other every morning...a lot of evenings...but I really spend some time before I go to bed just going through my feelings and trying to just be present, allow myself to feel difficult feelings...I like doing that kind of work, and I like being introspective, and I like working at hard things at myself and really challenging myself. And it turns out that that really helps me do my work better the more I do that, so it feels...It's how I increase my capacity to be of service to other people, is by really trying to keep growing and learning and also just taking care of myself. (p. 78)

It was fascinating to observe how each participant pursued growth and how that growth seemed to be integrated into their practices and their lives.

Value of Significant Relationships

The participants I interviewed cited how significant relationships with their mentors were central to their development as existential-humanistic practitioners. One described the influence his mentor had on him with the powerful analogy of a blacksmith, describing how aspects of his experience and character were melted down, molded, and hammered to create something new within himself and in his relationship with his mentor.

Another participant described how her work tended to be very creative and movement-centered, elements that didn't traditionally correspond to the family work she was doing. She expressed her appreciation that her mentor was empowering her to apply this creative approach.

> So I also specialized in marriage and family work ... And that work tends to be very creative. So using our bodies, moving around, doing a lot of those kinds of things. Using art for mediums, using writing and poetry. And Louis kind of showed me and kind of gave permission that that's a part that you can actually do and bring into the room ... and that is important. (p. 80)

For therapists, to experience a strong relationship with a mentor based on authenticity, humility, and empathy has a significant impact on their capacity to relate to their clients. My own mentor, Art, whom I discussed in the introduction to this chapter, mentioned that finding the right therapist is extremely important because seeing the right therapist can change one's whole life. In a similar way, it seems that finding the right mentor can change a therapist's life in their journey to become an existential–humanistic therapist.

Spirituality as Connected to the Existential–Humanistic Approach

Since my own spirituality of Buddhism has taken a central role in my journey to become an existential–humanistic therapist, I was especially excited to study how the theme of spirituality influenced the journeys of the participants I interviewed. One participant who has been engaged in spiritual practice for an extended period of time considers that people are normally in a "sleepwalking state of mind." She finds a lot of commonalities with the existential–humanistic approach:

> So I think that having had these 35 years of [spiritual] practice, of trying to know myself and to be with myself in the moment, to be present in my body, to be open to something higher or to the spiritual dimension, in an ordinary event ... All of those things are why I was drawn to E-H therapy, as a way to bring all those practices and values into my counseling. (p. 83)

As a spiritually inclined person, it is no surprise to me that spiritual values are revealed through all aspects of people's lives. In any case, the fact that the participants I interviewed so readily recognized these values suggests both something of their characters and their choice of this particular therapeutic approach.

Rewarding Work as a Therapist
One interesting theme that emerged from my interviews pertained to the rewarding aspects of working as an existential-humanistic therapist. One person described how the nature of the approach transformed hard work into very compelling activity:

> It changes it from work into something that's a really meaningful thing to do. I just find the clients so interesting and learning about the process that is going on. It is not like having a desk job in an office where you're adding up numbers. It is a place where you can be as real and authentic and present. (p. 85)

Participant B shared the profound value he places on being able to help people:

> I think when you've been able to connect with somebody in profound misery or suffering, and you've been able to connect with them and support them and attune to them or attend to them in a way which has helped them start to sort out their life and their experience and improve their quality of life, and to see that process unfold and people to move closer to the life they want to live, wow, that feels amazing to play a small part in. That's really beautiful. (p. 85)

This is important not only because of the sense of fulfillment on the part of the therapist, but also in the context of their ongoing work. Through their continuous effort to cultivate increased awareness of themselves and others, to connect, and to be attuned to existential and spiritual values, existential-humanistic therapists may be able to avoid "burning out" as might therapists who adhere to other approaches and who lack such resources.

After going through the findings of my study, it became clear that becoming an existential-humanistic therapist is a holistic process that involves the person of the therapist and their role as a therapist. These are closely interconnected for existential-humanistic therapists, and one informs the other. The findings show that the process of becoming an existential-humanistic therapist relies heavily on applying the value of the approach to the therapist's personal and professional life. This fosters a deep understanding of the healing power of presence; commitment to self-growth as a person as well as a therapist; meaningful relationships with mentors, supervisors, and family members; and a deep connection with a spirituality that shares common ground with the existential-humanistic approach. In the end, therapists find the journey to becoming existential-humanistic therapists as well as the therapeutic work to be highly rewarding.

A Comparison of the Two Studies
Both Claypool's (2010) study and my own (Park, 2020) examined the topic of the development of existential-humanistic therapists. Claypool concerned himself with the journeys of contemporary leaders in existential-humanistic psychology, while my study focused on the journeys of practicing existential-humanistic therapists.

Considering that the themes and methods of the studies were similar, it is not surprising that I uncovered significant common themes in both studies: an emphasis on presence (*ontological sensibility* in Claypool's study), self-growth (*commitment to personal growth* in Claypool's study), significant relationship with mentors, and spirituality (*spiritual sensibility* in Claypool's study).

At the same time, there are notable differences. Claypool reported that non-psychological influences such as philosophy and literature heavily influenced the shaping of existential-humanistic leaders at that time. In contrast, the therapists I studied did not note such an influence but, instead, highlighted the value therapists placed on having had rewarding experiences in their therapeutic work.

Another difference is Claypool's observation that values and experience in the lives of existential-humanistic leaders were particularly significant, while the therapists in my study stressed values and experience in the context of their specific therapeutic practice. For example, Claypool highlighted that presence was an important quality in the character of the seven existential-humanistic leaders, whereas those in my study only stressed presence in terms of its value as a healing component in the practice of therapy.

Such differences might emerge from the fundamental difference in design between Claypool's study, which aimed to understand the background and characters of established leaders, and mine, which aimed to examine the experience of practitioners of existential-humanistic therapy. Being in a different stage of their careers, and indeed, being at a different point in time with respect to established existential-humanistic literature could also have affected their outlooks. Even these differences do not represent sharp diversions. The two studies may be seen as complementary. With that in mind, both the convergent and divergent themes of the two studies provide support and validation that the journey to become an existential-humanistic therapist has a holistic nature, with fundamental themes that are shared among leaders and practitioners alike.

Reflections on the Journey of Existential-Humanistic Practitioners

From an early age I was attuned to existential sensibilities, sought happiness, and had a strong urge to help others. This has ultimately led me to pursue a career as a therapist. I was strongly drawn to existential-humanistic values and sought ways to better understand and practice it.

I am fortunate to have had the opportunity, presented through Claypool's research, to read of the experiences of leaders in the field of existential psychology. This illuminated essential elements that informed their character, perspectives, experience, and practice that, together, influenced their development. But reading Claypool's interviews only whetted my appetite; it made me curious as to the degree to which these elements were significant to a broader set of existential-humanistic therapists, and also how their values manifested themselves in the practice of actual therapy.

Ultimately, my study revealed to me that the practice of existential-humanistic psychology diverged from other therapeutic approaches in that it focuses on personal qualities embodied in the practitioner in order to engage and stimulate their clients' healing rather than relying on an intellectualized web of theory. These qualities include presence, mindfulness, existential awareness, and a striving for personal growth. Developing these qualities entails a sensitive education, connection with life experience, and recognition of spirituality or mystery.

As I was writing this chapter, I encountered my own existential fear of losing a loved one. At 3:00 in the morning, I had to bring my husband to the hospital emergency room. Leaving him there, I came back home with my children. After I comforted them back to sleep, I returned to writing this chapter. I was, of course, preoccupied. I was deeply aware of the fear of losing him and of concerns about how my life would be changed if he were to pass away. I was profoundly aware of my deep appreciation and love for him.

My husband was fine and came home after just a few hours, but I felt that my whole existence was shaken and awakened by this experience. I noticed that my capacity to be present in the moment was much more powerful than before. I believe this realization is connected to what Kirk Schneider (2009) refers to as the "awakening to awe"—a deeply significant recognition of the spirituality or mystery of being.

It is through the pursuit of such awakenings that leaders and practitioners of existential humanistic psychology aim to live more fully and help others to become freer. It is through the study of these people and how they pursue this objective that insight can be gained as to what qualities contribute to their ultimate success.

Ultimately, I see that the journeys of the leaders in existential-humanistic psychology and the practitioners in my study are closely aligned with my own journey. I deeply resonate with what I have learned through all the interviews and analysis. It is my hope that aspiring existential-humanistic therapists can gain valuable perspectives from these studies that will inspire and inform their own professional development.

References

Claypool, T. R. (2010). *On becoming an existential psychologist: The journeys of contemporary leaders* (Publication No. 3412340)[Doctoral dissertation, University of the Rockies]. Proquest Dissertations and Theses Global.

Greening, T., & Hobson, D. (1979). *Instant relief: The encyclopedia of self-help.*

Seaview Books.

Park, H. (2020). *The journey to become an existential-humanistic therapist* [Unpublished doctoral dissertation]. Saybrook University.

Schneider, K. J. (2009). *Awakening to awe: Personal stories of profound transformation.* Jason Aronson.

Serlin, I. A. (Ed.). (2007). *Whole person healthcare* (Vols. 1, 2, and 3). Praeger Publishers.

Chapter 2

Kirk Schneider's Path to Existential–Humanistic Psychology[1]

Kirk J. Schneider and Andrew M. Bland

Over the past 60 years, I have had the privilege of witnessing many poignant transformations. As a practicing psychologist, I have beheld them in state hospitals, in psychiatric emergency clinics, in drug and alcohol agencies, and in private practice; and as a youth, I experienced them in my own intensive psychotherapies. There is little "pretty" about these ordeals, but when they succeed, they are profoundly gratifying—life-changing.

Poignant transformations emerge from the depths of despair—but they result, if one is fortunate, in the heights of renewal. Certainly this was true for me and for many of the people I have known or worked with. What could be more precious than the gift of liberation from crippling despair, of being freed to pursue what deeply matters? What could be more critical than participating in—really grappling with—the rescue of one's soul?

Depth and existential therapy promote a hard-won coexistence between rivaling parts of ourselves—parts that sometimes agonize, yet in the long run shed light on the experience of being fully human, of being fully and richly alive. Put more formally, existential therapy emphasizes three major themes: (a) freedom to explore what deeply matters to oneself; (b) experiential or whole-bodied reflection on what deeply matters; and (c) responsibility or the ability to respond to, act on, and apply what deeply matters.

The depth psychologists and philosophers throughout history have

---

[1] Portions of this chapter are adapted from "The Awe of Being Alive" (Schneider, 2019) and from Schneider's contributions to *On Being a Master Therapist* (Kottler & Carlson, 2014). I also want to thank Andrew Bland for his superb collaboration on this chapter.

long centered on the holding of paradox as key to our individual and collective well-being (Schneider, 1990/1999). We might now say that the awe for life—for our smallness as well as greatness, our fragility as well as boldness—is one of the most enriching paradoxes that we can experience; it also is one of the most trying. Are we ready to grapple with such paradoxes in our everyday lives, within ourselves and among our fellow citizens? Are we ready to get out of our own way, to humble ourselves to the point of discomfort and open ourselves to the point of intrigue or even amazement at what we may learn? Are we ready to really "hear" and enable the contrasting voices within and without, to let them jostle and tumble about in order to—just possibly—find conciliation in those voices, a new synthesis that could expand and deepen our view?

When I work with a client, I see myself more as a fellow traveler, as the existential analyst Irv Yalom put it, rather than the formal "doctor" serving up a remedy. I attempt to be available as a person rather than an engineer; I attune to the needs of my human client, not to a bundle of electrochemical processes or a diagnostic label. That does not mean I will not try to support that client in whatever way might be helpful at any given time—for example, with a medical referral or a problem-solving strategy. But I will strive to be available to them at the most immediate, profound level of contact possible to address the feelings, body sensations, and images behind their words and explanations. All this involves attention to process, not just content. The approach supports a "whole-bodied" awareness of both what a client desires, as well as what blocks them from what is desired on the deepest of levels, often beyond words. In this way, any decision emerging from the therapy is energized by the whole body and that client's visceral core.

Not every client can or wants to work at that level, which explains my existential-*integrative* offering; but for those who can and do, the approach provides the opportunity for a life-changing shift. This shift bolsters one's capacity to experience the fuller ranges of one's thoughts, feelings, and sensations—one's whole-body encounter with life. Based on that foundation, it is possible to make bold, concrete, meaningful changes in one's life. Put another way, such clients are able to cultivate a deep and abiding presence for themselves and the world—and through that presence, to experience humility, wonder, and a sense of adventure toward living. This sense, for those who can really live it, fosters meaning and poignancy. It is the experience of life's paradoxes—the sliver of fear in a loving relationship, or the hint of sorrow in a moment of glee, or the taste of envy in the most admiring friendships—

Becoming an Existential–Humanistic Therapist

that lends life its zest, its pathos, and its intensity: its awe.

As discussed more in what follows and as a client in therapy myself, I have moved from positions of abject terror to gradual intrigue, to wonder about my life circumstances. For example, I have shifted from paralysis before the unpredictability of fate, to incremental trust, to curiosity, to fascination with what might be discovered, and to a growing capacity to love. Through their abiding presence, my therapists supported me to feel safe enough to face my inner battle. They "held a mirror" for me to see "close up" both how I was currently living as well as how I could live should I gradually step out of my cramped-yet-familiar world. These experiences proved integral to my attraction to existential-humanistic psychology.

Kirk with his Mother

I

I was born under hypnosis[2] on July 27, 1956, to astute, psychologically

---

[2] As far as I can gather, my mother was one of the few women to undergo this unique form of delivery, particularly for the 1950s. When I asked her about the process, she told me that, all things considered, it was quite pleasurable, and that the hypnotic

minded parents. I grew up in the Italian-German working-class neighborhood of Euclid, Ohio, a suburb of Cleveland, until I was nine; we were the only Jewish family in the vicinity. My father was a humanistic educator—a math and science teacher-turned-professor of education. He also was very philosophical, completed his dissertation on creativity in kids, and immersed himself in writings by E. Paul Torrance, Frank Barron, Abe Maslow, Carl Rogers, and Rollo May. Further, he wrote some unpublished essays on the psychological rigidity of conventional society and of parenting that stifled creativity and discovery in children and adults. My paternal line derived from Jewish priests, and my great-grandfather was apparently a *rebbe* (as noted on my grandfather's gravestone), a Jewish spiritual teacher or rabbi who may have been a mystic in Eastern Europe. Very little is known about my grandfather except that he probably immigrated from Russia, ran a malt and hops store in Brooklyn, and may have had some run-ins with the law. He died of a massive heart attack at age 39. Both my paternal uncle and my father also died the same way at ages 51 and 53, respectively. These upheavals had a major impact on my approach to life in that they taught me that I needed to not take life for granted, to "think outside the box," and to do all I can to live out the existential-humanistic sensibility toward "freedom" as distinct from fatalism (see May, 1981).[3]

My mother had a high school education and some college but was very bright and ambitious. She specialized in fashion design and then worked her way to become one of the top television spokespersons in Cleveland, landing jobs doing television commercials (a few of which I had the privilege to participate in, such as Smucker's jelly and Oscar Meyer Weiner—which was a surreal experience for a seven- or eight-year-old kid!). She also became the chief spokesperson for the Cleveland Illuminating Company and did radio programs for a CBS affiliate in Cleveland. My maternal grandfather (from a small town outside Kiev) was an extraordinarily self-educated plumber. His main area of interest was world history, and he fervently read the

---

induction appeared to work. On the other hand, whether or not the induction worked on me to date is up to readers to decide!

[3] On a practical level, I radically shifted my diet to plant-based, pursued a holistic path toward health and healing, and became much more proactive about self-care than I believe my forebears in their time could find the resources to practice effectively. I feel extremely fortunate to live in an era during which both conventional and holistic approaches to healthcare can have such positive effects, *if* one is willing—and has the means, of course—to engage them.

international journal *Foreign Affairs*. My maternal grandmother was a warm, vivacious, and socially active person who also had immigrated from Ukraine.

As sometimes happens with transformative experiences, the awe for life began for me with a tragedy, like a boulder smashing through a window. My earliest memory is a gauzy image of my parents weeping on the living room couch. I was two-and-a-half years old, and my seven-year-old brother Kelly had just died. It was 1959, and the combination of chicken pox and pneumonia proved too much for an otherwise radiant and vigorous child. The explosion of this event in the collective psyche of our family cannot be intellectually grasped. The most I can say is that the parents I knew before the event were dimly recognizable in its crushing aftermath. The warm and playful sibling I knew—the smiling leader—was vanquished, and in his place yawned a gaping void; a pit of rage, sorrow, and terror.

I had no idea what hit me. I was imploding. My defenses were all but expired. All I knew was that my parents were sobbing, my brother was gone, and life before and after were like night and day. This upending of reality threw me into a tailspin—a helpless and paranoid world. I wet my bed constantly, I had night terrors (images of witches and demons in my window), I went on crying jags for what seemed like days, and I threw temper tantrums to the point where I kicked my mother in the mouth once and she lost a tooth. At about four years old, I was in such dire shape that I seemed to be losing touch with consensual reality. My world was filled with monsters, I was horrified of germs, and death seemed ever-looming. At this point, I was much closer to terror toward life than awe.

Distraught as they were, my parents did all they could to talk me through my battles and, eventually, when I was five, they had the foresight and sense of urgency to refer me to a child psychoanalyst, Edwin Schiff. Dr. Schiff helped me to turn my life around; for although I continued to have profound fears and outbursts, he helped me to work through rather than mask over these potentially restorative maladies. Greatest of all, he was a rock-solid presence who enabled me to say or feel anything. I was hanging on by a thread, but he remained a pillar—steadfast and supportive—until I passed through the storm. His calmness and steadiness gave me a base from which to feel calmer and steadier myself. His ability to be present to me helped me to be more present to myself, to glimpse that I could survive the most horrific fears. Gradually, I began to feel safer to open up to my therapist and to my parents. I began to feel a freedom well up in me, a sense that I could step back, collect my breath, and see more to my circumstances than absolute destruction and death. Dr. Schiff challenged me to develop inner resources such as my creativity, curiosity, and imagination. He encouraged me to reflect on the bases for my fears and to move at my own pace. He respected me and my capacities, which in turn spurred me to create drawings, stories, and thoughts about life's puzzlements or to venture out into uncertain terrains, relationships, and ideas, which I eventually did after much tussling and even further therapy.

As I reflect on it, Dr. Schiff's presence helped me to enter a dimension that was bigger and more powerful than even death. This was the dimension of mystery. I realized that mystery eclipsed death because it is beyond anything that could be said or even felt about the state of being human. Mystery was the vast unknown, and the more that I learned to open to the unknown, the less I became paralyzed by fears and fantasies arising from my known world—the world of crying parents, helplessness, bodily threats, and radical changes in my environment.

II

These realizations led me to look at scary movies with some degree of fascination instead of just paralyzing fright. It was soon after that I became increasingly intrigued with science fiction and horror books and films. We had a horror show host in Cleveland who was very popular with kids. His name was Ghoulardi; he was like a mesmerizing beatnik, with a very funny beard and all kinds of skeletons, posters of monsters, and a lit-up face on a dimly lit set. His Friday night thriller movies sparked my interest in sci-fi and horror (most of it was campy but some was very fascinating—unveiling creative and imaginative characters, story lines, and monsters). I recall, for example, being petrified by a late-night horror film called *The Cyclops* when I was about seven years old. That night, I was so braced by fear that I tore out of my friend's house where I watched the film and ran straight back to my house, about a block away. The wind was whipping and the air was frigid as I dashed with my heart racing. The houses I passed looked downright evil, especially the one on the corner, with its peeling paint and dark windows. That was a traumatizing episode for me in many ways—which is partly why I recall it so vividly—and yet I felt a thrill about the episode, too. There was something of the fantastic about it, and my venture into the inky midnight air, the sense of something chasing me, stirred me to wonder what that "monster" might know or reveal.

I had many such admixtures of fear and fascination walking up and down my street, looking at the puzzling houses, gnarled trees, and blowing leaves, particularly in the evening or when charmed by a fairy tale or a show about the supernatural. What comes to mind are the many science fiction shows I watched, from *The Outer Limits* to *The Twilight Zone* to *One Step Beyond* (a serial about the paranormal), and the chills-yet-thrills they brought to my awakening consciousness about life and the world.

The theme that united many of these shows was a theme that united many of the facets of my psychological healing: a realization that the "alien" or "threat" or "monster" that appeared to be jeopardizing humanity (or my personal survival) was more like a messenger to an expanded consciousness. It was more like a shadowy guide unveiling a crisis that eventually might lead to a renewed understanding of life, the universe, or the unknown. Such stories and flights of fancy also led me to immerse myself in a rich fantasy world of self-created plays, stories, and a whole stable of movie characters that I would create scenes for during my playtime. By junior high, I was fascinated by short stories such as those by Edgar Allen Poe, whom I attempted to emulate with an outpouring of short stories of my own.

I was jarred by scary movies, and yet they opened me to alternative approaches to life, future possibilities, and my own imagination (see my later work in this area, *Horror and the Holy* [1993], as well as a chapter titled *From Despair and Fanaticism to Awe: A Post-traumatic Growth Perspective on Cinematic Horror* [2013]). This emerging perspective manifested in my increasing fascination with science fiction and creative play.

III

This era was the early 1960s, and although World War II had long ceased and the state of Israel was an inspiration to many, there was still a fair amount of bigotry in our neighborhood, and it showed up for me in a range of unnerving forms. One morning when I was about eight, my parents and I woke up to a shocking sight. An enormous black swastika was painted on our ping pong table hanging in the garage. This was the prod for one of many discussions—especially with my dad—about racism, antisemitism, and social justice. On several nightmarish occasions, I was chased, bullied, and beaten for being Jewish (a "Christ killer," "Kike," etc.) as well as just for being a sensitive, "different" kid. We had "greasers" and leather-clad motorcycle gangs in or near the neighborhood. Sometimes they also wore big, vintage crosses of the German military. I admired these characters in a strange way and certainly took notice of their girlfriends, but I was also terrified of them and astounded by their power, or what I took to be power.

There was also a time at about age seven when I crossed over to the "dark side" with the bullies and even bigots. Despite being reared on in-depth conversations about prejudice, politics, and "healthy societies," I buckled under and joined the hateful masses. A turning point in my life was the time I gave in to peer pressure and joined a gang of neighborhood kids who stalked a boy of color who had an intellectual disability. I remember actually liking the kid and having sympathy for him because he was often picked on by callous peers. Yet here I was, one of those callous kids myself, chasing him down the street, calling him names and generally threatening him. I lost my conscience and all I had been taught by my socially conscious parents that afternoon. How this happened I am not quite sure, as it was quite out of character for me. But it was most likely because I got particularly scared on that day—scared to oppose the crowd, the power of the tyrannical mind, the solace of conformity.

In the middle of that abomination, my father abruptly ran up to me, pulled me out of the crowd, and spanked me hard for several seconds. This was extremely rare (one of maybe two times he did this), as my parents practiced distinctly humanistic parenting skills, enabling me abundant room to express myself and to work through my own follies. But that afternoon was different, and my dad responded in kind; I emphasize "responded" here because he didn't just react or explode. He made me aware of how serious my transgression was, urging me to consider what it might have been like if I were the one chased. I never forgot that incident, which remains emblazoned in my conscience. It became the springboard to an ongoing conversation about the toxicity of prejudice and how we cut ourselves off from ourselves as much as from others in the process of debasing others. These ideas were already astir in our family environment growing up, but they became core, at least for me, from that time on.

Yet, for all its alien "otherness," much of my experience of that neighborhood was life-affirming. Although there were kids to emphatically avoid, there were also several with whom I had a great time. This group continually played in the street together and on small but trimmed lawns or in empty lots. We chased the ice cream truck together on sweltering summer days, met for Saturday afternoon movies, made up our own skits, flipped baseball cards, joined in neighborhood cookouts, played football and baseball, ventured into the woods, etc.

I also had the chance to discover the charms of Christmas. My best friend had a tree every year, and I remember how fun it was to see presents around it and to hear the Christmas stories. *A Christmas Carol* was one of my favorites, and I have a vivid memory of watching it with friends and at school. Christmas songs and television specials also had a spark for me. Here, again, was an illustration of the difference between abstract categories for the "other" (in this case, Christians) and details "on the ground"—engaging living people, ideas, and actions. I also learned that Christianity could be about love and generosity as much as rejection and bullying.

My parents *talked to me* and opened me to the bigger picture of life. They used stories such as *Zorba the Greek* and *The Wizard of Oz* and, later, films such as *To Kill a Mockingbird* and *Twelve Angry Men* as object lessons in recognizing the humanity in marginalized people and the integrity it takes to open to that humanity. Slowly, I began to see the many-sidedness of the people in my neighborhood and how, through talking, sports, and sharing holidays, we could find some wondrous qualities in one another.

IV

I became an average student in school—in some ways regressed and emotionally reticent, probably due to my early traumas—but I loved *certain* school events. These almost always related either to the arts or to sports. I loved field trips to the Cleveland Museum of Art and to Severance Hall to see our local orchestra. I also loved art class, social studies, and, to some extent, English—and by high school I excelled in these classes. I also loved running around and exploring the outdoors. I loved raw contact with nature, whether it was body surfing, skiing, or playing football in the mud and snow. I also loved to travel—especially to big cities like New York, from which my father and his family hailed and where he took us often.

I also had a very earthy, independent-minded uncle from New York who helped raise my dad. Uncle Henry was a very philosophical, loquacious vegetarian and health-minded bachelor—ahead of his time in some ways, but rather stifled when it came to intimate relationships. Still, he was a legend in our family, very good with my cousins and me, taking us to Coney Island, movies, and many sights in NYC. He also was a staunch liberal and humanist with socialist leanings. His life philosophy also seemed to fuel his longevity and vitality right up to his death at about 90—just two or three years after his last rounds of jogging on the beach and playing handball. Uncle Henry was an important link in my intellectual and humanistic lineage that emanated from the streets of New York to my dad and to a life of inquiry.

When I was ten, by that time living in Shaker Heights, my parents divorced. As I understand it, they basically were unsuited for each other from the time they got married when she was 18 and he was 22. It was a major blow, but I remember them sitting me down in our car and informing me, through my tears, in a very mature and straightforward way. They were especially clear that the divorce had nothing whatever to do with me and that it was for the best for each of us in the long run. This had some logic because I did see them bicker and to some degree devalue each other's outlooks and ways of doing things.

The 1960s had a largely liberating influence on my dad—and this impacted me, as well. I would visit him every week for an overnight, and we would often take long walks and have extensive, philosophically stimulating conversations or see movies together and talk them over. We would also take long drives and vacations together—especially to New York, the ocean, and other places along the Eastern seaboard. As I became an adolescent, we also sometimes went to discos together and met girls or women in our respective age groups—although Dad tended to pursue women distinctly younger than himself, and he prided himself on being a youthful 40-plus-year-old. He could pass as a handsome, athletic guy who was very active in sports as a young man. I am sure all this context related to some degree to the glamour, as I saw it, of the then-new humanistic psychology with its stress on mind, body, and spirit.

I should also mention that Dad was a strict atheist till the end of his life when he was beginning to acknowledge a kind of spiritual dimension. We even had some friendly arguments about this, as I became increasingly identified with spiritually oriented romantics and existentialists (such as R. D. Laing), whereas he remained a fairly staunch rationalist and secularist (like Carl Rogers and Albert Ellis). I just felt that the mystery of life, its untamable depths, beckoned for an inquiry that folks like Laing as well as Otto Rank, Paul Tillich, and Rollo May began to pioneer in psychology (for an elaboration, see Schneider, 1998).

I must admit that sometimes my Dad and I got a little reckless with our ventures. At age 15, in the face of a driving rainstorm, I almost drowned off the coast of Virginia Beach. Undaunted by the rain that day—as well as reports of a hurricane about 50 miles off the coast—Dad and I plunged gleefully into the surf. But that surf turned out to be treacherous, and while Dad prudently hovered near shore, I took a few more strides into deeper water. In a matter of minutes, I found myself besieged by waves, which crashed all about me. There simply was no direction to these waves, and the harder I fought, the more I got pulled into the maelstrom. I tried calling to Dad, who was by that time markedly anxious about me, but was incapable of getting past the wild surf that separated us. Finally, thankfully, I remembered a skill that I learned in swim class, which was to attempt to relax, take some deep breaths, and curl myself into a ball, à la the "jelly fish" position. This enabled me to regain some energy and go with the waves for a brief period until I could figure out what to do. Then it struck me. I'm a good diver, and so I plunged head-first under the waves, dove as deeply as I could, and used every ounce of my strength to stroke my way to the shore.

I should also mention in connection with the above that I became a fairly decent swimmer. I joined several swim clubs and swam for my junior high and high school swim teams. I also became a water safety instructor or lifeguard at a local Jewish Community Center. I find the swimming relevant because I learned strict discipline and concerted persistence given the miles of laps we swam per day in high school, both at 7:00 a.m. and again after school. Through these Spartan regimens, I learned the value of intensive exercise and conditioning, and such routines have informed my later graduate years and tough slogs in mental hospitals and clinics as well as academic and professional writings (13 authored and co-authored books and over 200 articles, chapters, and essays). This background in sports also gave me a deeper sense of community and colleagueship that has contributed significantly to my interest in and engagement with many aspects of my existential-humanistic therapy training and professional affairs. Again, the development of my capacity to be present and to "stay with" the challenges was core.

V

As I moved toward university, I became increasingly interested in being a creative writer, a philosopher, and a psychologist. My first semester at Ohio University (OU) in Athens, Ohio—where I ultimately majored in psychology and minored in philosophy—was a mind-blowing affirmation of that disposition. I met a magnetic philosophy graduate student my first or second day in fall of 1974. He spent about seven hours with me at a local McDonald's (of all places!) informing me about the existential greats Kierkegaard and Nietzsche, along with copious references to related writers and thinkers. Soon after, I began reading Maurice Friedman's (1964) *The Worlds of Existentialism* and Rollo May's (1958) *Existence*. I pursued them with zeal, and I regarded my early time at the university as a true wonderland of intellectual inquiry. I relished my walks around campus as well as several of my classes.

It is hard to describe my exhilaration with academic life at this time and how much it propelled me to write. I kept copious notes for future articles and potential books, along with a journal of dreams and reflections. (I have accumulated some 17 or 18 journals in my life and continue with them to this day). I was profoundly energized by my introductory psychology and philosophy professors at OU; they brought the subjects alive, showed how they mattered, and made them relevant to my own and others' lives. I also started reading Herman Hesse at the time, and books such as *Steppenwolf* (Hesse, 1927/1963) and *Demian* (Hesse, 1919/1969) struck at my core. It was essentially a magical time for me—a time of profound intellectual, emotional, and relational growth. I loved meeting women of similar inclinations and exploring sexual and romantic possibilities. I also became very close with a male friend, Jeff Bricker, who was a philosophy major and superlative student of Zen as well as of Henry David Thoreau. Jeff and I would talk philosophy for hours in our shared laundry room in the dorm, and two years later we backpacked through Europe together, which was one of the greatest journeys of my life. We visited eight countries, had many hikes and adventures, and stayed at youth hostels at a buck a night. We even spent a night on a mountain in Switzerland, which we had to abandon because we became so cold in the middle of the night. It was the summer of 1976, and much came up for me about the gifts as well as the challenges of our democratic way of life. I devoted an entire journal to that 50-day trip.

All these experiences increased my desire to become a humanistic and existential psychologist. I was very fortunate to know this from the start of my undergraduate career. I should also mention that as I experienced the rewards of a holistic lifestyle—a life of depth and meaning—I became increasingly skeptical of conventional culture and psychology. My father's openness and personal frustrations with the culture, particularly in terms of the rote and mechanical approaches of educational institutions, not least childrearing practices, was certainly an influence. In fact, he was so open that he gave me permission to conduct a brief (maybe 45 minutes) "psychoanalysis" on him during one of my early psychology classes. And it was through that analysis, along with other conversations we had, that I learned how he felt stifled not only because of social conventions but also because of his own personal trauma, having lost his father at age five. This realization about my dad spurred me all the more to pursue humanistic psychology and to attempt as best I could to go full bore into my life and career.

VI

The next major influence on my career path in existential-humanistic psychology concerned my revered professor, Bob Masek, at West Georgia College (WGC), where I completed master's studies. Bob took a liking to me, and I to him, but when he encouraged me to take an internship at a local mental hospital, I began to become anxious. This, in combination with being 22—very far away from my Cleveland home, having just visited with my dad and his new girlfriend (a year older than me), and having just watched a terrifying movie called *Magic*—led me into a deeper state of unease. And as if that weren't enough, seeing a horrifying note on my car saying that I would soon die and feeling emotionally raw from the remarkable psychospiritual discoveries I was making in the extraordinary humanistic psychology program at WGC—along with unfinished business from earlier traumas—set me off on what I could only call a nervous breakdown. It all began one late December night, and it felt like the roof caved in. I started experiencing major night terrors, early morning tremors, and a fear that I was going psychotic. I did actually experience frightening and intrusive thoughts as well as perceptual illusions at the time, but fortunately I had the wherewithal to realize that I was experiencing these things.

This turbulence led me to the psychoanalytically oriented existential therapist Ann Gustin (based on the referral of a deeply intuitive blind student in my class, Debbie Hazelton. You could say that Debbie fit the archetype of the "blind seer" because she was one). Ann was probably the most important healing influence in my life up to that time, and perhaps ever since. My nine-month-long "journey" with Ann was as life-changing as that which I experienced with Edwin Schiff when I was five, and the most important quality it taught me was to "stay with myself," no matter how turbulent the "storms."

Looking back, I view both therapies as lifesaving in some way. I'm sure I internalized these sensitive yet profound and supportive relationships that subsequently helped me to simply cope, and then a few years later, actually enabled me to become turned on by—fascinated with—the bigger questions of life. Back and forth I swung between terror and wonder; from quailing apprehension to incremental intrigue toward that which horrified; and from social withdrawal to energizing risks with my therapists and the world-at-large. Consequently, I was able to experience the fuller ranges of my thoughts, feelings, and sensations. I, like many of the people I have worked with, was freed to attain goals but also a greater presence to my life and to life itself. The result was that I became less identified with the old and crippling parts of life and more identified with the new and evolving parts—the parts that deeply mattered. The key to my own therapy, and indeed to depth-existential therapy as a whole, is that it supports the coexistence of emotional and intellectual contraries. I loved and I hated at the same time; I was terrified of death, and yet I was intrigued by its mystery, by the mystery of life.

While my transformation took a sustained period of time, of course, it taught me tremendously about the power of presence to heal—both from the standpoint of my therapist and what I learned to mobilize within. That therapy gifted me an inner freedom that cannot be measured or even articulated in words; it was simply felt and expressed in ways for which I have boundless gratitude. From that profound experience, I felt maximally liberated—not just intellectually, but with my whole bodily being—to pursue my humanistic theory/therapy interests, as well as my life, with as few undue barriers as possible.

It also freed me to work tirelessly on the writings and themes that had long entranced me—culminating in my first major article in the *Journal of Humanistic Psychology* in the mid-1980s, on Kierkegaard's "absolute paradox" and its relevance to clinical theory and to life (Schneider, 1986). That publication, as well as my discovery of Ernest Becker's work (Schneider, 2015), led to the book *The Paradoxical Self* (Schneider, 1990/1999), the premise of which can be detected throughout the entire corpus of my professional writing. The therapy with Ann also helped center me enough to be able to meet and work with some of the most remarkable scholars and indeed founders in our field. In addition to the deepening of my relationship with Bob Masek, I also came to know and work closely with his colleagues Don Rice and Mike Arons at WGC and eventually Stan Krippner, Rollo May, and Jim Bugental at Saybrook University, where I earned my doctorate. I really cannot underestimate the role that these mentors have played in my life.

Bob Masek, as I noted earlier, inspired me in some difficult and unnerving ways, but he also provided a banquet of psycho-philosophy through his teachings on existential-phenomenology, the British school of psychoanalysis, Merleau-Ponty, and the phenomenology of projective testing. Don Rice, another charismatic professor and former student of Stan Krippner, had just returned from a fellowship with R. D. Laing when I met him during my first semester at WGC. Don was also a graduate of the Humanistic Psychology Institute (now Saybrook University) and regaled me with his inspiring stories of having worked with Rollo May and Jim Bugental. I became (and remain) quite close with Don, who brought humanism to every facet of his teaching and life, so far as I could gather, and he gave me my first opportunity as a teaching assistant. He also held wonderful seminars on folks like Laing, Alan Watts, parapsychology, and multiculturalism, several of them in his and his wife Cheryl's welcoming home. Mike Arons, then chair of the psychology department at WGC, was also a creative and inspiring figure. Although I didn't get to know Mike as well as others I mention here, I took some fabulous seminars with him on French philosophy, depth psychology, and experiential group process. Having been a protégé and colleague of Abe Maslow, who recommended Mike as founder of the humanistic psychology orientation at WGC, Mike would pepper us with anecdotes about Abe, as well as works that evoked the heart of the humanistic vision.

I met Stanley Krippner one of my first days attending the Humanistic Psychology Institute in San Francisco. I became Stan's secretary as a work-study student in the early 1980s and gained a wealth of insights into everything from Stan's prodigious work output, to his superlative standards for writing and speaking, to his entrancing ventures into the worlds of altered states of consciousness, indigenous healing, and parapsychology. Stan even introduced me to the Grateful Dead's Mickey Hart and to Lucas Ranch, the famed compound of the film director George Lucas, where, thanks to the graces of Stan, I gave a lunchtime talk.

Jim Bugental and his wife, Elizabeth, were my core clinical mentors; I spent three years with them as my supervisors. Rollo May was my spiritual-philosophical mentor who also invited me to write a book with him (*The Psychology of Existence*; Schneider & May, 1995). It was they who helped me develop the tools to organize my thinking about therapy in a way that has been extremely valuable both to my professional development as a writer and teacher, as well as to my practical development as a clinician. Hence my belief that procuring a quality mentor and confidant is key to taking the raw material of personal therapy and marshaling it into a viable and cohesive therapeutic career.

Advice for Novices

I have been told that my gentle and respectful disposition, my soothing voice, and my appreciation for clients' hidden or shameful inner lives are significant for their willingness and ability to heal—or to put it in more professional parlance, for their capacity to become more integrated within themselves. For therapists to be (comparatively) centered or aligned within themselves, for them to experience an "inner home" to which they can return as needed, and for them to genuinely clear a space to provide the kind of healing that they themselves have undergone are all foundational for the work. This ideal does not preclude other more visible qualities such as intelligence, a professional and stable demeanor, and a knowledgeable skill set. But it means that those latter traits have become integrated in such a way as to have become "second nature" to therapists' overall approach, and certainly secondary to the prime qualities of a humane and present disposition. I know that Rollo May used to say that he rarely chose analytic training candidates for how good they looked on paper (e.g., for their grades or fine clothing), but on the basis of how much they seemed to have struggled in their own lives and whether they seemed to have come to a place of acceptance or appreciation for that struggle and the courage that is needed to face it in the here and now. I look for similar dispositions in those I train, or I help students work with those dispositions. From my own experience, it is vitally important to sense that therapists have somehow "been there" with clients—not in exactly the same place, but in a parallel place—and have found ways to work their way through. But this attainment should always come with profound humility. It should ever be attended by the acute realization that life can tear one down at any moment and that the best we can do is to draw on that realization by savoring the moments of our aliveness—our *possibilities*—while they are here.

There is simply no easy way around one's own "down and dirty" grappling with inner demons if a therapist is to provide the kind of care that is demanded by the deepest client struggles. This realization also highlights a growing problem with the kinds of training that are increasingly offered in our country. Such trainings tend to be overly focused on the mastery of techniques and woefully under-focused on trainees' own tumultuous lives, their own capacities to discover a "home" within those lives so that they can offer that template to others in profound distress. This means that we need more training that focuses on experiential (i.e., immediate, affective, and kinesthetic) aspects of therapy transactions as well as more focus on experiential forms of personal therapy for the candidates.

Rollo May once urged: learn everything you can about clinical psychology, therapeutic skills, and professional management, and then leave it at the office door the moment you greet your client. I resonate with much of this and would only repeat that it is critical to engage in your own personal, experiential therapy to provide a staging ground to facilitate such work (or work that is comparable) with a client.

Demand, therefore, that such therapy be provided. Try also to realize that in early stages of training there is likely to be much confusion, much fumbling for "getting it right," etc. That's a natural part of the learning process, and I see it all the time with my students. But also try to bear in mind that you are developing—and need to develop—your own organic style and that the fumbling will likely diminish in time and much will become second nature. But this leads to a third axiom, that practice (like in so many fields) is essential—and if you wish to become really accomplished, you need to avail yourself of as many quality training opportunities as possible, ideally with master experientially oriented therapists (Kottler & Carlson, 2014).

Also, learn to engage life. In my experience, becoming an excellent depth-experiential therapist is inseparable from living in a depth-experiential, awe-informed manner. Learn the classics and grapple with them. I think trainees as well as professional therapists need to spend a great deal more time with the arts and humanities, both in their schooling as well as in their avocational life. These are the realms that also help to sensitize therapists to the great therapeutic teachings of the past as well as present; for these teachings can sensitize, deepen, and inform all who heal. Finally, live life as fully and vitally as possible. Take up writing, painting, playing, contemplating, and loving. But don't do these things just to become an optimal therapist. Let your inner optimal therapist become a byproduct of your passion for life—or at the least, let the two inform and enhance each other. That's the best advice I can give.

Heading into the Future

As a coda, I just want to add that I am hopeful about the prospects of existential-humanistic therapy in the future. I don't know if it will continue to be called by that name, but I do know that there are surges of interest in existential-humanistic trends. Among these are the "I–Thou" relationship (Buber, 2000/1958), existential-integrative therapy, the spirituality of awe, and the application of existential theory to social problems. My hope is that readers of this chapter will take up the mantle in these areas and beyond; for abounding inquiry and enlarged vision have long been among existential-humanism's most treasured qualities.

References

Buber, M. (2000). *I and thou* (R. G. Smith, Trans.) Scribner Classics. (Original work published 1958)

Friedman, M. (1964). *The worlds of existentialism: A critical reader.* Random House.

Hesse, H. (1963). *Steppenwolf* (B. Creighton, Trans.). Bantam. (Original work published 1927)

Hesse, H. (1969). *Demian.* Bantam. (Original work published 1919)

Kottler, J., & Carlson, J. (2014). *On being a master therapist: Practicing what you preach.* Wiley.

May, R. (1958). The origins and significance of the existential movement in psychology. In R. May, E. Angel & H. F. Ellenberger (Eds.), *Existence: A new dimension in psychiatry and psychology* (pp. 3–36). Basic.

May, R. (1981). *Freedom and destiny.* Norton.

Schneider, K. J. (1986). Encountering and integrating Kierkegaard's absolute paradox. *Journal of Humanistic Psychology, 26*(3), 62–80. https://doi.org/10.1177/0022167886263005

Schneider, K. J. (1993). *Horror and the holy: Wisdom-teachings of the monster tale.* Open Court.

Schneider, K. J. (1998). Toward a science of the heart: Romanticism and the revival of psychology. *American Psychologist, 53*(3), 277–289. https://doi.org/10.1037/0003-066X.53.3.277

Schneider, K. J. (1999). *The paradoxical self: Toward an understanding of our contradictory nature.* Humanity. (Original work published 1990)

Schneider, K. (2013). From despair and fanaticism to awe: A post-traumatic growth perspective on cinematic horror. In J. Greenberg and D. Sullivan (Eds.) *Death in classic and contemporary film* (pp. 217–229). Pallgrave-Macmillan.

Schneider, K. J. (2015). My journey with Kierkegaard: From the paradoxical self to the
polarized mind. *Journal of Humanistic Psychology, 55*(4), 404-411. https://doi.org/10.1177%2F0022167814537889

Schneider, K. J. (2019, November 12). The awe of being alive. *Aeon.* https://aeon.co/essays/to-feel-the-awe-of-living-learn-to-live-with-terror-and-wonder

Schneider, K. J., & May, R. (1995). *The psychology of existence: An integrative, clinical perspective.* McGraw-Hill.

Chapter 3

My Existential Journey

Lisa Xochitl Vallejos

When I look back now, it seems as though the path to my becoming an existential-humanistic therapist was inevitable. If ever anything was fated, this was it.

I knew when I was very young that I would be a helper. It was innate in me; friends would confess their secrets to me in middle school and I would get them help. At the age of 13, I watched *Silence of the Lambs* and decided then that I would become a psychologist and someday work for the Federal Bureau of Investigation. Only the first half of that came true but I often marvel that, at such a tender age, I knew without doubt what I wanted to be when I grew up.

In the first class of my master's degree program, theories of counseling, my instructor made the recommendation that we read a book called *The Gift of Therapy* by Irvin Yalom (2002). I jotted it in my notebook and, when the weekend arrived, went in search of the book. I found it, grabbed some chipotle, a blanket, and some water, and parked myself in a quiet space under a tree. I started reading, and kept reading, and kept reading until the sun was creeping down and I started to get cold. I gathered my stuff, went home and continued to read. I finished the book that weekend, and when I was done, I was as clear as I had been when I was 13. I wasn't going to be just any old kind of therapist. I was going to be a therapist like Dr. Yalom. I didn't fully know what existentialism was, but when my peers were declaring their theoretical orientation as eclectic, I was fully committed to becoming an existential-humanistic therapist.

As I am prone to do, I became obsessive in my search to learn about this new passion. I purchased all of Yalom's books and devoured them—and when he named other existentialists, I bought their books, too. I purchased *Existential Psychotherapy* (Yalom, 1980) and, along with my trusty dictionary, began trying to understand the world of existential thinking. Sometimes it was really easy and I felt confident. Sometimes it was really hard and I felt completely out of my depth.

I was a first-generation college student and, although I was a voracious reader as a youth, I'd not been introduced to philosophy or much classic literature, so I had a lot to learn. When Yalom would reference ancient philosophers, I would feel a wince of shame that I recognized names and nothing more. I had no idea what he was talking about at times, and I would think I was in over my head and needed to choose something simpler, where therapy happens by a manual. In existential therapy, there is no manual. There is no one way or right way to do it; there are many ways, and each existential therapist interprets the process. Here I was, the first in my immediate family to enroll in a graduate program, and I chose the path without a clear map and was navigating it without a guide.

Lost as I felt, there were times when I would read something and my soul would leap with excitement—and it would affirm my choice. Yalom (1980), in discussing freedom, wrote about some of the following interventions in therapy:

- To a patient who insists that her behavior is controlled by her unconscious, a therapist says, "Whose unconscious is it?"
- A group leader has a "can't" bell that he rings whenever a patient in his group says, "I can't." The patient is asked to recant and then to restate the phrase as "I won't" (Yalom, 1980, p. 216).

As a young existentialist, statements like these both invigorated and terrified me. I was confronted with the ways in which I'd abdicated my freedom in my own life, by blaming bad choices on childhood trauma, or by refusing responsibility with "I can't" instead of owning my choice. I saw the ways in which I had passively chosen in my life, and with the passive choice became the victim of my own passivity. I realized how much taking full responsibility was terrifying but oddly liberating. What if I could choose to not be harmed by my childhood as an adult? What if I could easily say "I won't" instead of "I can't"?

Existentialism made sense to me. It made sense to me to approach life from a stance of not denying what is obvious, such as death. It made sense to me to face these things that seemed so terrifying in the dark because only then would we learn how to really live. It made sense to me that life isn't something to be wasted, but rather savored. We are only as free as we are responsible, and I loved the freedom in accepting that and letting everything else go. For much of my life, I'd sought answers in spirituality, encyclopedias, and wherever I could find them. I tried to find a moral code that fit me, but there was never something that felt just right. Existentialism—and taking responsibility for myself—allowed me to construct a code for living that worked for me.

Being an existential therapist started out as a mostly theoretical and intellectual exercise for me. When I read about the givens of existence, I felt they were logical. It was easy to understand that if we acknowledge we have limited time, we will be more likely to spend that time well. It was easy to grasp the idea that being free also meant being responsible. It wasn't until life hit me with a couple of hard doses of reality that I began to understand that being an existential therapist wasn't merely a philosophical exercise; it was a way of being.

In 2006, I was doing my post-master's licensing hours just outside of Houston. In January, my second nephew was born, and I visited Colorado for his birth. A few days later, I was dropped off at the airport and spent the whole flight crying softly, much to the chagrin of my seatmate. The pain of leaving made me realize that I only had a short time while my nieces and nephews were small, and being in another state was making me miss so much of their childhood. I decided by the time I landed that I would move to be closer. By March, I was back in Colorado, staying with my grandmother. She was up in age and down in health by this time. Much of my month with her was spent listening to her talking about her eventual death and telling me what she wanted, and didn't want, when she died. "Don't bring flowers to my grave when I'm dead and can't enjoy them; give them to me now, while I can," she said.

And so I did. I spent hours listening to her talk about her life, listening to her unfulfilled dreams and wishes for the future. She taught me how to listen fully even when my heart was breaking at the thought of life without her. She let me rub her aching feet and cook for her, like she'd done for me all those years ago when I was a child. I learned more about what it meant to be existential in that month, as I lived belly to belly with the knowledge that I wouldn't have many more opportunities to be with her like this.

This time in my life was necessary preparation for what was to come next. Only a year later, I would give birth to a baby boy who had a congenital heart defect and for whom the prognosis wasn't great. It was then that I turned to something unexpected, but something that would ultimately save my life while I was fighting to save his—*Existential Psychotherapy* by Irvin Yalom (1980). In the darkest moment of my despair, when I was worrying about whether my boy would die and how

I could possibly survive that, I read a line that arrested my borderline suicidal thoughts. The line was "though the physicality of death destroys us, the idea of it saves us" (p. 40). Looking at this tiny baby lying in my lap, those words pierced through my fog of pain and I felt relief. All of the existential reading I'd done up to that point suddenly traveled the six inches down from my head and took residence in my heart.

In that moment, reading that line, I realized I had a choice: I could choose to live fully or I could choose to die slowly. Option one meant that I had to release the fears of my son dying, which I couldn't even imagine at that time. Option two meant that I would live in a small little bubble of fear and never again take a chance. That felt like a terrible existence, hardly a life—and so I took a deep breath and chose to embrace life.

It was hard at first, but with practice, I began to learn to face and conquer my fears. I took my son swimming and to the park. I started taking classes toward my doctorate degree and decided to start a private practice. My perspective on counseling was different than it was before I'd faced my own terror. I was able to meet my clients in deep places without feeling the need to distance from the pain. Instead of running from the unknown, now I ran toward it. I learned how to help my clients sit with their discomfort because I was familiar with sitting with my own.

Rollo May (1981) said that "the aim of psychotherapy is to set people free" (p. 19), and Schneider (2008) says that "freedom is the capacity to choose within the natural limits of life" (p. 35). In my journey to becoming an existential-humanistic psychotherapist, that meant there are certain things I will never be able to change, no matter how much I wish I could. I will never be able to make my son not have a life-threatening illness. I will never not be the daughter of my parents, and I will never be more than 5'4" except when I wear heels. There are many things that I will never be able to control or change, so my freedom lies in that which I can. It reminds me of the Serenity prayer: "God grant me the serenity to accept the things I cannot change, the courage to change the things I can and the wisdom to know the difference" (in Sifton, 2003).

Getting my degree at Saybrook University was a significant turning point for my evolution as a therapist. I was able to sit at the table with people such as Tom Greening, one of the first practitioners of existential psychotherapy, who kindly took me under his wing. My first professional presentation was with Dr. Greening on the topic of existential shattering. Some of my most cherished moments were sitting with Dr. Greening late into the evenings, listening to him talk about his life and his experiences. It was as though I was transported into his world, where he shared office space with James F. T. Bugental, another leader in the existential field, as he regaled me with stories of days past. I felt like a fly on the wall, listening to the hours of conversations and consultations that ended up as an approach to psychotherapy that others, like me, could follow.

I was fortunate to be able to engage in therapy with one of the fathers of the tradition, and the person whose words altered the course of my life at one point, and then saved my life at another—Irvin Yalom. On a whim, I reached out to Dr. Yalom on the off chance that he might have an opening to take on another client. To my surprise, he did, and within weeks, I was sitting in his office. Many people have heroes and idols who can be found in *People* magazine or on *Sports Center*. My hero was a small but powerful man in a sweater, with kind, intense eyes, whose gentle questions would guide me to the core of my deepest fears and then help set me free.

Every book I read, every class I took, every seminar I attended changed me ever so slightly and it showed up in my work. When my clients would start to go off into the woods in session, I would bring them back to the now with questions such as, "How does it feel when you talk about your dad?" Sometimes it would be me pointing out my own feelings, such as "I really felt that in my stomach when you said that, and I'm wondering if you felt something as well?" At other times, the past would show up in the counseling session, but only as much as it was alive in the present moment.

I had the great fortune of completing a certificate in the foundations of existential-humanistic therapy from the Existential–Humanistic Institute and learned from Orah Krug, Nader Shabahangi, and many more luminaries in the field. From each, I took a different lesson and experience. I learned how to be deeply present from Kirk Schneider, whose compassion and deep caring helped me to attune to my own deep feelings. I learned from Orah Krug how to understand my own context—my own foundations and the ground upon which I built—that in turn helped me to understand my clients and their experiences in a much deeper way. From Nader Shabahangi, I learned the quantum dance—the ways in which I could dance between my experience and that of another to further my understanding, compassion, and consciousness.

Being present with my clients in this manner made a difference in innumerable ways. Being attuned to my own experience and being willing to risk sharing those experiences unlocked deeper levels in the clients that were often surprising. My initial training as a counselor was oriented largely on how to make a client better, or how to alleviate some concern. Learning to work as an existential therapist was a departure in that the focus was now on helping clients to "clarify, reflect upon and understand life" (van Deurzen, 2002, p. 18) instead of the medical model of cure. Life was no longer a problem to solve but a mystery to understand. It was my job not to guide as an expert, but rather to be a co-pilot on a sometimes complex path.

Fundamentally, existential therapy is coming to life on life's terms and learning to take responsibility for making the changes we are able to make. When an individual accepts things that are unchangeable, they will be able to create a life worth living. We can't change the past; we will all eventually die; there are givens of existence (death, isolation, meaninglessness, and freedom), and none of us can escape them (Yalom, 1980). My work as an existential therapist is about helping people face those givens and their resistance to them in order to uncover what it really means to live a meaningful life. I believe that when we have the courage to face life as it is, and take our power back, then we begin to truly live. We can then create a life where we aren't rife with resistance, numbing the pain of being alive, but one where we embrace the pain as a part of living fully. It is when we accept that love will also come with loss, that we can embrace love coming to us without fear. On the other side of life is death, and if we spend our whole life fearful of death we won't ever know what it is to genuinely live. However, when we embrace death as an inevitable part of being alive, we then become liberated from fear. I like to see death as a gentle reminder to live while I still have the chance.

When I work with clients, I work with what's present in the moment. What's in the room with us; what's alive right now that we can address? How can my feelings be a guide for what might be happening with and for the client? Unlike the popular idea that therapists should maintain a blank slate, I reject that notion in favor of authenticity and a real relationship. I care for my clients, and they know it. While I believe in the importance of maintaining ethical boundaries, I also believe in the power of authentic human connection. When I became a student of existential therapy, the one thing that always stood out to me was the humanity present in the connections I made and in the case studies I read. In the many years I've been a therapist, I'd never read a case study that made me cry, but when I started reading existential case studies that changed. I could feel, in my own body, the transformative power that was at work in these stories. What I've learned is that as I trust myself and my training, following my gut is usually the right path, even when it seems strange.

Sometimes I think I am the most unlikely existentialist; I am a Latina woman who was born into poverty, the daughter of a young single mother and an addict father. I spent my formative years in the projects (low-income housing), subsisting on welfare, commodities, and food stamps. I grew up poor and never considered myself a candidate for college until as high school graduation approached I had no plans for what to do afterward. I enrolled in a community college, lacking the self-confidence to believe I could be successful. Then, one class at a time, I began to transform. The further I went in my academic career, the more I believed it was possible to be something bigger than my past would have predicted. Under the guidance of people like Louis Hoffman, I began to blossom, and the little girl from the projects became a scholar–practitioner.

In the course of my career, I have become an advocate for social and racial justice. I was reluctant at first to do this work because in addressing these issues I felt as though I would be pigeonholed. It seems to fall mostly on Black and Indigenous people, and People of Color, to be the advocates and voices for racial justice—and it is difficult work. It is hard enough being a Latina woman in a racist world, and I didn't want to feel stuck in this role, as though I were voluntarily carrying the additional burden of trying to convince people of my humanity.

Eventually—with a series of events that were seemingly unrelated but, in looking back, were absolutely connected—I began to realize that my not being vocal about justice issues was a luxury I couldn't afford. Being true to existential roots meant that I had the responsibility to face what was before me if I truly wanted to be free. The reality was that I was always going to be carrying an additional burden simply by being me. My bronze skin and black hair will always make me an "other" in a White world. How I choose to carry the reality of being relegated to the margins is the only thing I can control. While I had always been involved in multicultural and justice work, at least to a small degree, I realized that my personal intersections and professional experience offered a lens that was invaluable and necessary. I joined with others who were also passionate about justice in social issues and mental health, becoming an active participant in community efforts and social and political advocacy. To me, justice, equity, and inclusivity are values deeply congruent with existential-humanistic principles. To confront the givens of existence means to address things such as racism, sexism, classism, cisheterosexism, and ableism, and to recognize that it is our collective responsibility to change those systems. It is also important to recognize those issues in a mental health context because being impacted by systems of oppression has a definite impact on mental wellness. Until we can honestly reckon with the impact of social systems and racism on mental health and wellness, we risk being foot soldiers of systemic oppression and the status quo.

I used to think of being an existential therapist as a theoretical orientation, but I've come to believe that it is not a theory but a way of being. Being an existentialist isn't something to put on when in session; it becomes how you live everything. Existentialism has permeated my life in the best and most meaningful ways. I no longer shy away from having hard talks, such as asking my elderly father if he has his affairs in order. I tend to turn away from my own pain more often than I like;

yet, I've learned to practice kindness and compassion for myself.

Bugental (1978) said of the existential-humanistic therapy journey: "hard won wisdom says that the person who goes on the journey can never be the one who returns from it" (p. 32). I fully agree. When I began this journey, I was a bright-eyed young woman, with some life experience and a lot of naivety. I had no idea that life would take me on a journey that at times forced me to my knees in grief and pain. At the beginning, when I set out on this path, I imagined myself in a café in France, walking in the steps of the greats. Now, the dreams of French cafés are distant as I sit in my basement office writing, the sounds of my family permeating the air. I have learned along the way that dreaming of some far-off future keeps me from being here, present with myself and with my life. There are few things that existentialists all agree upon, but one of those things is the value of presence. The realization that life may end at any moment means that the luxury of putting off until tomorrow is not a viable choice.

I sit with the realization that I am not my past; nor is there a future I need be concerned with. I am only the choices I make today, and I become what I choose. Working with my clients from these perspectives and helping them create a life worth living—one about which they are passionate and feel no need to escape—is a gift. I get to work with people and let them know that they are not broken, or wrong, and that they can create this life they desire in the choices they make. They don't have to remain a victim of life's circumstances but can assume responsibility and exercise their free will in the ways in which they are able. Then they become the actor of their own life, the master of their own universe—and thus, find themselves free.

Last year, I visited my hometown and returned to the projects, to the tiny two-bedroom unit where we lived when I was born. I walked the steps I walked as a child and thought about how much my life has changed since that time. No one, least of all me, would have ever predicted that the little girl with tangled hair and deep emotions would someday be called doctor and would help many people out of their own personal hells. Had someone told 16-year-old me that I would someday be an author, a speaker, and someone to whom people look for inspiration, I wouldn't have believed them. I often need to pause and be reminded that it has been my own choices that have led me to where I am. The choice I made to read Yalom's book and to follow my conscience to Saybrook University—all of those choices have led to this moment, to this person, to this life. As winding and challenging as it has been, I wouldn't have changed a thing. I grew from an impossible place and managed to thrive. I have no doubt that finding the lifeline of existential therapy made all the difference.

> Did you hear about the rose that grew from a crack in the concrete?
> Proving nature's laws wrong, it learned to walk without having feet.
> Funny, it seems to by keeping its dreams; it learned to breathe fresh air.
> Long live the rose that grew from concrete when no one else even cared. (Tupac Shakur, 1999, p.3)

References

Bugental, J. F. T. (1978). *Psychotherapy and process: The fundamentals of an existential-humanistic approach*. McGraw-Hill.

May, R. (1981). *Freedom and destiny*. Norton.

Schneider, K. J. (Ed.). (2008). *Existential-integrative psychotherapy: Guideposts to the core of practice*. Rutledge.

Shakur, T. (2009). *The rose that grew from concrete*. MTV Books.

Sifton, E. (2003). *The serenity prayer: Faith and politics in times of peace and war*. Norton.

Van Deurzen, E. (2002). *Existential counseling and psychotherapy in practice* (2nd ed.). Sage.

Yalom, I. D. (1980). *Existential Psychotherapy*. Basic Books.

Yalom, I. D. (2002). *The gift of therapy: An open letter to a new generation of therapists and their patients*. HarperCollins Publishing.

Chapter 4

Middle Europe: Journey and Madrash

Ed Mendelowitz

> In their precise tracings-out and subtle causations, the strongest and fiercest emotions of life defy all analytical insight. We see the cloud, and feel its bolt, but meteorology only idly essays a critical scrutiny as to how that cloud became charged, and how this bolt so stuns. The metaphysical writers confess, that the most impressive, sudden, and overwhelming event, as well as the minutest, is but the product of an infinite series of infinitely involved and untraceable foregoing occurrences. Just so with every motion of the heart.
> *Pierre; or The Ambiguities* (Melville, 1995, p.96)

This, I must say, is a rather difficult assignment. I am not particularly enticed by the thought of writing about myself, though my essays over time include, inevitably, quite personal reflections upon my own story. I am reminded of Kierkegaard's (2013) ironical observation: "Those who bore others are the plebians, the crowd, the endless train of humanity in general; those who bore themselves are the chosen ones, the nobility" (p. 53). Kierkegaard goes on to observe that those who are not bored with themselves are generally "busy in the world in one way or another" and, for that very reason, "the most boring of all, the most unbearable" (p. 53). Fortunately, as the melancholy Dane also notes, the bored thinker may find copious entertainment in the play of reverie and thought. Hopefully, my ambivalence in taking on this assignment implies some modicum of Kierkegaardian reserve. Hopefully, too, certain readers will be interested and, possibly, edified by what I have to say. Still, as novelist Chaim Potok (1875) once mused, "all beginnings are hard" (p.3).

In the Beginning

I grew up in a village about twenty miles up the Hudson line from downtown Manhattan where I was born. The second of seven children in an assimilated Jewish family with parents who bore this ethnocultural difference quietly but proudly, I think that the experience of difference was significant in some fundamental way; a psychology of not wholly fitting was more or less implicit from the start. It was a family defined by an almost primordial Jewish matriarchy, a state of being and mind that would seem to be virtually archetypal in the world's collective unconscious. Not unlike the professional scenes, differences were tolerated, albeit only so far. To this day, each of my siblings save one lives within a 15-mile radius of the town in which I was raised.

Intelligent and hypersensitive, I suppose, I saw, in considerable respects, into family dynamics and circumstances with increasing clarity during an emotionally challenging adolescence. Rollo May professed a belief that the psychotherapist was, first and foremost, psychologist in their own family. I did not, upon first hearing this conception of things, think that the observation especially applied; caught up in my own ordeal, I did not take on at that time an especially therapeutic stance toward other family members. As I grew older, however, I realized the relevance of Rollo's insight. It is not that I functioned as guide or even confidante for others during my turbulent youth but, rather, that I suffered quietly, watched intently, and struggled in earnest—each of these, indeed, out of existential imperative. Kafka, quoted in Hannah Arendt's introduction to a volume of Walter Benjamin's (1968) essays, wrote in his diary:

> Anyone who cannot cope with life while he is alive needs one hand to ward off a little his despair over his fate... but with his other hand he can jot down what he sees among the ruins, for he sees different and more things than the others: after all, he is dead in his own lifetime and the real survivor. (p. 19)

Although I could write only as a sort of intelligent schoolboy in those early days, it was, I imagine, something vaguely like this. I was something of an outsider at home no less than in the world at large. "Art," I recall Rollo subsequently saying one evening, "comes out of the pain of adolescent loneliness." He elaborated immediately: "—and I don't think it comes out of anything less" (personal communication). I had been a fairly well-adjusted child, I recall, until the shadowy underpinnings of life became increasingly apparent over time.

I became an astute observer of interpersonal dynamics and differences. It would indeed seem to be the artistic type's calling and, arguably, that of the effective psychotherapist as well. I discerned family patterns and politics in a manner that none of my siblings seemed to do. Looking back, it makes intuitive sense that I would be drawn eventually to psychology, this replacing earlier thoughts I had entertained of becoming a rabbi. The rabbi at the synagogue I attended in my childhood (the only one I have ever attended on any regular basis) was a decent enough man but failed to particularly inspire as I progressed into adolescence. A friend of my parents (an extremely gifted abstract artist who had studied at legendary Black Mountain College with the German-American artist Josef Albers) and I became increasingly close as I grew into early adulthood. I think this unique bond with, and endorsement of, a significantly older man whose life was devoted to creative pursuit and artistic expression was a crucial part of my own increasingly aesthetic outlook over time. Life, proclaims Nietzsche (1993/1872) in *The Birth of Tragedy out of the Spirit of Music*, is only justified as an aesthetic experience. It was from my late friend that I learned about the nuances of beauty, color, tension, and form—a collage-like integration of disparate elements.

My undergraduate pursuit of psychology, though formal, was half-hearted at best. After excelling academically in high school for no special reason that I can reasonably discern aside from the fact that I possessed the apparent aptitude to do so, I seem to have declared a sort of tacit moratorium on academia during my college years. I pursued coursework in education as well as psychology, as though looking for clues as to where things had gone wrong and how what appeared to be a tortuous system might be reasonably improved. In an unpublished afterword to a 1997 essay entitled "Psychology, Science, and the Sea," I set down the following recounting of events:

> This essay on psychology and science addresses some concerns I have been thinking about for a long time, issues that, I am glad to remind myself, have concerned seemingly all the deep thinkers in our field whom I have most admired. Depth and subtlety are, indeed, the thing. From the moment psychologists take their earliest academic steps, they are handed Skinner boxes and statistical tables and taught to compute. As human nature is thus dissected and enumerated, these students of

psychology (who, as a rule, have too little feeling for art, literature, philosophy, or religion and forget that a man like Henry Murray, creator of the Thematic Apperception Test, had—like William James before him—given up medicine for psychology, venerating Melville as its greatest exemplar) develop a false sense of confidence in their calculations as they jab at one test tube or cage after another. It is the adolescent's pride in the shining sword of method. As full-fledged professionals, psychologists as a rule proceed myopically; like our clients, we have a hard time changing.

For some strange reason, I possessed an aptitude for mathematics and the sciences in my youth, enough so that I came to an awareness, through logic, of their inherent insufficiencies in shedding ultimate light on the complexities of existence. (If I had been really smart, I might have drifted further into the humanities, where I would likely have found more kindred spirits, better psychologists.) To be thus exiled from the main artery of the profession (by now a slick and fast-paced autobahn) from an early point in my learning was not easy and led to significant distress. Looking back, I see myself strung along for years in back rows of lecture halls in which various spokespersons sold their atrophied wares, while reading, covertly, dog-eared copies of Hesse, Kafka, Maslow, and Laing. The exceptional interesting course did little to mitigate the field's overall aridity. Eventually and thoroughly jaded by the scene, I started in with education courses to try and get a fix on where things had gone wrong. By college graduation, I had read much of the literature in humanistic education current at the time and even received teaching credentials for the primary grades.

When I moved to Berkeley in the late '70s in order to pursue my original interests in psychology more seriously than I had on the East Coast (to study "real" psychology), I found myself yet again frustrated, often disconsolate. Though the rooms were smaller and the students more wily and willful, I still found myself drifting toward those seats in the rear and the used bookshops along Telegraph Avenue. (At least by now I had some company: California has its advantages.) My most influential professors were a philosopher (a Jewish man who was uncommonly bright, awkwardly compulsive, and who evidenced uncommon integrity in enacting his beliefs through involvement in various causes, opposition to racism and inner-city violence, for example) and a social worker (a brilliant, bipolar African-American man who could ramble on maniacally about, seemingly, almost any topic and played Leadbelly on a 12-string, though not, as I recall, simultaneously—a man who was one of the more memorable and decent people affiliated with that amorphous institution and who, years later, would take his own life). Outsiders of sorts, working within the system; certainly not organization men. I read, in addition to my assignments, Freud, Jung, and the existentialists and worked in the least coveted internships (residential homes for schizophrenics, inner-city clinics, and prisons). Later on, having read more assiduously into Eastern thought, I discovered that I had been practicing, unwittingly, a cornerstone of Taoist wisdom: avoidance of authority and egoism in the interests of integrity and the more legitimate pursuit.

During my 2nd year, I was surprised to find myself with renewed vigor as I now donned the general intentionality and frenzy of my peers in jumping through administrative hoops of all sorts in order to take a course offered once a year and taught out of his Tiburon home by Rollo May. May was in his early seventies at that time; his books and stature were surpassing. There was a presence about him, a genuineness, to which I felt immediately drawn. I listened attentively for a change and, no less unusual, found myself volunteering my own thoughts in response. More impressive even than his staggering literacy and accomplishment was Rollo's very person: wise and dogged in its essence, with an abiding moral sensibility for once and none of the sham of image-building one finds too often among the stars. I came to develop a friendship with May, one based on a student's reverence for his teacher and a teacher's affection for his student (transference is universal, after all, and metaphysical in its origins: "unaccommodated man" is such a "bare, forked animal," as Shakespeare has said) that continued, with decreasing regularity, until Rollo's death in 1994. It was this mentoring relationship that has inspired a more committed, as opposed to half-hearted (though, God knows, the struggle is never wholly won), devotion to "real" psychology, that is to say, depth psychology—depth that does not let itself get bogged down in hypertrophied systematizing. "Thinking is great fun," Rollo mused one evening in class, "if you know how to do it."

In many ways, I have remained, like Ishmael, something of an outsider as an act of sheer survival. Nonetheless, I have learned a thing or two over the years, considered the problems of existence with some avidity, plied my trade under the imagined eyes of a pantheon of elders, pondered the wisdom literature of our field, resonated with the sublime voices, and meditated with some earnestness on psychology and its relationship to professionalism, science, and the broader humanities. My essay is an outcome of these processes, a bit of Nietzschean "joyful" science that argues for a broader conception of human nature than the present-day practice of psychology will allow. It is the outsider's insight, perhaps, but perhaps, too, a position of some advantage when psychologists at large do often seem to be little more than schoolboys and handmaids, well-trained women and men who may have accumulated theories and facts of all sorts but tend to understand poorly. These reflections are meant to be evocative, even provocative, are intended also to entertain the careful reader, and yet are deadly earnest in the end: the concerns addressed are paramount in significance. If there seems no way of stopping the unrepentant advance of the locomotive that had already intruded upon Thoreau's Walden silence and had defined Ahab's essential madness, at least the Kierkegaardian few can carry forth a tradition of truth-telling that, as Melville himself had observed, has not made for popularity.

> I am he who walks the States with a barb'd tongue, questioning everyone I meet,
> Who are you that wanted only to be told what you knew before?
> Who are you that wanted only a book to join you in your nonsense?
> Walt Whitman (1904), *By Blue Ontario's Shore* (p. 265)

Amerika, or the Man Who Disappeared

. . . he suddenly saw the Statue of Liberty, which had already been in view for some time, as though in an

> intenser sunlight. The sword in her hand seemed only just to have been raised aloft, and the unchained winds blew about her form.
> 'So high,' he said to himself, and quite forgetting to disembark, he found himself gradually pushed up against the railing by the massing throng of porters.
>
> Franz Kafka (1996), *Amerika (The Man Who Disappeared;* p.3)

On September 29, 1912, Kafka's friend Max Brod (cited in Kafka, 1996, p. vii) wrote in his diary: "'Kafka in ecstasy, writing all night. A novel set in America." Two days later, Brod wrote again: "Kafka in incredible ecstasy." And two days after this: "Kafka, continuing very inspired. A chapter finished. I am happy for him."

Running into Rollo May was a little like dropping blotter acid, something I also did on several occasions during that period of time. The influence and effect of my relationship with Rollo have proven to be long-lasting over the decades and years. I have encountered no one quite like him before or since, and I have met pretty much all of the prominent players in this arena. There would appear to be aspects of existence that may be accessed only through human encounter and example. We are, in the end, all-too-human creatures not suited for transcendence on everlasting arrangements. "Remain faithful to the earth," cautions Nietzsche (1954, p. 125). My lateral move to Berkeley from the East Coast in the late '70s was, psychologically speaking, an exodus of sorts from a kind of pharaonic Egypt of routine and convention, unwitting confinement.

In Rollo, I found the exemplar and mentor that I had been seeking with varying levels of awareness throughout early adulthood. He spotted me the very first night of class, squeezed between several others into a cramped alcove on the far side of his Tiburon living room. Rollo was instinctively predisposed toward those "wise, silent ones in the corners," as he put it that evening. It was his emphatic belief, I came to understand, that turbulence, legitimate suffering, were integral in the development of the effective psychotherapist and, by extension, effective personhood as well. Rollo was pervasively attentive to matters of character that inhere both before and beyond literacy and technique. Indeed, I pondered his conception of technique as "protection from consciousness," questioning him about these and other things in our earliest interactions. "You should learn all the theories," he told me, "but leave them at the door to your office." Encounter lies beyond the foreground of theory and didactics.

The Castle

It was late evening when K. arrived. The village lay under deep snow. There was no sign of the Castle hill, fog and darkness surrounded it, not even the faintest gleam of light suggested the large Castle. K. stood a long time on the wooden bridge that leads from the main road to the village, gazing upward into the seeming emptiness.

Franz Kafka (1998), *The Castle* (p. 1)

That essay of mine, "Psychology, Science, and the Sea," was a good one. I could not get it published, however, as it seemed too different from the familiar format and fare. One reviewer was wildly enthusiastic; another adamant that my writing, admittedly skillful, belonged in a literary journal rather than one associated with the APA; a third reviewer was agnostic and unable to make up their mind. The editor did the conservative thing and punted: My essay was rejected. I recall being somewhat disappointed yet also alerted to unease I would continue to feel even within the hallways of existential-humanistic psychology. During a weekend visit to my artist friend (who summered in a Thoreauvian cottage on the Block Island coastline, a place I visited a regularly after returning to the East Coast), we created a masthead for a self-published series:

 HUMANITAS

Volume 1, Issue 2
Spring 1997

Reflections on psyche, craft, and the doings and sufferings of the enduring self

I published the essay on my own, illustrating it with Indian ink sketches of the friend who had impressed upon me the concordance between message and medium. The aesthetics and presentation of things had become, for me, an abiding concern. Over time, I have come to size others up by the manner in which they themselves move through time and space. Only if they do this well do I find myself especially interested in what they have to say. "Form in movement," muses Beckett, an Irishman who excelled in just these realms.

Eugene Taylor (who once confided to me that transpersonal psychology was a pimple on the derrière of existential-humanistic psychology) was, patently, our historian. No one knew the liturgy nearly so well as he. I met Eugene in passing many years ago at one of the annual American Psychological Association conventions, finding him initially somewhat brusque, though his vast erudition was self-evident from the start; we did not keep in touch. My involvement with the professional divisions was inconsistent at best, whereas Eugene knew everyone and appeared to be everywhere affiliated. When we met ten years later, there was an immediate connection. ("Kafka—he's the one who wrote that story about the man who turns into a bug?" Eugene was turned on by idiosyncratic minds, and especially by excellence.) I recall sitting across from him at a restaurant in the Boston suburbs along with several colleagues as he talked about Melville's *Pierre; or The Ambiguities*—a book that fascinated me and which I had never heard another psychologist so much as mention. I learned a lot from listening in on that monologue yet recall a colleague being put off by Eugene's somewhat pedantic tone. I, however, was transfixed. Eugene's knowledge was staggering, his take on things irrepressibly turned-on. We became good friends during the final years of his life.

Kafka never completed his final novel. Indeed, not one of his three novels (all now recognized as masterpieces of modernist 20th century literature) was ever finished; many of his stories were left similarly incomplete. *The Castle* in particular leaves off, rather strikingly, mid-sentence, as though the author had simply lost interest and was not thinking primarily about notoriety or sharing publicly what he had to say. "Kafka," writes Stephen Dowden (1995), "showed no... faith in the larger redemptive potency of art, politics, or religion" and, hence, was not "driven by metaphysical need to embrace false gods" (p.86). Speaking more specifically about *The Castle*, Dowden (p. 92) notes:

> Most of the novel's characters, especially K. but not only K., invest an effort of virtually talmudic density in trying to interpret castle messages correctly. The task is futile. Even if the message can be found, the chances of excavating its meaning are so remote as to be negligible.

A radical ambiguity reminiscent of Melville, do you see? "The secret doctrine of Kafka's mysticism," Dowden (1995) concludes, "is its refusal to yield to exegesis" (p. 97). If ultimate concerns remain opaque even in a life of genius, can it be so different in our own?

Days after Eugene's passing, I wrote:

> About a week after Eugene's death I had a dream. I was sitting with him in what appeared to be a hotel room. (We are all travelers, after all, are we not?) We were discussing psychology and our shared visions about what our discipline might one day conceivably be. I said something to him about a requisite yet compact lexicon that would not succumb to clichés or hackneying, one that pointed upward and outward toward where we needed more nearly to be. Eugene responded with genuine enthusiasm, as he often would to my somewhat less scholastically derived yet simpatico hopes and ideals. A woman entered the room who seemed vaguely familiar to me. I realized she was there to learn from a master. Eugene suddenly spun around in his chair to a writing desk and, like the energetic teacher of old, scanned his laptop computer with joyful alertness. Opening an electronic file to "the third chapter" (telling us what he was doing as he did so), he took off from what had now become my original point of departure to instruct us on finer points only he himself knew. (Yes, Eugene always knew exactly where to find in the liturgy just what he wanted to convey.) Behind him, I now beheld an entire wall of books. I am happy, I thought, that Reb Taylor is still with us. And then I woke up to find he was gone.

Stan Krippner was right in expressing a premonition that with Eugene's passing we were losing something irreplaceable. By banishing bona fide brilliance to the hinterlands simply because it is rough around its edges, we risk losing those Jamesean frontiers that have inspired our most surpassing exemplars and works.

Upon receiving the Society for Humanistic Psychology's Rollo May Award several years ago, I jotted down some other thoughts:

> I would like in my talk to reflect on my own personal acquaintance with Rollo May, an affectionate mentoring relationship, even friendship, that continued until his death and that, many years later, I continue to think about a great deal. I would like especially to speak to what was unique in May's very person—his quietly charismatic way of being in the world and gracefully admirable character, his toughness and exquisitely sensitive core. I would like to reflect on what was most special and unique in all this and what may be in it for the rest of us, for psychology more broadly. Rollo was fond of quoting this passage out of the fragments of Heraclitus: "They do not understand how that which differs with itself is in agreement: harmony consists of opposing tension, like that of bow and the lyre." Rollo himself was a bundle of contradictions who—true to Heraclitus' evocation—forged out of these tensions and paradoxes one of the most beautiful human beings I have ever known.

It was my wife, Khanh, who lobbied on my behalf for that award. In my late 50s, I married a lovely, spontaneous, willful Vietnamese woman whom I met while lecturing on Rollo's legacy and work in Seoul. Khanh relies on intuition in life to a remarkable degree. Her instincts in these realms are, likewise, remarkable, though, God knows, no one bats one thousand in these realms. I think, though, that she correctly discerned that I was contributing to a literary psychology uniquely honoring the man by which it had been informed. It was the Korean translator of William James's *Varieties of Religious Experience* and Ernest Becker's *The Denial of Death* (a religion professor met through Eugene) who invited me to speak. Khanh maintains that our meeting was fated, and there were, no doubt, strange occurrences attending it that are hard to rationally fathom. I live, as I always have, with the radical mystery of things. I have little idea about greater designs and, like Melville and James, remain agnostic before those ultimate ambiguities that can never be precisely pinned down. It has occasionally crossed my mind that no one else would have advocated for my receipt of that award, though once it was proffered its support was apparently uncontested. Existential-humanistic psychology will lose a great deal and perhaps its soul if it ever foregoes its outsider sentiments and visions, those "wise, silent ones in the corner."

Budapest

For the better part of a decade, I served on the faculty of a film and psychology program co-sponsored by the Boston Institute of Psychotherapy and Lesley University taking place in a theater just outside Harvard Square. I tended to bring unfamiliar filmmakers and films, preponderantly European, into the mix. One year this annual series touted "Gender and Identity" as its theme. I suggested a Hungarian film by Ildikó Enyedi, a little known artist from Budapest whose extraordinary *My Twentieth Century* (1989)—a quirky and uproariously playful first feature—would go on to win the esteemed Caméra d'Or award at Cannes later that year. I received predictable skepticism from other faculty for whom the film's non-linear narrative and poetic renderings appeared mystifying. Perhaps even the idiosyncratic dialogue put them off. (Can there be a stranger language on the face of the planet than Hungarian, the native tongue of my grandmother?) Interestingly, the most simpatico response came, as it often would during my tenure with this group, from the Venezuelan projectionist—like myself, an aesthete at heart.

I pointed out to my colleagues that their film series had been ongoing for a decade before my arrival and yet, despite having included a mix of women and men on the faculty roster, oddly, had never included a film by a female director. I found it fascinating that this gathering of Cambridge psychologists appeared less disconcerted by my observation than by the free-spirited artwork itself. Mainstream psychology, sophisticated or otherwise, leans inexorably toward the left hemisphere. Enyedi's film plays, unrestrainedly and doggedly, with the tensions between masculine and feminine world energies in the wake of Edison's light bulb and numerous other inventions, deftly juxtaposing a "mass murdering century" with the effervescent miracle of existence itself. Even a metaphorically patriarchal and patronizing early psychiatry is delightfully lampooned en route. The admixture of humor, pathos, and history in its myriad manifestations against a backdrop of sheer imaginative joy—this is what I eventually attempted to convey to an audience accustomed to more predictable things.

I have followed Enyedi's subsequent films over the years. She does not make many, and those she does one typically goes out of one's way to track down and see. I recall even sharing a quick exchange of chat messages when I had a fleeting presence on Facebook and was, more recently, delighted to find she had bookmarked an essay of mine on one of the academic sites.

I was overjoyed one recent day to discover that Enyedi's (2017) *Body and Soul* (her first feature film in 18 long years!) can now be streamed conveniently on Netflix. This newest film is quintessential Enyedi—resplendent with wit and wisdom, death and transcendence, a terror and beauty that accrue at life's boundaries. Two awkward souls, Endre and Maria, employed in a slaughterhouse are drawn together despite timidity, habit, and everyday routine, guided by the dreams that they share in common while sleeping. Everything is here: humdrum reality and its horrors as well, dream and luminescence, isolation and love. Despite all-too-human frailties, the two protagonists discover through happenstance that they share identical dreams of becoming, respectively, a stag and doe deep in the Hungarian forest. Hesitantly, the two would-be lovers let themselves be guided by their dreams.

In an *American Cinematographer* (Benjamin, 2018) interview, Enyedi reflects eloquently:

> This is a Simone Weil film. She makes a distinction, and Rilke has it too, between the holy—the transcendent—and morality. The transcendent is on another level; it is a very direct connection to the elementary forces of nature. The transcendent is wider, truer and more basic than morality, which is trying to set a code for social life.
>
> The film wants to communicate, to anybody who is watching it, that everyday life is missing something. We are very politely softening the edges and covering the essence because it's too strong, too powerful. The film is about discovering that essence.

It is not too much to point out that this, in brief, is what the literature and work of existential-humanistic psychology, at its best, is all about. In this instance, we are deftly escorted by a master of storytelling, nuance, and metaphysical speculation.

The Unbearable Lightness of Being

There is a destination but no way there; what we refer to as way is hesitation.
Franz Kafka, (2006), *The Zürau Aphorisms* (No. 26, p. 26)

My father, I know, pondered silently throughout the course of a ninety-five-year life the family his mother left behind in Central Europe, half of the members of which would not survive. In 1935, as a child of ten, he traveled by ship and rail with his mother and younger brother to the Jewish quarter in Bratislava where she was born. There were train stations along the way where they were not allowed to disembark because they were Jews. It was the only time my father would ever see his grandparents along with several aunts and uncles. Years before, at the age of seventeen, my grandmother, the eldest of eight, emigrated with her next oldest sister to the States. The two girls were accompanied by my great-grandfather who brought them to Yonkers, New York with a plan to return to Bratislava once they were sufficiently settled in order to retrieve the rest of the family and also relocate them to the New World. In the end, he was unable to adjust to what he perceived of as the secular world of America and, so, returned to Central Europe. My great-grandfather perished in Auschwitz, a matter I do not recall my father ever mentioning, though it quietly haunted him throughout his years. He described his grandfather as a watchmaker but also as a self-educated, learned man within his community. When I moved to California at the age of twenty-five to pursue my interests in psychology more avidly, my father observed that, had the family remained somehow in Middle Europe, I would have become "a scribe." He was speaking of existential callings and codes, I now realize, and linking me to a forebear I would never know.

I recall as a child meeting excitedly a great-uncle who had emigrated from that darkening world to Palestine-becoming-Israel (a land that has become, in certain respects, also menacing and dark) and absorbing stories about how he had at the age of thirteen been hidden from the Gestapo by nuns. Those nuns, who couldn't have cared less about being remembered, composed a group to which I aspire to belong—individuals abiding by Elijah's "still small voice" of conscience, each trying to do her part before moving gracefully along. In the waning pages of an essay that some years ago morphed into a book, I quote the Polish filmmaker, Krzysztof Kieslowski (cited in Insdorf, 1999): "A train is going somewhere . . . the car of film is very crowded. In order for others to get on, someone has to get off, to make room" (p. 185). As I age, I feel increasingly simpatico with those who chase neither fame nor public immortality. From the sanatorium in which he died, Kafka wrote his friend with the request that his unpublished work be burned; those several volumes already in print he could do nothing about, but he felt the world could survive without especial privation were his numerous other writings destroyed in a holocaust of words. It is our good fortune that Brod, who by no means got everything right, did not comply.

I do not define myself as an "Existential-Humanistic" psychotherapist, though my identity and work as a psychotherapist and writer is intimately related to the Existential-Humanistic domains. I am doubtful that the mentors I hold in highest regard would easily locate themselves amid our current acronyms and cliques. My suspicion is that, even more than I, most would remain outsiders amid these minions. I think of Rollo May spotting me in that faraway alcove in Tiburon so long ago. Somehow, there is both succor and poetic valence in that distant gesture and evocation. Intuiting the inexorable pull of gravity and our overarching postmodernist ethos ("many people, few gestures," muses Kundera [1991] in his novel *Immortality*), I find fulfillment in relations closer to home—in my wife and daughter, in simple acts of kindness transacted in the daily round, in a headful of memories of teachers, friends, and family members whose lives have already come and gone. "If there is a supreme value in Kundera's universe," notes Trevor Cribben Merrill (2013), "perhaps it is attachment to and respect for loved ones dead and gone" (p. 166). I confess to feeling an affinity for such a wistful conception of things. As I peruse a volume of correspondence between Arendt and Jaspers (1992) gifted by my parents on my 40th birthday long ago, I think about my late mother and a wizened father who will follow her very soon. "Everyone would do well," Arendt writes her mentor and friend, to "examine his life in the light of yours"; "You are one of these people I count among the great gifts of this world," writes Jaspers in return. I find fulfillment in books, films, and artworks, and in those rarified encounters and friendships that occur far from the madding crowd.

Word has it (though I cannot be sure) that, along with my Vietnamese wife and daughter Miryam, I am on my way to Los Angeles. West Hollywood—a very long way from that Jewish quarter in Middle Europe.

Immortality

> From a certain point, there is no more turning back. That is the point that must be reached.
> Franz Kafka (2006), *The Zürau Aphorisms* (No. 5, p. 7)

Thrilling moments. Martin Luther King's "Beyond Vietnam" speech delivered at Riverside Church one year to the day before he died in Memphis. *Democracy Now!* broadcasts it now in its entirety on the anniversary of King's birthday earlier this winter. King's breathtaking commingling of the myriad psychological, political, and spiritual planes as he reaches out to glimpse and touch those ultimate realms of transcendence and convergence is riveting to hear. Another *Democracy Now!* episode addresses the ongoing saga of the Canadian government and pipeline versus the Native American community of the Northwest. A young Wet'sawet'en woman confronts the authorities, an officer's rifle pointing directly at her: "We are here for humanity. For life. We are unarmed. We are peaceful. You are killers. You are genocidal maniacs."

In many ways, I have been an almost unwitting adherent of the philosophical reflection articulated by Karl Jaspers. Five years ago, I traveled to Vancouver with my wife and very young daughter, picking up an old friend in Portland along the way. I had been invited to a meeting of the American Philosophical Association in order to provide commentary on German scholar Matthias Bormuth's (2006) *Life Conduct in Modern Times*, a study of Jaspers's philosophical and psychiatric conceptions amidst an increasingly critical stance toward psychoanalysis. I was looking for new blood, different epistemologies and perspectives; with advancing time and maturity, humanistic psychology had become, for me personally, increasingly redundant and often dull. Psychology, metaphysically inclined, was articulated by James well over a century ago. James's metaphysics, however, did not shy away from science; rather, what he opposed was "the ever-narrowing definition of science itself" (Taylor, 1996). Matthias and I connected at once. We met over lunch and several beers the next day and have become increasingly close friends ever since.

Healing Through Meeting

> The indestructible is one thing; at one and the same time it is each individual, and it is something common to all;

hence the uniquely indissoluble connections among mankind.

Franz Kafka (2006), *The Zürau Aphorisms* (No. 70/71, p. 70)

Like my late friend Eugene, I have always been enthralled by James's abiding attentiveness to "pure experience." (The German-Jewish literary critic Walter Benjamin [cited in Leslie, 2007, p. 40] bemoaned Kant's categorical definition of experience as "lifeless," as imposing a kind of finitude on the infinite, pointing instead toward "manifestations of the 'absolute' in space and time.") In Zen, it is called "direct pointing"—the thing itself as opposed to displays of superfluous abstraction or faux authenticity. Authenticity is King at the Riverside Church and in Memphis. Authenticity is Malcom X in Harlem or, earlier on in his own psycho-spiritual quest here in Boston. Authenticity is that Wet'sawet'en woman who tells it like it is. We are less likely to find such feats of integration at gatherings of health professionals in Carmel-by-the-Sea. Arguably, it is a lot to ask of any professional organization to match them. Still, these might constitute a high bar by which we are inspired and to which we ourselves aspire.

A client of mine with whom I have worked during several stretches of time wrote about the nature of this work and relationship some years ago. Entitling her book *Sculpting the Darkness* (in homage to Russian filmmaker Andrei Tarkovsky's *Sculpting in Time* on the themes of creative endeavor both broadly and, more specifically, in film), Lori (Golzmane, 2012) elegantly recounts:

> I have always intuitively understood the connection between art and inner exploration. Discussing film and literature is, of course, a primary means by which I share myself with Dr. M; I feel as if I am inextricably wedded to certain artworks such that they are part of me just as my heart or my blood is part of me as well. These works deal with themes similar to those that I face, but it is the very nature of art that truly promotes such a union. The artist enters a vast and tortuous realm to engage in the process of creation, but the reader, viewer, or listener also enters such a realm to absorb the creation. There is an aspect of trust involved in both cases; each party forges a relationship with creativity itself and must surrender to its mystery in order to gain any reward from the experience. It is when some part of me recognizes that this seemingly external inspiration—the

words written by another, the painting fashioned by another's hand—is also found within myself that I truly connect with the artwork, and by extension with the open expanse of possibility. (pp. 138–139)

And,

Just as film or poetry or music allows the ineffable self to flow outward, to fill the spaces that exist in conscious awareness, the psychotherapeutic relationship ought to do the same; it should encourage the self to flow outward, to expand, to find expression for the tiniest, quietest corners of the mind. The loud cries are important, but it is the softness, the silence within me that requires the most care. When I reflect on my relationship with Dr. M, it is his nurturing of these quiet spaces that I most often think of. The subtlety of his understanding is not informed by the *Diagnostic and Statistical Manual of Mental Disorders* or the American Psychological Association, but rather by the true observers and philosophers of human experience, the artists. There is an art to relationship as well, and I have honed my ability to appreciate this throughout the time that I've known him. Our relationship, just like any relationship, is a mutual creation; it is mysterious and synergistic, and its healing nature derives from these qualities. I am able to recognize my role in co-creating and maintaining this intricate entity that moves with grace and sensitivity and, also, my contribution to its beauty. It is from this recognition that I draw courage.

"Healing through meeting," as Martin Buber would say. Also, I and Thou. Both parties are engaged and altered in ways that cannot be anticipated and will never be wholly spelled out. There are as many theories of psychotherapy, Otto Rank (1978) once mused, as there are psychotherapeutic relations. Healing is reciprocal at its core.

The Impossibility of Crows

The crows like to insist a single crow is enough to destroy heaven. This is incontestably true, but it says nothing about heaven, because heaven is just another way of saying: the impossibility of crows.
Franz Kafka (2006), *The Zürau Aphorisms* (No. 32, p. 32)

Kafka's Zürau aphorisms were posthumously published under the title: *Reflections on Sin, Suffering, Hope, and the True Way*. Although the title was Brod's, there can be little doubt that Kafka's mind was especially set upon the sacred realms during several months while visiting his sister, Ottla, in the Bohemian countryside. Roberto Calasso, working on his remarkable study *K.* and immersed in the student notebooks in which Kafka hand wrote his final novel, chanced upon the *Zürau Aphorisms* accidentally, each fragment, carefully numbered, written on a separate sheet of onion skin paper. "Like shards of meteorites," observed Colasso (cited in Kafka, 2006, p. viii) obeisantly, "fallen in a barren land"; here, "the scenery had changed utterly" (p. viii).

I wonder if existential-humanistic psychology might not benefit from the equivalent of those hallowed scraps of paper—a "new Kabbala" of the sort that Kafka imagined someone more capable than he might one day write. We might engage in Bohemian meditations in relative solitude of a sort Jaspers referred to as "existence-philosophical reflection" so as to contribute more convincingly to a planetary literature and conscience going forth. I refer not to the training endeavors of "masters" or "experts"—terms and conceptions Jaspers found abhorrent. "Serviceable," Jaspers chides (cited in Bormuth, 2006), "are those who can be trained" (p. 119).

If enough of us are able individually to do this, we might pick up somewhere in the vicinity where overarching spirits like James, Jaspers, and May suggestively left off—that of esoteric artworks and understandings. What is "truly innovative" in Jaspers, notes Matthias (Bormuth, 2006) resides "in the unusual reception of the humanities as a scholarly tradition" (p. 13) and its application to scientific discourse. It is ludicrous to think that an illumined rapprochement with science will somehow attenuate our humanistic stirrings or roots. "God is the sum of all possibility," muses Isaac Bashevis Singer (cited in Harley, 2009), "and Time is the mechanism through which potentiality achieves sequence" (p. 10). Although the unadulterated "objective look" is wholly insufficient, its wholesale avoidance is by no means where it's at.

The Goddess of Happiness

> Two tasks of the beginning of life: to keep reducing your circle, and to keep making sure you're not hiding somewhere outside it.   Franz Kafka (2006), *The Zürau Aphorisms* (No. 94, p. 93)

Exactly one year ago as a consequence of a routine annual physical, I went through a sequence of examinations and procedures and was diagnosed with, and subsequently treated for, cancer. Mortality has, for me, never been an especially distant thought. Still, the immediate encounter differs from its philosophical or abstract counterparts. Treatment has gone well, the British radiologist (with whom in idle moments I discuss the novels of Huxley) tells me. I am to be monitored every six months with the odds tilted entirely in my favor. I experience a quiet joy in this, as do my wife and several friends and family members. There is a heightened sense of poignancy, of the brevity and oftentimes beauty of life—a "loan," as Rank (1978) opined, for which eventual "repayment" is inevitable. As I reminisce, I feel fortunate to have been born into a complex and difficult set of circumstances counterposed by a hypersensitive, intelligent constitution. ("Shoulders are from God," writes Singer [1953] in one his stories; "and burdens too" [p.11].) I feel especially grateful for having had just enough guides and guidance through my formative years to start on a path that seems to have been there all along.

I am, by this point in time, a very occasional essayist. Humanitas, I am pleased to say, has morphed into a column for the Society of Humanistic Psychology—a personal Madrash in which I provide commentary on our organization's broader themes. I remain passionately devoted to the literature and work of existential-humanistic psychology; it remains the place in which I locate my professional self, a historical lineage and sphere about which I continue to think deeply. Still, I am not at all sure that I have ever felt entirely at home in this collective arena—less so, I think, as the years pass and the various sub-specialties become increasingly branded and popularized. In quintessential ways, I remain an outsider sitting contemplatively in the remotest corner of the room. Nevertheless, insofar as one dons an identity of any sort in order to be located by others with greater ease, existential-humanistic psychology encompasses the general domain in which I live and breathe. Here one finds a literature and sensibility that reaches back through the ages—at least as far as the Biblical authors and ancient Greeks, indeed to the earliest stirrings of consciousness.

Rollo often lamented the fact that students participating in his case conferences on psychotherapy rarely, if ever, brought in dreams or associations—fragments from the subconscious depths that, at the further reaches of consciousness, merge with the upper octaves of experience and insight. In her book, Lori Golzmane (2012) sets down this moving reverie about fear, encounter, courage, and advance:

The other day, I was standing in my kitchen when, in a moment of stillness, I suddenly perceived the chasm, the inner darkness that I so often write about. Awareness of it sliced through conscious thought with a pang of anxiety and I instantly felt dizzy with the intensity of it. Despite its unpleasantness, I didn't immediately push it away or attempt to blanket it with more mundane concerns. Within seconds, I found myself plummeting into its depths.

After the initial shock of panic—which was significant—my attention slowly began to shift; I found myself focusing less on the sensation of falling and more on the particularities of what was happening to me. I then began to wonder how I would convey this experience to Dr. M. What did it feel like to be here at this precise moment? How would I describe my surroundings? As I endeavored to shape the anxiety into an image and thus began to notice its subtler qualities, I realized that I was no longer falling; I was in fact back on the ledge, standing beside Dr. M. Wishing to show him the monstrous nature of what I faced, I pointed to the abyss. He followed the line of my finger, past the cold mist clinging to the perimeter, deep into the dizzying blackness below. I watched as he gazed into it for several minutes, carefully surveying the landscape of the dark. Part of me feared that he would be appalled or frightened by its size, its menacing appearance, even though I had surely stood here with him many times before. Perhaps he would see something he had not previously perceived, some fatal flaw, some hidden edge of corruption.

Eventually, he turned to look at me and gently nodded. His face did not display shock or disgust; it was instead receptive, as if to say, Yes, I am here, Lori. I turned back to look out into the vastness, and as he and I continued to stand there, I became aware of the horizon beyond the chasm, the line where the land met the sky. Some distance off, there was what looked to be a meadow of some kind, with a verdant copse of trees and a vibrant river that wound its way around the circumference of the land. The sky itself was rich and deep, with hues of every shade feathering into another infinity altogether. After a time, I noticed a desire to tread further on, to see what lay beyond the void, beyond my current line of sight. I felt anxious, particularly since I remembered the last time I had ventured out only to be dragged back to this pit. Still, there seemed to be so much more out there; it seemed a shame to remain here forever, stuck in this one place. I turned to Dr. M and he nodded again, almost imperceptibly. I smiled quietly in acknowledgment and, after shutting my eyes for a brief moment, began to walk. (Golzmane, 2012, pp. 139–141)

Rollo liked to trace the word "existence" to its Latin root, "ex-sistere"—literally, to stand out, to emerge—and, in *The Courage to Create* (May, 1975) pointed to its resonance with "ex-stasis" (p. 48) or ecstasy. Shortly after his arrival at Zürau, Kafka (2006) set down a reverie of his own: "O beautiful hour, masterful state, garden gone wild. You turn from the house and see, rushing toward you on the garden path, the goddess of happiness" (p. 114). The Czech poet mentioned encountering this elusive deity only once, but there is no reason to doubt the veracity of his vision and words.

In memory of Wilma Saberski Mendelowitz (June 7, 1926 – May 14, 2019) and
Stanley Morton Mendelowitz (January 1, 1925 – April 17, 2020)

References

Arendt, H., & Jaspers, K. (1992). *Correspondence: 1926–1969* (R. & R. Kimber, Trans.). Harcourt Brace Jovanovich.
Benjamin, B. (2018). On Body and Soul: Interview with Ildikó Enyedi. In *American Cinematographer*. https://ascmag.com/blog/the-film-book/on-body-and-soul-director-ildiko-enyedi
Benjamin, W. (1968). *Illuminations: Essays and reflections* (H. Arendt, Ed.). Harcourt, Brace and Janovich, Inc.
Bormuth, M. (2006). *Life conduct in modern times: Karl Jaspers and psychoanalysis* (S. Nurmi-Schomers, Trans.). Springer.
Dowden, S. D. (1995). *Kafka's Castle and the critical imagination*. Camden House, Inc.
Enyedi, I. (1989). *My 20th century*. Budapest Stúdió Vállalat, Feihändler Filmproduktion GmbH, Magyar Filmgyártó Vállalat.
Enyedi, I. (2017). *Body and soul*. Hungary: Films Boutique and Inforg—M & M Film.
Golzmane, L. (2012). *Sculpting the darkness: A memoir of psychotherapy*. Self-published manuscript.
Hartley, M. (2009). *Guide to the works of Isaac Bashevis Singer*. Vantage Press.
Insdorf, A. (1999). *Double lives, second chances: The cinema of Krzyzstof Kieslowski*. Hyperion.

Kafka, F. (1996). *Amerika (The man who disappeared)* (M. Hofmann, Trans.). New Directions Books.

Kafka, F. (1998). *The castle* (M. Harman, Trans.). Schocken Books. (Original work published 1926)

Kafka, F. (2006). *The Zürau aphorisms* (R. Calasso, Ed.. M. Hofmann, Trans.) Schocken Books.

Kundera, M. (1991). *Immortality* (P. Kussi, Trans.). Grove Weidenfeld.

Kierkegaard, S. (2013). Either/Or, A fragment of life. In H. V. Hong & E. H. Hong (Eds.), *The essential Kierkegaard*. Princeton University Press. (Original work published 1843)

Leslie, E. (2007). *Critical lives: Walter Benjamin.* Reaktion Books.

May, R. (1975). *The Courage to create*. Norton.

Melville, H. (1995). *Pierre; or the ambiguities*. HarperCollins. (Original work published 1852)

Merrill, T. C. (2013). *The book of imitation and desire: Reading Milan Kundera with René Girard*. Bloomsbury Publishing Inc.

Nietzsche, F. (1993). *The birth of tragedy out of the spirit of music* (S. Whiteside, Trans.). Penguin Books. (Original work published 1872)

Nietzsche, F. (1954). Thus spake Zarathustra: A book for all or not. In *The portable Nietzsche* (W. Kaufmann, Trans.). Viking Press. (Original work published 1883)

Potok, C. (1975). *In the beginning*. Fawcett Books.

Rank, O. (1978). *Will therapy* (J. Taft, Trans.). Norton. (Original work published 1929, 1931)

Singer, I. B. (1953). *Gimpel the fool and other stories*. Farrar, Straus and Giroux.

Taylor, E. (1996). *William James on Consciousness beyond the margin*. Princeton University Press.

Whitman, W. (1904). *Leaves of Grass*. Small, Maynard & Company.

Chapter 5

Becoming an Existential–Humanistic Therapist

Katerina Zymnis

Deciding to Become a Therapist

The catalyst that prompted me to embark upon training as a psychotherapist 27 years ago was my two-year old son, Sophocles, developing a speech problem at the age of two. I decided to seek help and luckily came across an experienced speech therapist who suggested that I engage in therapeutic work as well. I immediately joined a parenting group offered at my older children's school. A few months later, I decided to begin group therapy, which lasted for about five years—and that experience became the starting point of my journey toward becoming a therapist.

Right from the start, I was thrilled with the results psychotherapy was having on me and the "miracle" that was unfolding within my family and in my entire life. I soon realized that, as I was changing, everything was changing around me. This is not to say that my son's difficulty was magically disappearing, although it ultimately disappeared completely. But as usually happens in therapy, my initial presenting problem shifted in line with the new discoveries and challenges I was encountering as my inner processes evolved. Psychotherapy was helping me to discover a new world of possibilities and personal meaning. It was bizarre: Although everything appeared to remain the same (same three kids, same partner, same family of origin, same friends, same country), I felt that my life was turning upside down for the better and that I was finding—or possibly creating—a new pattern in life's never-ending chaos. I felt that I had begun a profound and exploratory journey with no return.

One year before I finally decided to end my group therapy sessions, I caught myself observing, even scrutinizing, what my therapist was doing. I knew by then that I wanted to learn ways to help people ignite their own "miracles" and find their own potential to create a fulfilling life. This soon led me to the realization that observing my therapist, learning from her, and appreciating the benefits of effective psychotherapy was a necessary but not sufficient condition for becoming a psychotherapist. I became fully aware that I was facing new decisions that had to be thoroughly examined once again in my life. I realized that if I was to become a psychotherapist, I needed to seriously consider my will to commit to a thorough and lengthy educational program in psychology that would be followed by specialized training in psychotherapeutic practice.

I was aware that the road would be long. Being a married mother of three and having a different educational background, a first university degree in economics, kept me stuck in my inner search for some months. Overthinking and fear prevented me from taking a final decision. I felt overwhelmed by the time demands that I imagined a university degree in psychology would require from me and apprehensive about the impact of a radical career change on my "organized" life. Nevertheless, therapy's "miracle effect" was so intense, pervasive, and persistent that it helped me not only confront my fears but also savor the process of deconstructing and reconstructing my structured life from scratch. I was able to keep what really mattered and embark on the uncharted territories of a new profession. I decided to begin my new path taking one step at a time and allowing the process to unfold organically. I had learned by then to listen to my inner wisdom—which led me to trust myself and feel the courage to make my dream happen—while never ceasing to imagine the kind of therapist I wanted to become. Moreover, I had unconditional support from my lifelong partner, Thomas, and my three kids, Argyris, Despina, and Sophocles, who always encouraged me (sometimes with incredible patience) along the way.

Starting a Degree and Training in Psychotherapeutic Practice

I finally decided to enroll in a master's program in counseling psychology, followed by a four-year training in Adlerian Individual Psychotherapy and a ten-year training program in Systemic Family and Group psychotherapy. Going back to university as a young adult was a very interesting experience. My eagerness and curiosity to dive into each psychology course was genuine and profound. Throughout the course of my studies, I was feeling that I had finally found my place on earth and that new horizons were constantly opening for me.

At university, I met professors and classmates who were to become close friends and co-workers later in life. As an example, I met my dear professor, Evy Dallas, who introduced me to the seminal work of Rollo May, Viktor Frankl, and Irvin Yalom during our class on theories of counseling. Evy became a fellow traveler on my route of knowledge and later became a dear friend in life. Yalom's books, *Existential Psychotherapy* (1980) and *Theory and Practice of Group Psychotherapy* (Yalom & Leszcz, 2005), had a definitive impact on my future professional development, along with Rollo May's *Existence* (1994) and Viktor Frankl's *Man's Search for Meaning* (1985). During the same course, I was also intrigued and deeply influenced by the Systemic approach to helping families and couples and by the theories of Alfred Adler (2013) and Carl Rogers (1967).

While studying at the university, I was thrilled to meet Evgenia Georganda, our professor while training in group therapy with Michael Fakinos. I also met Alexis Harisiadis, a superb classmate who introduced me to James Bugental's *The Art of the Psychotherapist* (1987) and *Psychotherapy Isn't What You Think: Bringing the Therapeutic Engagement Into the Living Moment* (1999). In 2004, both Evgenia and Alexis were to become, along with Evy Dallas and myself, the initial founding group of *gignesthai*—The Hellenic Association for Existential Psychology.

After completing my master's degree in counseling psychology, the eagerness to learn and explore the field of psychotherapy became stronger. I decided to begin my training in Adlerian Psychology, taught by visiting professors from Florida Atlantic University and the American Adlerian Training Institute. I still remember a thought-provoking dialogue with Dr. Len Sperry on the helping factors in psychotherapy. I recall Professor Sperry holding the first edition of *The Heart and Soul of Change* (Hubble, Duncan, & Miller, 1999) and asking himself out loud what it was that really allowed change to happen. I recall him saying: "I would be deeply grateful if someone could provide an answer to what factors contribute to the complex process of change. There are no answers yet." The question of what helps in psychotherapy was to become, 20 years later, the focus of investigation in my doctoral thesis, to which I will refer later.

Along with the study of the Adlerian approach, I decided to enroll in a thorough program in Systemic Family and Group Psychotherapy at the Athenian Institute of Anthropos (AKMA). The program had a strong emphasis on experiential learning. Working with my teachers and mentors over more than ten years was a constant source of inspiration, knowledge, and experience. I was blessed to have met in my life important teachers such as Vaso Vassiliou, Dionysis Sakkas, Salvador

Minuchin, Ken Gergen, and Karl Tomm (to name a few), along with all the trainers, classmates, and supervisors who prepared us for such an important endeavor: to help families thrive. The Systemic approach to psychotherapy trained me to observe the processes that unfold in human systems while, at the same time, as observer-therapist, becoming a fundamental, active part of the therapeutic system. As I participated in and worked with various psychotherapeutic groups and families, I was able to discern alliances in families and couples, dysfunctional patterns of communication, and transgenerational patterns of dysfunction both in genograms and in the communication processes taking place in the "here and now" therapeutic encounters. I became particularly keen on observing boundary issues among family members, challenges that arise due to multiculturalism and new family formats, the effect of traditional values in society, and the value gap frequently experienced in a rapidly changing and globalized world.

Looking for the Individual Within a Larger Context

Discovering my Existential Identity

Parallel to my deep enthusiasm for the study of human systems, I began to feel that I was losing sight of the individual and their capacity for transcending the challenging situations and dysfunctional family systems into which they were "thrown" in life. Understanding the processes and patterns that took place within human systems could not, for me, capture the wholeness of each human being and their unique personal choices when faced with the givens of life. And as usually happens when we are aware and open to our internal experience and needs, I found myself facing a new professional challenge that brought forth that deep interest in the existential approach ignited during my university years.

During that time, I was president of the board of the Greek Society for Adlerian Psychology and was invited to lead a psychotherapy group in the women's prison in Athens. I accepted the position, completely aware that what I knew about leading groups till then was not enough. I searched for articles and books at a time when the professional literature was not as accessible as it is today. I found no help from my teachers, who tended to discourage me from assuming such a difficult endeavor, but I refused to succumb to the anxiety created in me by my lack of experience in working with marginal populations. I was fully aware that my skills in observing dysfunctional communication processes and in session-planning based on hypothesis formation, the definition of clear therapeutic goals, and the use of techniques and protocols would not be enough for my work in the prison environment. All my knowledge until then seemed inadequate to me. I was preparing myself to face a new professional challenge colored by extreme unpredictability and uncertainty. I knew deep down that what really mattered was my presence and—most important—my genuine attitude as a human being who was humbly aware of my finitude and the daimonic side of human beings, and their suffering and pain. These qualities, along with my capability to communicate honestly with an open stance toward the other, I recognized as foundational.

I also knew that in order to begin my work with a disciplined and professional stance I needed a theoretical framework. I decided to, once again, dive into my favorite university books authored by Irvin Yalom (1980), Viktor Frankl (1985), Rollo May (1958, 1994, 20009), Martin Buber (1996; Buber et al., 1997), and Albert Camus (2013) as a start. I suspected that these authors would help me create a working frame of reference. Having these thinkers as supportive guides, wise mentors, and constant sources of knowledge, I managed to lead a three-hour weekly psychotherapy support group of 25 imprisoned women for about three years.

The group at the prison worked mainly experientially, allowing triggering exercises to highlight existential themes and open the process of individual change. Themes related to freedom, destiny, finiteness, limitations, choice, and responsibility kept emerging in each session, bringing to the surface many challenging aspects of the human condition. We addressed these themes in an indirect way while working and experimenting with art, poetry, theatrical expression, body sculpting, and role plays. The concepts of destiny and the freedom to choose a personal and responsible stance toward the current situation of living in prison, and the prospect of a daunting future after the release from prison, continuously manifested itself in our work. It was paradoxical and at times surreal to work enthusiastically on personal choice when confronted with the givens of life in a physical environment (the prison building) surrounded by iron bars.

Looking back, I know today that what helped me the most to do my best as a therapist was my authentic stance and my honest presence as a human being. I also know that once trust had been established the women who took part wholeheartedly in the group had captured my genuine interest in meeting their stories and my deep and sincere respect for them and their lives. The group participants sensed that I was very far from judging them and that I genuinely believed that they had the power to change if they decided to do so. The validation of their therapist meant a lot to them. For some, it was the first time that another human being showed any kind of faith and trust in their capacity to lead a functioning life. I soon realized that people in extreme conditions, such as incarceration, are alert to the nonverbal cues of communication and feel the other's presence intensely without overthinking. It is a paradoxical situation: I understood that human beings who in the majority have a shattered personal history of abuse, betrayal, and deprivation and who have committed crimes of several kinds, are very sensitive, welcoming, and receptive to the cues of truthfulness and authenticity. In many instances, I felt that the members of my group responded to my authentic and genuine stance of openness and acceptance with trust.

Moreover, I was beginning to realize that what I was learning from our group work, in a purely experiential way, was the foundation of the existential-humanistic approach to psychotherapy. I began to perceive that human beings are capable of deciding what to do with their givens and, in many cases, to decide to strive for growth, even when trapped in (or, perhaps, even because of) boundary situations and givens such as prison incarceration or the confrontation with death.

Working with this group changed me profoundly. I felt genuinely honored by the group participants who waited for me wearing clean and elegant clothes, always with a cup of aromatic coffee for me to share and to savor in the warm, welcoming atmosphere they took care to create. Each Thursday afternoon, while leaving the prison after my morning work, I felt like a better person, enriched by the experiences and feelings shared in our group. Most of the time and despite challenges that never ceased to emerge, I felt that working with these women was a blessing. The group participants enriched and widened my soul. I felt that life had been worth living every time that I left the prison building. Some of the group members whom I had the honor to meet after their release managed to find their own meaning in life, to reignite their lost faith in others and in themselves, along with hope for a better tomorrow.

Unfortunately, the group was abruptly terminated by the prison authorities due to problems created by drug trafficking within the establishment. One of our group members had been held responsible for organizing the plot. Once again, I realized that polarities are inevitable in life. I began to accept once again that reality, and therefore professional life as well, are colored by a never-ending interaction of contrasting experiences of joy and disappointment, of death and rebirth.

Continuing My Journey as an Existential Therapist
The abrupt ending of our work was a big loss for all of us. I felt very sad and disappointed. Group members did not have time for closure or to say goodbye to each other, much as occurs in a sudden death. Nevertheless, looking back to that period, it is fascinating for me to observe today the synergy that takes place in life's unfolding processes. I knew after working with the prison group that my journey toward becoming an existential therapist had begun and that there was no way back to older ways of seeing the therapy world.

During that time, I began to encounter other colleagues who shared the same enthusiasm toward the existential approach. I met these people through different and unexpected roads and places. As an example, I met Orah Krug at a wedding on the Greek island of Rhodes back in 2001. Our encounter was as dazzling as it was unexpected. Each of us had been invited respectively by the bride or the groom, and therefore did not know each other. We sat at the same table during dinner, and it only took a word uttered by one of us to ignite a sort of existential stardust current between the two of us. Being aware of the other people's lack of interest in our bizarre topics of conversation, especially at a wedding, we managed to change the initial sitting arrangement and spent all night talking side by side about existentialism. Orah's very close acquaintance with Irvin Yalom, her thorough study of James Bugental, and her research (Krug, 2009) on the paramount work of both master therapists introduced me in an immediate, experiential way to the existential-humanistic approach developed in the United States of America. I was intrigued to dive into

Yalom's interpersonal approach to therapy along with Bugental's intrapersonal client's process perspective. Orah introduced me to the work performed by the Existential Humanistic Institute in San Francisco and to Kirk Schneider's contribution, among others. The seminal works of Yalom, Bugental, Krug, and Schneider on psychotherapy modalities and processes were to become important pillars of the psychotherapy training program at our institute in Athens some years later.

My deep connection and friendship with Orah Krug are a blessing for me today. We keep meeting each other frequently due to another turn in my life: My frequent visits during the past sixteen years to my elder son, Argyris, who decided to move to San Francisco after completing his studies at Stanford University. On one of my visits to San Francisco, Orah Krug introduced me to Kirk Schneider.

Meeting Kirk became and still is another blessing in my life. Our friendship is colored by our sincere mutual respect, our love for our profession and our deep interest in existential theory and research. Kirk Schneider's groundbreaking work on the existential-integrative approach, along with the development of the concept of awe, the paradoxical nature of human beings, and the polarization of human minds and relationships shed light on new aspects of the process of healing. This perspective brought me closer once again to the work of Rollo May, Kirk's mentor and close friend. The word "integrative" resonated with my need to integrate and make good use of my previously "epigenetically" acquired therapeutic skills and my newer fervor for the existential approach.

During the same period in which I met Orah Krug and Kirk Schneider, I encountered dear friends from my university studies in Athens who invited me to become part of their exploration of the existential approach. My encounter with Evy Dallas, Evgenia Georganda, and Alexis Harisiadis after graduating from university was another blessing for which I am grateful. The four of us began to gather for hours at least once per week at Evgenia's welcoming office. Initially, the main purpose of our meetings was to talk about our shared interest in the concepts developed by the various existential approaches to psychotherapy. All of us had been trained in different therapeutic modalities. Nevertheless, the four of us shared the bond of our university years and our common enthusiasm for the existential views on therapy.

Becoming an Existential Trainer
Our weekly relaxed talks soon became deep and passionate dialogues during which we enjoyed coffee and our company while exchanging

theory, experiences, dreams, and plans as they made their subtle and later intense and pervasive appearance in our group. After some months, we decided to open our group and invited some close colleagues and psychology students to participate in these evening dialogues. We soon realized that our encounters were becoming seminars. Students were asking us, if possible, to teach them theory and to train them in this new fascinating modality of work. Immediately, the four of us became aware of our need to study the existential approach further and in an even more structured way.

As a first step, we reached Emmy van Deurzen, founder of the New School and the Existential Academy in the United Kingdom, and Ernesto Spinelli, whom we had first met as a presenter at a seminar given by Irvin Yalom in London. London was very appealing for us since Evy Dallas had a flat in the city that soon became our existential training nest. The four of us travelled for a while, managing to train in existential modalities and to create an even stronger bond among ourselves that laid the solid foundations for the birth of The Hellenic Society for Existential Psychology, Gignesthai, in 2004.

Nowadays Gignesthai is a well-known training institute, located in Athens, Greece, which offers a four-year training program in existential psychotherapy and has been accredited by the European Association for Psychotherapy (EAP). Greek students are, in the majority, well versed in the English language. Nevertheless, we embarked on the translation into the Greek languages of important works authored by Emmy van Deurzen (1988), Ernesto Spinelli (2004, 2005, 2007), Mick Cooper (2016), Kirk Schneider (1995, 2009, 2010, 2016), and Orah Krug (2009). All of them have enriched our training program not only with their writings but also with their teachings and their presence in Athens.

We are proud of our students and graduates who complete their studies and feel prepared for the profession, equipped with therapeutic skills and a deep knowledge of what it means to be a therapist, along with the responsibility that the role implies. Our training is theoretical and experiential and, as such, requires a thorough commitment from all of us teachers and students. It is based on theory, practice, and experiential workshops and is also deliberately enriched with all forms of art, such as drawing, cinema, theater, poetry, and literature. Experiential work, along with theoretical material, is mainly directed to the therapist's inner preparation for becoming a fellow traveler, accompanying their client in their journey toward healing.

Gignesthai's teaching staff, together with the founding members, has formed a working group that keeps developing ideas, thus making contributions to the existential field. As an example of our institute's contribution to the existential approach, our research team has developed the concept of "*Oistros* for life," an idea elaborated on in our study of Greek philosophy and contemporary literature. The concept of Oistros is linked to the transforming power that death awareness may effect upon human beings. Fear of death is transformed into a love for life and all that it can bring. The acknowledgment of our human destiny and our limitations (especially the fact that everything changes, and everything is finite) propels us into a stance of living life intensely and fully. In this courageous stance of being, we cherish every moment and become fully aware of the precious value of life. Oistros leads to a life full of passion, energy, and creativity, helping us to achieve the Epicurean dictum that "To live well and to die well is the same task" (Dallas et al., 2013).

Our work was presented at the Second International Conference on Existential Psychology hosted by the University of Fudan in Shanghai eight years ago. Introducing our work in China was a very meaningful experience that had an impact on me for several reasons. First, I was immersed in a different culture by Chinese psychology professors and students who played an active welcoming role in the conference, always eager to interact with all presenters. We had lunch together and shared coffee breaks in which we were all open to learn from one another how we live in our own different cultures. Second, I met colleagues from different parts of the world who showed me their way of working with existential concepts. As an example, I was impressed by the work of Xuefu Wang (Wang, 2011), who presented his work on *zhi mian*, a concept thoroughly elaborated by the Chinese Institute of Existential Psychology that is highly related to the previously mentioned concept of Oistros of life. Zhi mian means to face life directly and to have the courage to face our existential concerns with no pretenses. Oistros is linked to the awakening that drives human beings to change when stung by death awareness. The connection of both concepts corroborated the interrelation that takes place in knowledge and the epigenetic character of concept formation across time and civilizations. Zhi mian and Oistros became for me the symbol for building bridges among cultures and concepts in our profession. Third, I was blessed to meet in China two great colleagues: Erik Craig and Louis Hoffman. I was intrigued and deeply impressed by Erik's work on the *Tao, dasein,* and *psyche* (Craig, 2009), among other concepts. I discovered a bridge that connected oriental concepts with Heideggerian ideas finely elaborated by an American author who turns the intricate, theoretical postulations of

German thinkers into accessible and deep conceptualizations applicable to therapeutic practice.

Louis Hoffman's thorough work on existential psychology in a cross-cultural context (Hoffman et al., 2009; Hoffman et al., 2019), his elaboration on poetry and existential practice, and his prolific contribution as a writer and researcher has never ceased to impress me. Lately, I was honored to be part of a panel that included Erik and Louis, in which we presented work related to research in the existential field at the Second World Conference on Existential Psychotherapy that took place in Buenos Aires, Argentina in May 2019.

I presented at that panel some of the findings of my doctoral thesis; the title of my presentation was "The Existentiality of Therapeutic Factors. The main findings of my transtheoretical research refer to concepts that forge bridges between different approaches to psychotherapy and research. My early interest in the helping factors in psychotherapy followed me throughout my professional formation. The more I delved into clinical practice, the more I needed to see what contributed to change in the therapeutic endeavor. I knew that it was the time for me to dive into research.

I met Anastasios (Tassos) Stalikas during the time Gignesthai was forming. Tassos is a prominent psychology professor, therapist, and researcher at the Panteion University of Social and Political Sciences in Greece; he trained in Canada, where he taught for nearly two decades at McGill University. Meeting Tassos was another blessing in my life that opened a twofold road for me. As an existential-experiential therapist who had trained with Al Mahrer (1996) in Canada, Dr. Stalikas was thoroughly interested in psychotherapy process and outcome research. He was also immersed in the realm of positive psychology, which had driven him to found and become first president of the Hellenic Society for Positive Psychology.

Dr. Stalikas accepted me as a doctoral student, and I soon became part of his research team at the university. We designed a study that explored the presence of helping factors taking place in psychotherapy experienced from the client's perspective. More precisely, our work explored client-specific changes and therapeutic interventions from the client's point of view. We were aware that the importance of the client's perspective has been acknowledged during the last decades by the professional community (Bohart & Tallman, 1999; Lambert & Ogles, 2004; 2009; Elliott, 2010; Elliott et al., 2004). Nevertheless, the number of process research studies based solely on the client's perspective is still scant. Our study brings to the foreground the subjective experience of the client and, therefore, the imperative need to include it in the integral study of psychotherapy process research. The client's account of therapy contributes to the thorough exploration of psychotherapeutic processes and to the clarification of the therapeutic factors that lead to change.

Our research examined 10 semi-structured interviews held with clients who had successfully completed psychotherapy based on a variety of widely accepted therapeutic approaches. Grounded theory was used to analyze the interviews. Results led to a theoretical model that depicts the process of change in psychotherapy and the therapeutic factors that take place within that process. This theoretical model of change reveals the client's and the therapist's role, along with the role of their working alliance as basic factors of therapeutic change. Findings underscore the importance of the co-construction of a therapeutic world of new possibilities and different choices for the client: The creation of a safe and trustworthy environment; the human integrity and professional and accepting stance of the therapist; the client's intentionality for change and hard work; and a solid therapist and client working alliance as necessary conditions for successful psychotherapy. I soon realized that our findings underscored the existential character of the helping factors found in all the therapeutic modalities included in the study.

Working with Professor Stalikas, being part of his research group, and becoming a co-founder and active member of his newly formed society was a privilege for me. I was invited to give classes at the university in graduate and undergraduate courses. I took part in numerous conference presentations in Greece and around the world, in which we presented our findings as they were developing in our thesis. But most of all, I met remarkable colleagues who have become dear friends today.

I was introduced to the world of positive psychology and its development through the twenty years since its conception in 1998 by Martin Seligman (2002). Delving into the existential approach and positive psychology at the same time was a source of constant inspiration and deep, challenging questioning while dealing with seemingly contrasting ideas. I was mainly asked to teach topics related to the widespread concepts of *meaning in life* as part of several university courses. The field I was lecturing on was obviously becoming the natural bridge that connected both perspectives while concurrently contributing to my path toward my professional integration. Positive psychology's development toward its second wave (Wong, 2013; Ivtzan et al., 2015) has brought existential-humanistic and positive psychology nearer, helping me reconcile these two seemingly different perspectives, at least on a theoretical level. Thorough work needs to be done in both fields regarding research methodology because positive psychology and the existential approach rely on different, and at times conceptualized as competing, research methodologies.

At last positive psychology has turned its gaze toward the dark side of life and thus the acknowledgment of restrictions and difficulties that could, at times, become triggers for thriving. The existential-humanistic approach has always acknowledged, along with the givens and finitude of life, the value of a positive attitude and trust in the possibility for responsible choice inherent in human beings. The existential-humanistic perspective is enriched as well by the concepts of awe (Schneider, 2009), Oistros (Dallas et al. 2013), and zhi mian (Wang, 2011) that contribute to the creation of a fulfilling and functional life. These compatible concepts from both approaches build up to my continuous search for professional integration.

What is the Existential–Humanistic Approach for Me?

Existential-humanistic therapy resonates with my multicultural background. I was born and raised in Argentina. My family's origin is Greek, and I was educated in a school founded by the British community in Buenos Aires, a cosmopolitan city formed by immigrants from a Europe devastated by war, seeking to settle and create roots. My parents left Greece, fleeing from the horrors of World War II and the Greek Civil War that had devastated the country, creating an atmosphere of division and hatred within the population. My parents were young people who did not give up when confronted with death and despair, never lost hope in a brighter future, and dared to seek new paths for creating a fulfilling life. It is within this family nest that I was born, brought up in an atmosphere of never-ending possibility and strength to face life's horrors, with responsibility toward ourselves and society.

At the age of twelve, as I began secondary school, I was introduced to group work facilitated by psychologists who were at the time deeply influenced by Carl Rogers's encounter group movement. Our religion class had been replaced by a "Personal Formation" weekly encounter group, followed by spiritual retreats where I learned the magic of inner search combined with community sharing. Our educators, many of them Catholic nuns who were devoted to social work as well, ran an affluent girls' school situated in the outskirts of Buenos Aires. They prompted us pupils to work in the heavily populated urban area characterized by substandard housing and extremely difficult living conditions. I feel deep respect for my teachers, especially towards Sister Patricia Carney, who inspired us by her stance, her faith, and her commitment. We worked in groups with poor families, helping them to take care of their kids, change diapers, and feed children. It was not about a duty to be charitable and become philanthropists. Our endeavor contributed to forming our social conscience, becoming exposed to human struggling and learning to discern and inspire possibility and hope amidst difficult conditions. It was about seeing the whole of life and becoming aware of the challenging side of human beings and society.

My high school teachers' presence, stance, and support is a source of inspiration even today, many years after high school graduation. I have learned since adolescence that givens can be extremely harsh for some people. I began to see by then that it is what a human being makes out of their difficulties and challenges that matters. Our work with marginal populations was illuminated by our deep faith in the capacity of human beings for thriving and growing through pain. I saw that difficulties can be overcome when human beings are aware of their condition, validated by their people, and encouraged to search individually for possibilities. I was dazzled by this eye-opening search for personal freedom within extreme situations. Hence, it is not a surprise for me to have felt familiar with the existential-humanistic approach and its basic tenets as soon as I encountered it as a student.

It is while writing these lines that I realize that the seed of existential-humanistic therapy was incubating in me since adolescence. And I feel grateful for this. I can now understand as an adult why existential-humanistic therapy felt so familiar the first time I was exposed to its theoretical background in Evy Dallas's course on theories of counseling in my master's degree. The existential-humanistic approach carries the awareness of life's finitude along with possibility and hope within its basic premises. I contend that hope is not a magic-imbued, wishful-thinking word. It is a process that entails a plan based on new prospects and a sense of self-efficacy embedded in the individual who strives to make something good out of his restrictions (Snyder, 2002). The prospect of striving for the Aristotelian concept of the good life, a life colored by meaning and values, that most existential-humanistic writers propose differs from a long-held contemplative, pathetic stance of despair and alienation. The search for new possibilities and setting human beings free is a never-ending process that requires commitment, will, courage, wisdom, temperance, and justice toward ourselves and society. Looking for new ways to deal with life implies an active stance that helps human beings confront and deal with the fear of finitude and eventually the fear of an unlived life. Staying forever contemplating and becoming fully aware of despair and human misery is not enough for living a meaningful life. Probably it is a good starting point of awakening.

Existential-humanistic therapy was introduced in the United States by Rollo May with the publication of *Existence: A New Dimension in Psychiatry and Psychology* (May et al., 1958). May had spent several years teaching English language in Thessaloniki's Anatolia College in Greece before the book's publication. While travelling through Europe during his summer vacations, he became acquainted with the ideas of a post-war generation of existential thinkers highly influenced by despair and the horrors of World War II. Rollo May returned to his homeland enriched by his experience in Europe, ready to express his own stance and synthesis of what existentialism meant for him. He was highly influenced by the works of Soren Kierkegaard (2013) and Friedrich Nietzsche (2002). After his return to the United States, he completed his doctoral thesis (and later book) with the title *The Meaning of Anxiety* (1977), under the supervision of his mentor Paul Tillich (1999). Rollo May created lifelong links with James Bugental, Irvin Yalom, and Kirk Schneider, a group of thinkers that gave birth to the existential-humanistic approach in the United States, a field constantly enriched by the contributions of Orah Krug, Louis Hoffman, and Nathaniel Granger among other thinkers.

Existentialism in the New Continent carries its own intrinsic characteristics. It is imbued with the hope of never-ending possibilities along with the need for assuming individual responsibility toward life's challenges. This stance is congruent with the way American countries were conceived. Every immigrant was responsible for themselves in order to be able to survive and construct a life in the new land. On the contrary, European countries were able to endure across thousands of years by creating a strong sense of interdependence among their population. As an example, Greece as a country managed to survive 400 years of Turkish occupation as a result of creating strong bonds among families and local communities that remained united against the invader. European existentialism is about absolute interrelation and being with others in the world. The existential-humanistic stance is about assuming personal responsibility for each individual choice in life. My position is to create a synthesis of both stances (since I myself am a result of both continents and cultures), which means being responsible for my choices while being aware of my interdependence with others. I contend that a combination of both approaches creates a realistic way for setting people free. Anyway, life has a magical way of teaching us, if we have eyes to see. As an example, the COVID-19 pandemic has shown us in a brutal way that human beings are interrelated more than we thought we were, I dare say. And it has taught us that if we are to survive as a world population, we need to assume individual responsibility along with a stronger sense of interrelatedness and care for the welfare of others.

Existential–Humanistic Psychotherapy Changes Me

How Does Existential–Humanistic Therapy Change Me as a Person?

Becoming an existential-humanistic therapist is a never-ending process that makes me a better person. Such an ongoing transformation helps me to welcome uncertainty and to somehow get ready for the unexpected challenges and difficulties of life. Regarding my personal life, being fully present, one of the basic premises of the existential-humanistic approach, helps me savor and appreciate my people and the good things that happen in everydayness. It helps me to be able "to see a world in a grain of sand" (Blake, 2008), keeping some of the innocence of childhood years. Existential-humanistic principles help me feel comfortable with constant change, with chaos, with unforeseen events, and to accept life as it is with courage and hope. Moreover, my existential worldview helps me assume full responsibility for my choices and avoid blaming others for my mistakes. I have learned to treat myself with compassion and respect, even when I fail. Today, living in a world infected by the COVID-19 pandemic, I am even more aware of life's givens and harsh restrictions. Illness, suffering, fear, and despair bring forth in a brutal manner our limitations and vulnerability as a human species. I strongly agree with Sartre (Sartre & Mairet, 1960) that we are our choices, even when confronted with extreme limitations, and with Merleau-Ponty (Merleau-Ponty & Smith, 1962, who underpins that we are our bodies. I feel humble when facing life, death, and the human condition, assuming at the same time a responsible and active stance toward doing my best to protect my own health and the health of other human beings in the world community.

Today, more than ever in my life, I am fully aware that I only have one chance to live this one life that was given to me as a present, which I am blessed to have received and which I have no intention of throwing away by adopting any kind of antagonistic attitudes toward others. Becoming an existential-humanistic therapist is a constant reminder to be brave, and to choose responsibly among the possibilities that unveil themselves to me or that I am called upon to create. Looking at life through the lens of existential-humanism means being able to forge paths amidst chaos, to find new routes when roads seem blocked. Existential-humanism carries within it hope and creativity and is a constant reminder that the human condition does not doom us to darkness and despair. Being conscious of my finiteness helps me live life to the fullest and be grateful for the blessings that I constantly encounter as I walk my way.

How Does Existential-Humanism Change My Psychotherapeutic Practice and My Work as a Trainer?

The existential-humanistic approach has a continuous influence on my development as a human being who is also a therapist, a trainer, and a supervisor. The existential view of life has helped to strengthen my faith in human beings and our capacity for choice, growth, and the creation of possibilities. I strongly encourage clients to express the way they are experiencing therapy and our relationship in the moment and to become aware of their individual internal process. Experiencing the present moment is a mindful attitude that becomes one of the most precious tools for delving through therapy and life. Both for clients and for therapists!

The existential encounter is a real act taking place between two human beings in a real relationship. The client is seeking help. The therapist is willing to accompany a wounded person on their way toward healing with their whole being and, of course, their expertise. According to Jerome Frank (Frank & Frank, 1961), the therapeutic bond is nested in a contract based on the therapist's rationale and thorough expertise. Therapists are responsible for taking care to instill hope in the therapeutic endeavor. The expert therapist is not a blank screen and cannot hide behind a mask of aloofness and detachment. The therapist is called to be fully present and create an I–Thou relationship (Buber, 1996; Buber et al., 1997) as a sensitive human being who has the knowledge and will to create a holding environment for the client who seeks help. As Yalom (1980) wisely says, "it is the relationship that heals" (p. 401). Within the therapeutic relationship, the therapist is exposed to another human being and does not have anywhere to hide. Existential-humanistic therapists do not hide behind a mirror and therapy is not regarded as a sort of medicine given to a person in order to cure an illness. Hence the lack of techniques and specialized manuals and protocols in the existential-humanistic approach. Psychiatric diagnoses are not regarded as dictums carved in stone that turn into constraints toward healing. Clients who have been diagnosed by a medicalized health system are viewed as whole beings who are alive and mean much more than their *Diagnostic and Statistical Manual* (DSM) classification. Diagnosed clients are individuals who have a history of pain that needs to be healed. Existential-humanistic therapists need to place their required knowledge to one side, transcending their own need for the security offered by categorizations and readymade techniques described in manuals, while communicating with a client who has been categorized as dysfunctional. Being aware of our common humanness while working therapeutically with clients becomes an act of ultimate democracy that requires courage, respect, thorough professional preparation and, mainly, deep *agape* from the practitioner's side toward the human condition.

I conceive successful therapy as the co-creation of a therapeutic world in which the client, the therapist, and the relationship that they form create the conditions for change to happen. A strong therapeutic alliance based on the sincere and welcoming stance of the therapist is a powerful factor in promoting therapeutic change. The therapist's presence is conducive to the client's openness and will to share their concerns. Once trust is established in the relationship, a constant dynamic interaction emerges between client and therapist. This shared interaction creates the ground for new meanings and possibilities to emerge. The therapist who dares to be wholly present in the therapeutic endeavor will create the necessary conditions for change and healing to occur.

The therapeutic relationship is an ongoing kinesthetic process of cognitive and emotional interaction taking place between the therapist and the client. The processes that take place have an impact on the client and affect the therapist's choice of interventions as well. Being present as a therapist is a profound and powerful intervention. Existential-humanistic practitioners who are fully present for their clients need to be aware of the therapeutic process taking place in the here and now. As an example, decisions on how to deal with the client's defenses (the client's need to protect their well known, though probably dysfunctional, way of leading their lives) need to be attuned to the client's needs. By being fully present and aware of their intrapersonal experience, existential-humanistic therapists are called to look after the therapeutic endeavor. I agree that the client is the most important factor of change (Bohart & Tallman, 1999); nevertheless, the therapist has undoubtedly the ultimate responsibility for the process leading to change. Hence the need for us practitioners to assume responsibility as professionals in the field.

How Do I Visualize Existential–Humanistic Therapy in the Future?
The existential-humanistic approach is highly regarded by the humanistic approaches to therapy and has been positioned on solid ground cultivated by generations of thinkers and practitioners who have wisely worked on the basic premises that made the approach grow. Regarding the future, I envision existential-humanistic therapy thriving and on its way to becoming a humanitarian haven in a rapidly changing world—one characterized by efficient and quick communication that often seems unable to connect human hearts, especially among people in need. I visualize the existential-humanistic approach to therapy as an embracing ground for people seeking to be heard with respect and dignity while searching for new ways that allow them to lead a meaningful life.

A first suggestion for existential-humanistic psychology to develop further and strengthen its establishment in the therapeutic field is that thinkers and practitioners need to work on research. We need to generate thorough studies related to the process and outcome of existential-humanistic therapy if our approach is to survive and eventually thrive in a world in which national health systems tend to medicalize the helping professions, treating psychotherapy as a medicine to be imparted to patients according to protocols. I propose that existential-humanistic practitioners and thinkers leave aside older preconceptions and negative attitudes toward research. Studies that explore aspects of our practice, such as listening to the voice of our clients and the processes of change taking place in the therapeutic endeavor, are scarce. Research in our field can show that the humanistic approaches are as effective as the so-called "accepted forms of intervention" by the national health services of most countries. It is time for humanistic practitioners to leave aside their aversion (and probably lack of knowledge) toward statistical formulas. Besides, qualitative methods of research, preferred by most humanistic practitioners, have developed and evolved during the last decades, allowing researchers to explore human experience in depth as well as in breadth (Elliott, 2010).

As a second suggestion, I stress the need to carefully craft training curricula for psychotherapists that take into consideration the characteristics of trainees and are not readymade programs for mass consumption. Psychotherapy training programs must stress the responsibility that a psychotherapist assumes when relating with a client and must focus on experiential work, theory, and thorough knowledge of ethical codes and guidelines stated by professional organizations. Trainees need to be exposed to working with clients and receiving personalized supervision during their formation. One of the challenges that I face while training psychotherapists, especially during the first years of their programs, is the fear that students encounter when they realize that we do not teach "techniques." Most of the therapists-in-training ask to be taught a protocol and a step-by-step guide for doing therapy. They need a guiding map. Becoming familiar with the uncertainty of the therapeutic encounter takes time and practice. Clients who seek help need to find in their psychotherapists a person who will accept and listen to them in an unconditional way, helping them create a renewed sense of meaning and hope for new possibilities. Therefore, psychotherapists' training programs should focus on the personal skills development of each trainee. Theory and techniques are not enough.

As a third suggestion, and taking into consideration the lack of so-called techniques in existential practice, I address the need to build bridges with other approaches that might seem compatible with our principles and could shed light on aspects of the therapeutic endeavor that the existential-humanistic approach cannot cover in some cases. As an example, I find some aspects of the systemic approach precious even while working with individuals (Bertrando, 2018). Trying to visualize my client's life within the system that they are currently immersed in is helpful and conducive to a healthy understanding of their life situation. I strongly contend that it is time to leave behind rivalry between approaches, even between perspectives within the existential umbrella, and to strive for a profession in which practitioners collaborate toward a common goal, which is to help human beings live meaningful lives. As I expressed in earlier paragraphs, the ongoing interaction of the client, the therapist, and the relationship that they co-construct together creates the ground for achieving therapeutic change and healing. The clients' needs and active participation, paired with the therapist's professional stance and humanness, inspire the client who learns how to find new ways to live a functional life. As found in research (Zymnis & Stalikas, 2017), clients contend that all their therapists will be present in the client's life "forever."

Epilogue

Writing about my journey toward becoming an existential-humanistic therapist was a new blessing for me. It was an important opportunity to look with love and respect at the ongoing development of my professional life. It is with deep joy that I realize that many of the people who had an impact on my life are fellow travelers today. Meaningful relationships that persist through time are never-ending blessings. I honor the people who have left, feeling indebted for their unconditional support. I am deeply grateful to the editors of this volume, especially to Louis Hoffman, for inviting me to share my path of professional discovery. I encourage young therapists to dare, to leave obstacles aside, and to dive into the existential-humanistic approach, the premises of which will help them deal with the challenges that will be encountered in their lives.

References

Adler, A. (2013). *The practice and theory of individual psychology* (Vol. 133). Routledge.

Bertrando, P. (2018). *Systemic therapy with individuals*. Routledge.

Blake, W. (2008). *Auguries of Innocence: The complete poetry and prose of William Blake*. University of California Press.

Bohart, A. C., & Tallman, K. (1999). *How clients make therapy work: The process of active self- healing*. American Psychological Association.

Buber, M. (1996). *The letters of Martin Buber: A life of dialogue*. Syracuse University Press.

Buber, M., Cissna, K. N., Rogers, C. R., Anderson, R., & Cissna, K. N. (1997). *The Martin Buber-Carl Rogers dialogue: A new transcript with commentary*. SUNY Press.

Bugental, J. F. (1987). *The art of the psychotherapist: How to develop the skills that take psychotherapy beyond science*. W.W. Norton & Company.

Bugental, J. F. (1999). *Psychotherapy isn't what you think: Bringing the psychotherapeutic engagement into the living moment*. Zeig Tucker & Theisen Publishers.

Camus, A. (2013). *The myth of Sisyphus*. Penguin UK.

Craig, E. (2009). Tao, dasein, and psyche: Shared grounds for depth psychotherapy. American Psychological Association Annual Convention, 2006, New Orleans, LA.

Dallas, E., Georganda, E. T., Harisiadis, A., & Zymnis-Georgalos, K. (2013). Zhi mian and "Oistros" of life. *Journal of Humanistic Psychology, 53*(2), 252–260.

Elliott, R. (2010). Psychotherapy change process research: Realizing the promise. *Psychotherapy Research, 20*(2), 123–135.

Elliott, R. K., Greenberg, L. S., & Lietaer, G. (2004). Research on experiential psychotherapies. In M. J. Lambert (Ed.), *Bergin and Garfield's handbook of psychotherapy and behavior change* (5th ed., pp. 493–539). Wiley.

Frank, J. D., & Frank, J. B. (1961). *Persuasion and healing: A comprehensive study of psychotherapy*. Johns Hopkins University.

Frankl, V. E. (1985). *Man's search for meaning*. Simon and Schuster.

Hoffman, L. E., Yang, M. E., Kaklauskas, F. J., & Chan, A. E. (2009). *Existential psychology East-West*. University of the Rockies Press.

Hoffman, L. E., Yang, M. E, Mansilla, M., Dias, J., Moats, M., & Claypool, T. (2019). *Existential psychology East-West* (Vol .2). University Professors Press.

Hubble, M. A., Duncan, B. L., & Miller, S. D. (1999). *The heart and soul of change: What works in therapy*. American Psychological Association.

Ivtzan, I., Lomas, T., Hefferon, K., & Worth, P. (2015). *Second wave positive psychology: Embracing the dark side of life*. Routledge.

Kierkegaard, S. (2013). *Kierkegaard's writings: Stages on life's way* (Vol. 11). Princeton University Press.

Krug, O. T. (2009). James Bugental and Irvin Yalom: Two masters of existential therapy cultivate presence in the therapeutic encounter. *Journal of Humanistic Psychology, 49*(3), 329–354.

Lambert, M.J., & Ogles, B.M. (2004). The efficacy and effectiveness of psychotherapy. In M.J. Lambert (Ed.), *Bergin and Garfield's handbook of psychotherapy and behavior change* (5th ed., pp. 139-193. Wiley.

Lambert, M. J., & Ogles, B. M. (2009). Using clinical significance in psychotherapy outcome research: The need for a common procedure and validity data. *Psychotherapy Research, 19*(4–5), 493–501.

Mahrer, A. R. (1996). Studying distinguished practitioners: A humanistic approach to discovering how to do psychotherapy. *Journal of Humanistic Psychology, 36*(3), 31–48.

May, R. (1977). *The meaning of anxiety* (Revised ed.). W. W. Norton.

May, R. (1994). *Existence*. Jason Aronson.

May, R. (2009). *Man's search for himself*. WW Norton & Company.

May, R. E., Angel, E. E., & Ellenberger, H. F. (1958). *Existence: A new dimension in psychiatry and psychology*. Basic Books.

Merleau-Ponty, M., & Smith, C. T. (1966). *Phenomenology of perception* (C. Smith, Trans.). Routledge.

Nietzsche, F. (2002). *Nietzsche: Beyond good and evil: Prelude to a philosophy of the future*. Cambridge University Press.

Rogers, C. R. (1967). *On becoming a person: A therapist's view of psychotherapy*. Constable.

Sartre, J. P., & Mairet, P. (1960). *Existentialism and humanism*. Methuen.

Schneider, K. J. (2016). Existential-integrative therapy: Foundational implications for integrative practice. *Journal of Psychotherapy Integration, 26*(1), 49.

Schneider, K. J. (2009). *Awakening to awe: Personal stories of profound transformation*. Jason Aronson.

Schneider, K. J., & Krug, O. T. (2010). *Existential-humanistic therapy*. American Psychological Association.

Schneider, K. J., & May, R. (1995). *The psychology of existence: An integrative,*

clinical perspective. McGraw-Hill.
Seligman, M. E. (2002). Positive psychology, positive prevention, and positive therapy. In C. R. Snyder & S. J. Lopez (Eds.), *Handbook of positive psychology*, (pp. 3–9). Oxford University Press.
Snyder, C. R. (2002). Hope theory: Rainbows in the mind. *Psychological inquiry, 13*(4), 249–275.
Spinelli, E. (2005). *The interpreted world: An introduction to phenomenological psychology*. Sage.
Spinelli, E. (2007). *Practising existential psychotherapy: The relational world*. Sage.
Spinelli, E. (2004). *The mirror and the hammer*. Sage.
Stalikas, A., & Fitzpatrick, M. R. (2008). Positive emotions in psychotherapy theory, research, and practice: New kid on the block? *Journal of Psychotherapy Integration, 18*(2), 155.
Tillich, P. (1999). *The Essential Tillich*. University of Chicago Press.
van Deurzen-Smith, E. (1988). *Existential counselling in practice*. Sage Publications.
Wang, X. (2011). Zhi Mian and existential psychology. *The Humanistic Psychologist, 39*(3), 240–246.
Wong, P. T. (Ed.). (2013). *The human quest for meaning: Theories, research, and applications*. Routledge.
Yalom, I. D. (1980). *Existential psychotherapy*. Basic Books.
Yalom, I. D., & Leszcz, M. (2005). *Theory and practice of group psychotherapy*. Basic Books.
Zymnis, K., & Stalikas, A. (2017). *A grounded theory of therapeutic change from the client's perspective*. Doctoral Thesis. Panteion University of Political and Social Sciences. Athens, Greece.

Chapter 6

An Existentialist for Eternity

Mark Yang

A "Plan B" Psychologist

My dream was not to become a psychologist. Becoming a pilot was my first love. I'm still a plane spotter and occasionally fantasize about being in that captain's chair soaring above the clouds. So what did I do? I enrolled in college and declared computer engineering as my major. I decided to study computer engineering because I enjoyed computers and did not have the grades to become an aeronautical engineer, the closest thing to a pilot that I could think of. Computer engineering felt like a good compromise. Most important, I needed security and opted for the safe choice of a career path as a computer engineer. Becoming an engineer was an acceptable choice toward my family's pursuit of the Chinese-American dream. My path was set and I was safely on my way . . . except . . . I was a lousy engineer. Though I did well in mathematics in high school and even competed in a few tournaments, I reached my limit in college. A very humbling and painful initial encounter with finitude. I was forced to admit to myself and others that I did not have the right stuff. My classmates were the real engineers. They were better at engineering and mathematics. So, reluctantly, I switched my major to psychology and eventually became a psychologist. For a while, psychology felt second best. I am a plan B psychologist because plan A did not work out. Thank God!

My Three Wise Men

The decision to get off the conventional and safe path was painful and filled with fear. One of the things that I enjoyed about being a computer engineering major was that my path was well laid out. I now understand that as my *"escape from freedom."* All I had to do was to bury myself in my studies, walk that gilded path one step at a time and I would eventually arrive at the promised land. My engineering courses were pre-selected and I did not have to deal with the confusion and anxiety of class selection every semester. I pitied those who were not "on the path" and had to struggle for their indeterminate existence. I was one of the privileged few who did not have to enter the morass and fight for admission into the classes in the humanities that were often overcrowded. But due to my failure, I became one of the pitiful, lost, directionless souls. My future was all of a sudden filled with uncertainty. What should I study? How would I get to the promised land now that I was not good enough to traverse that gilded path? I was curious about psychology, but I did not think it would lead me to the promised land. I was lost and troubled. So I sought counsel.

The first "wise man" I sought out was Dr. Michael Tanner, the director of my computer engineering program. He'd been to the promised land. He worked for IBM and looked like he had the right stuff. Surely he would have good advice for me. He learned of my interest in psychology and suggested the field of artificial intelligence (AI), as it combined my interest in computers and psychology, a logical choice that made a lot of sense. Ah, if I'd only taken his advice back then. I'd be raking in the bucks now given how AI is currently all the rage. But something was missing. Though still unclear as to what I wanted, at least I knew what I did not want. The integration of computers with psychology felt like a compromise to me. I now know that for every *yes*, there co-exists a multitude of *nos*. I now know that the process of finding what one wants involves negation, becoming clear about what one does not want.

Then, I went to the second "wise man" who was a "counselor" in the department of psychology. Still thinking like an engineer, I was logical and systematic in conducting my due diligence. The counselor was true to his title and task, for he advised me on the courses that I needed to take in psychology if I were to change majors and graduate on time. He did his job as an "academic counselor" but was unfortunately effective in persuading me away from psychology, for he failed to perceive my inner needs. Psychology felt dry and uninspiring as embodied by this representative.

Desperate and directionless, I ventured into the office of Dr. Ralph Quinn, the hippy professor who taught humanistic psychology, my first college-level course away from the gilded path. Looking back, his was, sadly, the only formal course in humanistic psychology that was available in both my undergraduate and graduate programs. Ralph, who preferred that all his students call him by his first name, was totally cool. I remember him seducing us with talk of sex by promising us to show slides of nude encounter groups during one of his classes. Sure enough, the large lecture hall was filled with over 400 students two days later. He turned off the lights and began showing us pictures of elephant seals battling for supremacy, throwing their considerable weight around the beaches of Santa Cruz. The lecture hall erupted in boos, but Ralph took it in stride. I was captivated by his charisma and his warmth. Thus I ventured into his office during office hours and presented him with my life's dilemma. Ralph offered no advice or suggestions that day. What he did was care for me through listening intently to my pain and struggles. It is only now that I'm able to fully understand, appreciate, and describe to you the wisdom of his companionship—how he embodied existential-humanistic psychology for me in the midst of my despair. He provided an experience that was much more meaningful than any counsel he was to give.

As you can tell, that experience has stayed with me till now. At that time, as a lost twenty-year old, I had no idea what took place. But it felt right. I remember walking out of his office in a comfortable daze, a daze that I now understand as a shift in consciousness. Unwittingly, I had experienced companionship and faith. He offered me no sage advice but, rather, the experience of being heard and trusted. His wisdom was embodied. Nothing was solved, for I still did not know if psychology was the right choice for me. I would not know for a long time. But Ralph's companionship helped me to experience that unknowing was okay. I did not have to figure it all out then. Important things took time. He did not tell me these things directly. He embodied them for me. He did not tell me about psychology; he helped me to experience it. So even though I did not walk out of his office with a clear, rational sense of what I was to do with one of the most important decisions in my life, intuitively, my body, spirit, and soul came to realize that the experience I had just encountered was what I was after. I eventually chose to pursue psychology whole-heartedly and left behind artificial intelligence, a compromise, and computer information sciences, a derivative of the original secure path. That single thirty-minute conversation with Ralph changed my life, though I certainly did not know it at the time.

Ralph's companionship reminded me of a poem titled *My Old Jungian Therapist* written by Dave Elkins (1998), another mentor of mine on my journey to becoming, and an existential-humanistic psychologist. Dave wrote this poem as a tribute to his mentor and many of the words resonated with my experience. In the poem, Dave wrote of how his wise 73- year-old mentor had the patience to be lost with him as he struggled on his own dark, labyrinthine path, offering Dave nothing but his faith that had taken a lifetime to build. Now the mentorship provided to me by Ralph and Dave, as described in the poem, ripples on as I, too, do my best to embody and pass on what I've experienced during the lost periods of my own journey.

Fast-forward 25 years and I once again visited my old college campus. Unfortunately, I was unable to get in touch with my old professor. However, I found out how fortunate I was when I heard similar stories of Ralph's impact from a number of colleagues who attended the same workshop. Upon hearing the stories, I felt extremely fortunate to be one of Ralph's first students as he was just a rookie professor at the time of my counsel. He was far from perfect for he began his second career as a middle-aged single father with a butt-load of debt! Yet, he was perfect for me and many others since. What I learned was that for 25 years and counting, anonymously, Ralph humbly committed himself to his teaching at the local university. But his work ripples on through myself and numerous others he touched. Without fanfare, he impacted a number of us at critical developmental junctures of our lives. Through his example and companionship, he mentored us through critical times of uncertainty and helped us to have the faith to find ourselves in our own life journeys. His spirit ripples on through the words on this page. Ralph's humble dedication in the "backwaters" of a local university embodies the moral of the following Taoist parable of an unpretentious tortoise who chooses to drag his tail in the mud.

> Zhuangzi with his bamboo pole
> Was fishing in Pu river.
>
> The Prince of Chu
> Sent two vice-chancellors
> With a formal document:
> "We hereby appoint you
> Prime Minister."
>
> Zhuangzi held his bamboo pole.
> Still watching Pu river,
> He said:
> "I am told there is a sacred tortoise,
> Offered and canonized
> Three thousand years ago,

> Venerated by the prince,
> Wrapped in silk,
> In a precious shrine
> On an altar
> In the Temple.
>
> "What do you think:
> Is it better to give up one's life
> And leave a sacred shell
> As an object of cult
> In a cloud of incense
> Three thousand years,
> Or better to live
> As a plain turtle
> Dragging its tail in the mud?"
>
> "For the turtle," said the Vice-Chancellor,
> "Better to live
> And drag its tail in the mud!"
>
> "Go home!" said Zhuangzi.
> "Leave me here
> To drag my tail in the mud!" (Merton, 2010, pp. 93–94)

Even though I eventually decided to switch majors and traverse the less secure path that is psychology, the times of uncertainty were far from over. At the time of graduation, I once again faced a difficult choice. Many of my friends were looking forward to graduation and entering the workforce or ministry, other paths that were well traveled. The choice facing me was whether to continue my studies in psychology. I knew that an advanced degree was necessary if I wanted to make a career in psychology but the prospect of another four or five years of studies was daunting to me. Did I really want to engage in four or five years of additional studies after just completing four years of university studies? Furthermore, one year of graduate school tuition equaled four years of undergraduate tuition! Most of my friends thought that I was masochistic for considering additional studies. Though I didn't understand it at the time, I was faced with existential isolation. Despite the belongingness and support I felt from my college Christian fellowship, my decision about the future was mine and mine alone. The companionship and values of the fellowship helped me to transition from an engineer to a psychologist. The values of ministry, caring for the soul, were initially nurtured in the fellowship when I was a neophyte person of care. But now, in order to continue my growth as a *Seelsorger* (German for care of the soul), I needed to leave my spiritual and emotional home. In the words of James Bugental (1987), I needed to struggle with how much am I to be a-part-of, and how much am I apart-from the crowd. Most of my closest friends chose volunteer ministry, but I heard a different call. I was torn, so I returned to Ralph for counsel.

This time around was different. I encountered a thoughtful *shifu* (master) who offered his opinion that, if it were up to him, the study of psychology would take on an apprentice model where the apprentice would learn the trade from their shifu through living together. Ralph taught me to respect our field and that becoming a good therapist is a life-long pursuit. So, of course, one should invest at least four to five years to earn an advanced degree. Curiously, rather than feeling intimidated, I became inspired. Once again, I knew in my bones that Ralph was right. I made the decision to walk the road less travelled and take my chances in applying for graduate school.

The Learning Never Ends

Fast-forward four years and you would find me taking a walk with my mentor from graduate school. Dr. Winston Gooden was a popular professor, so many competed for his time. Inviting him out for walks was my way of ensuring time with him. During our last walk before leaving for my final year of internship, Winston shared with me, off the cuff, that he had recently read that seasoned clinicians were ten years in the making post-graduation. Exasperated, I shared with Winston the counsel I received from Ralph near the end of my undergraduate studies. I pleaded with Winston, "I was asked to commit to four to five years of dedicated studies after my undergraduate degree and now, near graduation, you tell me that another ten years is minimally required to become a seasoned clinician! Are you kidding me? Is this a sham? How is it that the period of professional growth becomes lengthier the higher one climbs? This shit never ends!" I pressed on and asked Winston what's to be said ten years after graduating with my doctorate, a supposed "terminal degree?" Winston simply laughed and said, "Your clients will offer you a simple 'Thanks'." I could not deny that Winston was speaking the truth. This recalls the beginning of verse 41 of the *Tao Te Ching*, which states that:

> When a superior man hears of the Tao,
> he immediately begins to embody it.
> When an average man hears of the Tao,
> he half believes it, half doubts it.
> When a foolish man hears of the Tao,
> he laughs out loud.
> If he didn't laugh,
> it wouldn't be the Tao. (Lao Tzu, 1995)

I was beginning to emerge from my foolishness to understand that the Way of the Tao is a life-long pursuit, a way of life.

It is now 23 years since that walk with Winston, and I am on the other side of the mentoring relationship. I found myself sharing with my own doctoral students that the four years they've invested in obtaining their doctorate in clinical psychology serves only as an introduction. For how much can you learn about psychodynamic, CBT, family systems, or humanistic psychology in a 40-hour class? I know that my students understand this intellectually just as I did. Yet, I can also imagine them thinking, "I spent all this money and time for just an introduction! Foolishness!" Yet truth passes the test of time. Now I have the honor of getting together with graduates, and they share with me that they understand better now what I shared with them. They find that there is so much to learn and too little time. They are passing along the same message to their students and colleagues. Now, like Winston and Ralph, I'm the one who is smiling and nodding for I, too, am on this life-long journey of learning.

Applied Philosophy. No More Statistics, Please!

My first opportunity to formally learn about existential psychology was in graduate school, which offered a two-unit elective course (half of a full-course) titled "Existential Psychology." I didn't take it. In fact, my buddy, a fellow student in the program, encouraged me to take the course, saying that it was right up my alley. I dismissed his recommendation, telling him that I was disinterested because of all that philosophy. How ironic! Looking back, I now see that I was not yet mature enough to appreciate the importance of philosophy, the type of philosophy that is grounded in everyday life. In regard to this, I have Irvin Yalom to thank for presenting existential philosophy and psychology in a way that is not so abstract and esoteric. I'm grateful for Yalom and others who embody existential psychology as lived-meaning rather than abstract theory. In fact, now I'm the champion for applied philosophy. I think graduate programs in psychology should follow the Catholic tradition of requiring those entering priesthood to have a good foundation in philosophy, recognizing its importance in caring for the soul. If it were up to me, I'd have my students study at least one year of philosophy in place of statistics. A foolish proposal, I recognize, in the face of empiricism as the dominant philosophy of the current era.

I cannot remember for sure, but most likely it was Winston who taught that short course on existential psychology. The funny thing is, I took all of Winston's courses except for his course on existential psychology. I even conducted an independent studies course with him focused on self-psychology, the closest thing I could find to humanistic psychology at the time. Though humanistic psychology was never offered, its spirit was still alive in my soul. Though I did not formally take the course on existential psychology with Winston, I soaked it in from him because of his way of being and because of how he nurtured me through our relationship. He is no longer an idol but will always remain a mentor of mine. His erudite elegance will forever be something I aspire to, even though I realize that I have my own unique way of being.

As is the case with most mentoring relationships, in order to continue to grow, the protégé needs to individuate and progress beyond the mentor. This was certainly my case as well, for I found the Winston within me after leaving him. I remember an episode during my internship training where I shocked myself and internally jumped for joy when I found myself sounding like Winston during one of my group sessions. It was an out-of-body experience. As time passed, my idealization of Winston diminished and we became more collegial. Part of the diminishment is the natural evolution of becoming not Winston, but the internalized Winston in the form of Mark, as I mentor my own students. Winston's spirit ripples on through me and I'm still ever so grateful. The end of idolization took place during one of my last visits with Winston post-graduation. I sat in his office after lunch and once again shared my life with Winston as I always have. I noticed that he was tired and struggling to keep attentive. I immediately harkened back to how I, too, was struggling with holding attention during a recent afternoon supervision session I conducted. We are human, all too human. It pained me to see that Winston had aged. Along with love, finitude was also in the room. During that moment, I realized once again that Winston, Ralph, my students, my clients, and I are all fellow travelers, each living out different roles throughout our individual and shared journeys through existence.

Existential Psychology: A Calling

A question that I've pondered and have been asked numerous times is, "When did you become an existential psychologist?" The short answer is after graduate school when I had time to read Irvin Yalom and finally found the type of psychology I was looking for. The truth is, I was quite disillusioned and disappointed in my graduate education. I chose to attend Fuller Seminary because I wanted to integrate my Christian faith with the study of psychology. In place of integration, I found deconstruction. My classmates and I joked sarcastically that seminary rhymed with cemetery, a place where we come to bury our faiths. A similar warning was given about how one risked losing one's humanity in the course of studying clinical psychology. People became cases and human experience turned into syndromes. Sadly, the psyche, the soul, was desperately missing in my study of both theology and psychology. This was not true across the board. I'm grateful for the few professors, Winston among them, who kept me from total disillusionment. But overall, I longed for a psychology of awe that took seriously the *Noos* (Greek for Spirit) in addition to the Psyche.

So for a long while, I was soaking in bitter discontent while paying back my considerable student loans. Why was I still paying for a program that I found disappointing? Yet with time, as I compared my program with others, I eventually came around and appreciated the quality education that I did receive in clinical psychology at Fuller Seminary. Fuller enjoyed a good reputation in the psychology circles around Southern California for training responsible, competent, and ethical psychologists. I eventually came to appreciate being part of that community and took on part of the responsibility for maintaining that reputation. On the other hand, it may just be that I've mellowed out as I've gotten older. In the end, what helped to redeem my graduate education and gave me meaning was when I began to learn about Logotherapy.

I've always been curious and concerned about the big questions in life, one of which was how do we make sense of suffering? I recall going to my pastor during high school and asking him the same question that my English teacher proposed to us in a written assignment: "Why did God let innocent babies die?" I do not recall the full answer given by my pastor. What I took with me was that there are big answers to big questions and that God had a wider perspective than us all. I agreed but was still searching.

Ten years later, I had the occasion to attend a talk given by a Holocaust survivor. Here was another opportunity to find some answers to the big questions I had always had. I was in the midst of my graduate studies at that time, so naturally I wanted to know about the psychological makeup of Holocaust survivors. What were the secret elements that led to resilience? To my disappointment, the speaker told me that he was only a child during the Holocaust and that he survived by not thinking too much about the big questions in life. He shielded himself from trauma through distancing. Who can blame him? I left the workshop disappointed and remained so until I encountered the writings of Victor Frankl. At last, someone made sense and found meaning out of the tremendous suffering he endured in the concentration camps.

While my gathering disappointment regarding my graduate education cannot begin to compare to the suffering that Frankl endured, his writings inspired me and helped me to find a way out of my disenchantment. What was I to do with the disappointment, the sunken costs in the form of tuition paid for the disillusionment that was my graduate studies? The time had passed and the money was already spent. I was still paying back my student loans at that point and I was sulking in despondency. Beyond brooding and complaining, what could I do? In the midst of my despair, Frankl's writings spoke to me. I learned from *Man's Search for Meaning* that:

> What was really needed was a fundamental change in attitude toward life. We had to learn ourselves, and, furthermore, we had

to teach the despairing men, that *it did not really matter what we expected from life, but rather what life expected from us.* We needed to stop asking about the meaning of life, and instead to think of ourselves as those who were being questioned by life – daily and hourly. Our answer must consist, not in talk and meditation, but in right action and in right conduct. Life ultimately means taking responsibility to find the right answers to its problems and to fulfill the tasks which it constantly sets for each individual. (Frankl, 1985, p. 98)

This harkens back to that famous speech by President Kennedy in which he said, "Ask not what your country can do for you, but what you can do for your country!" Victor Frankl's own experience from surviving the concentration camps bore witness to his theory. Frankl (1985) wrote that he and many of the prisoners had long passed the stage of asking about the meaning of life, a naïve query that understands life as the attainment of some aim through the active creation of something of value. Instead, what helped him survive the camps was turning the question around and living for a purpose, of responding to the question himself of what his life asked and expected of him!

I later learned that logotherapists call this a "Copernican Turn." Brilliant! The universe does not revolve around me. What was important was finding *my* place in the universe. All was not lost. While I could not turn back the clock, I could respond and make a better future for others. Even though I did not find the psychology that I desired in graduate school, I can still do my best to ensure that this experience is not repeated with others. This is why I choose to remain in Asia to teach the next generation of psychology trainees the principles of existential-humanistic psychology. Ultimately, it is up to each trainee to select the orientation that suits them most, but at least they will have been exposed to existential-humanistic psychology at some point along their journey. And I know there will be a subset of kindred spirits for whom the existential-humanistic tradition will be home. In many ways, following in the footsteps of Ralph 35 years later, I am creating my own "Introduction to Humanistic Psychology" to a crop of fresh-faced students who are curious and searching for something more in the field of psychology.

So back to the question of when I became an existential psychologist. When do any of us become an existential psychologist? How do we know that existential psychology is the path for us? I believe that I'm not alone in sharing that we were existentialists all along. I'd argue that we'd known it and known it all along. James Hillman (1997), in *The Soul's Code: In Search of Character and Calling*, wrote, "A calling may be postponed, avoided, intermittently missed. It may also possess you completely. Whatever; eventually it will out. It makes its claim. The daimon does not go away" (p. 8). My existential way of being was always there, long before I encountered the writings of Yalom, Nietzsche, or Kierkegaard. I recall "vegging" sessions with a few of my nerd buddies during high school. While others were carousing at keg parties, our delight was to sit in the backyard and gaze upon the stars, talking "nonsense" while pondering the big questions in life. This put quite a dent in our dating lives or the lack thereof.

These teenage philosophical discourses were my first foray into philosophy. Philosophy felt alive and embodied, central to our state of being. Fortunately, this affinity was not entirely killed off by the way in which philosophy was taught in graduate school. The esoteric philosophical dialogues we'd have in a few of our classes were anything but enlightening and inspiring. The discussions were abstract and hairsplitting. Philosophy seemed the antithesis of applied psychology. Again, it was not until I encountered Irvin Yalom and other existential writers that I discovered that philosophy need not be so abstract and esoteric. That the gifted philosopher is one who is grounded; or, in Chinese, we'd say that they *Jiēdìqì* (接地气). Now that I'm farther along on the journey, I see that there are those who are called to extend the field of existential philosophy and that is their gift and their delight. As for me, I am an existential psychologist whose delight is to ponder and extend embodied applications of existential philosophy. To each their own. So, like Jonah, I accepted my fate and eventually made my way to Ninevah and am now an evangelist for both existential philosophy and existential-humanistic psychology.

The irony continues, for an evangelist proclaiming the Gospel (the good news) of existential-humanistic psychology is the best description for what I do and how I live my life. The thing is, I'm strongly turned off by televangelists, and yet, ironically, the apostolic language of "The Great Commission" (King James Bible, 1769/2017, Matthew 28: 16-20) and the life of the missionary is what I most identify with. Evangelists are "called" to their missions. My identification as an existential psychologist comes as a calling to me, and the agency and will as to what I do can be best described as a mission. I believe that we have a choice. We can surrender, follow our destinies, and journey down the river of life in flow with the currents. Or we can deny our fate and swim upriver against the currents. Either way, the river will carry us downstream to our eventual destinations. In writing this, I wonder if Sartre and the branch of the atheistic existentialists would accuse me of escaping freedom, for existence precedes essence (Sartre, 2007). That there is no essential Mark that was meant to be. That the meaning that Mark is making out of his thrownness is entirely his own, and there is nothing predestined. As for me, I'm more aligned with Kierkegaard and the theists in believing that I was created by a creator with a mission in mind and that a destiny awaits me—a destiny that I am doing my best to live out through faith. To go against it and the potential that lies within me would result in existential guilt. In the end, it's all a great mystery to me and I am certainly filled with questions for the great beyond. The big questions are always there. For now, I know that I am an existentialist who is doing his best to create meaning in the midst of groundlessness and follow a calling that can only be perceived through the heart.

The idea of a calling is not unique to existential psychology. James Hillman (1997), a prominent Jungian analyst, believes that we all possess a personal calling, a destiny unique to us alone. Our primary purpose in life is to follow this calling and fulfill our destiny. This idea was promoted by Plato in the Myth of Er, presented at the end of his masterpiece, *The Republic* (ca. 375 B.C.E.). The story includes an account of the cosmos and the afterlife that greatly influenced religious, philosophical, and scientific thought for many centuries. The story begins with Er dying in battle. Yet his body did not decompose and he tells others of his journey in the afterlife. Toward the end of his journey, Er and the other souls arrive at the Spindle of Necessity, which is attended by sirens and the three daughters of the goddess Necessity. The daughters are known collectively as the Fates, white-robed incarnations of destiny. The souls, except for Er, were each given a lottery token. Then, in the order in which their lottery tokens were chosen, each soul was required to come forward to choose his or her next life. After this, each soul was assigned a Daimon, a guardian spirit to help him or her through their life. They traveled then to the Plane of Oblivion, where the River of Forgetfulness flowed. Each soul was required to drink some of the water, causing them to forget everything; again, Er only watched. Finally, as they lay down at night to sleep, each soul was lifted up into the night in various directions for rebirth, completing their journey.

The notion that a daimon accompanies us in life as a "carrier of our destiny" was promoted by Heraclitus, who preceded Plato. For Heraclitus, a person's daimon was their fate. Hillman adopted the concept of the daimon to account for the urge we all feel to discover and align our life with a personal calling, unique to our individuality and interests, and to which we can passionately devote our life. In line with this idea, Robert Greene (2013), author of the book *Mastery*, noted that throughout history many geniuses have spoken of a daimon, or inner voice, that accompanied them throughout life:

> For Napoleon Bonaparte it was his "star" that he always felt in ascendance when he made the right move. For Socrates, it was his daimon, a voice that he heard…which inevitably spoke to him in the negative, telling him what to avoid. For Goethe, he also called it a daimon, a kind of spirit that dwelled within him and compelled him to fulfill his destiny. In more modern times, Albert Einstein talked of a kind of inner voice that shaped the direction of his speculations. All of these are variations on what Leonardo da Vinci experienced with his own sense of fate. (p. 25)

In the end, the debate is an illusion. Whether I'm predestined to live out a destiny that was appointed or self-selected prior to my birth, or pointed forward with agency and will toward a future that I'm responsible for creating, it's all encapsulated under the Tao, the one and only existence. It is more apt to understand that my predestined calling and the future becoming present are not dichotomous but inseparable parts of myself. Medard Boss (1977) reminded us that the past and future always exist in a person's present. Herman Hesse (1951) portrayed this beautifully in the following passage from his magnum opus *Siddhartha*. The protagonist Siddhartha, after a life-long pursuit, settled down with a master who was anything but a simple river guide helping others to cross the river of life. This wise teacher urged Siddhartha to meditate and learn from the river. After much contemplation, Siddhartha realized:

> The secret from the river is that there is no time. The river is everywhere at once, at the source and at the mouth, at the waterfall, at the ferry, at the rapids, in the sea, in the mountains, everywhere at once, and that there is only the present time for it, not the shadow of the past, not the shadow of the future. "This it is," said Siddhartha. "And when I had learned it, I looked at my life, and it was also a river, and the boy Siddhartha was only separated from the man Siddhartha and from the old man

Siddhartha by a shadow, not by something real. Also, Siddhartha's previous births were no past, and his death and his return to Brahma was no future. Nothing was, nothing will be; everything is, everything has existence and is present." (Hesse, 2012, p. 60)

So when did I become an existentialist? I now say, "I've always been an existentialist!" I was, am, and am becoming the existentialist that is uniquely me. Knowing this helps me to feel grounded with a sense of awe and responsibility. I also feel very fortunate to know who I am in this regard as it is the guiding light as I live out my existence.

I'm not sure what others will take away from the story of my journey of learning. One thing that I hope to convey is that the process of becoming a good therapist is not about the mastery of skills or the attainment of knowledge along the lines of achievement and conquests. Instead, it is more a matter of attunement, alignment, and reverence. It is the recognition that the art of therapy is much too profound to be mastered. There are no master clinicians. We are all on the path of learning. There is nothing to be conquered, for when we climb, it is the mountain as much as our own legs that lifts us upward. Ed Viesturs (2007), who has climbed all 14 of the 8,000-meter peaks in the world without supplemental oxygen, learned humility and respect from the Sherpas who taught him to tread lightly and gently while climbing these magnificent peaks. We can only take what the mountains give us. As in therapy, we must have patience and be prepared. Perhaps then the mountains, like our clients, may permit us to reach their highest peaks. If we have learned indeed to "trust the process," we'd recognize that it is the process that is the master and that there is a force greater than oneself at work. The delight is in the journey and not the destination, for to travel well is better than to arrive. We are all existentialists on our journeys whether we know it or not.

References

Boss, M. (1977). *Existential foundations of medicine and* psychology. Jason Aronson, Inc.
Bugental, J. F. T. (1987). *The art of the psychotherapist.* W.W. Norton & Company.
Elkins, D. (1998). My old Jungian analyst. *Journal of Humanistic Psychology*: *38* (1), 41. https://doi.org/10.1177%2F00221678980381005
Frankl, V. (1985). *Man's search for meaning.* Pocket Books.
Greene, R. (2013). *Mastery.* Penguin Books.

Hesse, H. (2012). *Siddhartha.* Harper Collins Publishers, Ltd. (Original work published 1951)

Hillman, J. (1997). *The soul's code: In search of character and calling.* Warner Books, Inc.

King James Bible. (2017). King James Bible Online (Original work published 1979). https://www.kingjamesbible online.org/

Lao Tzu (1995). *Tao Te Ching* (S. Mitchell, Trans.). Retrieved May 2, 2019, from http://albanycomplementaryhealth.com/wp-content/uploads/2016/07/TaoTeChing-LaoTzu-StephenMitchellTranslation-33p.pdf

Merton, T. (2010). *The way of Chuang Tzu.* New Directions Publishing Corporation.

Plato. (2016). *The Republic* (B. Jowett, Trans.). Digireads.com Publishing. (original work written ca. 375 B.C.E.)

Sartre, J-P. (2007). *Existentialism is a humanism* (C. Macomber, Trans.). Yale University Press. (Original work published 1945)

Viesturs, E. (2007). *No shortcuts to the top: Climbing the world's 14 highest peaks.* Broadway Books.

Chapter 7

Looking Over My Shoulder

Myrtle Heery

I know what you want. You want a story that won't surprise you. That will confirm what you already know. That won't make you see higher or further or differently. You want a flat story. An immobile story. You want dry, yeastless factuality. *Life of Pi*, (Martel, 2001, p. 302)

The objective world can be dry, yeastless factuality. Such as I am writing, which involves my fingers touching letters on the keyboard of a computer; and in a broader view of the objective reality, it is a spring day in California in the year 2020. I am now sheltering in place along with all Californians due to the COVID-19 pandemic. How is this objective reality affecting me?

My isolation due to COVID-19 is bringing my subjective reality into sharp focus on my whole life and my existential questions about living and dying. I sit in silence to touch my feelings and find the words to express these feelings. It absolutely sucks watching the news on TV and learning that thousands of people are dying every day all over the world from this virus. No one I know personally has died yet, but I am sure I will know someone soon enough. And I could be one of those who dies. At age 73, I am part of the more vulnerable older population, and my chances of dying are greater if I should contract the virus.

This reality is harsh, yet paradoxically comforting to know that everyone on the planet is going through this experience together. I share this immediate focus with you, the reader, to bring you into my actual moment as I write. As you read these words, part of your objective reality is that you are holding a book and reading it or listening to this book on an auditory device. Part of your subjective reality is that what you are reading or listening to is stirring feelings, impressions, images, and other unknown dimensions of your subjective world. The objective world touches us harshly, humorously, sweetly in so many ways—and stirs up our subjective world.

The inner world of each person is immense, perhaps larger than will ever be consciously known to yourself or to others. This vast unknown territory is the landscape through which I accompany my clients on their psychotherapeutic journeys. To talk *about* me or a client is to make me or the client an *object* of observation, of speculation, or of report. Human objects are not to be confused with human *subjects*. The very fact of human subjectivity is the most distinguishing and salient feature of human life (Bugental, 1999). We have the paradox of the human as simultaneously being both subject and object. This paradoxical distinction is crucial and is at the root of existential-humanistic psychotherapy. Thus, this recognition of limitation—which I am now writing about and you are now reading about or listening to—applies to what I am saying right now.

What do we hold when our lives are threatened? What is the meaning of living? What do we hold to be true as we pass through great hardships? These questions and more are critical to me in these heightened, unpredictable moments. I contemplate these questions in the following pages and invite you to accompany me on my objective and subjective journey in becoming and being, first and foremost, an existential-humanistic person, and second, in sharing the great honor of accompanying others on their sacred journey of being, belonging, and becoming through psychotherapy.

Honoring Grannie Wisdom

I have no clue what my Grannie would say or do if she lived in these times of thousands of people dying from a virus. She lived through the Spanish flu pandemic, World War I, the Great Depression, World War II, and the polio epidemic. These tragedies I know contributed immensely to who she became.

My Grannie was tiny, maybe five feet tall, with piercing blue eyes that seemed from my perspective to see right into my soul. In other words, no lies to Grannie! She crocheted a lot. I would sit at her feet and stare at her fingers quickly moving the thin threads with a tiny needle in and out, forming the most beautiful placemats, hats, gloves, and even huge tablecloths. The thread was either pure white or light brown. Whether she chose one color over the other depended on whom she was giving the item to and for what use. When she would drop a stitch and go back and pick it up, I would look closely at how she made the correction. She quickly picked the stitch up, moving her fingers and needle back to the dropped stitch.

Those blue eyes never strayed from the work of her fingers. The mistakes were quickly corrected with ease and sometimes while humming an old gospel hymn. She showed me how to be patient, how to correct mistakes, and how to let go. Sitting at her feet, watching her hands working, and rarely talking was the setting for the more-than-weekly lessons building the foundation of who I became. When she did speak, it was profound. I remember asking Grannie what were those funny purple things peeking through the skin on her hands.

"Child, those are veins the good Lord shows to us as we grow older, reminding us that our time here is limited."

"When will the Lord show veins on my hands?"

"In time, little one, in time. Don't worry yourself; it happens to everyone."

"What does it mean that time is limited, Grannie?"

"Now that is a big subject I will answer when you are older. For now, remember to use your wonderful giggle no matter what happens. Promise me?"

"I promise, Grannie."

We never had that talk about time being limited. Instead, she would tell me regularly, "Remember to giggle, because you will need it."

The power of Grannie wisdom comes as a great balance with the tragedies I, along with millions of others, are living through with COVID-19. She was right; laughing at times helps me tremendously right now. Not to diminish the immense losses both physically and economically, but to assist in bringing hope into the moment and the future.

Grannie was the first existential-humanist I knew. She walked her talk. I am sure she never knew the term existential-humanist and would probably laugh to see those words beside her name. I remember the veins on my grandmother's hands, and I see the veins on my own hands steadily showing and marking time. My hands are like a faithful old clock, reminding me daily that I am aging and more vulnerable emotionally and physically. As I look over my shoulder at my life, I see it with older eyes, hopefully with wise eyes similar to my Grannie's.

White Privilege

I was born into a middle-class white family in Savannah, Georgia, in 1946. My father was Judge of the Family Court. Anyone could call him at home and they did. There were no cell phones, and the Judge's home number was in the phone book, making him an easy contact for everyone. People called regularly, and as soon as I could reach that phone, I pleaded to answer it. Daddy did not want to take the court calls at home and agreed to have me basically appease the caller. He instructed me to tell whoever was calling that he would talk with them by phone tomorrow at his office. There was the caveat that if this was an emergency, they should hang up and call 911 for the police.

I was so excited to answer the phone using the most adult voice I could find in my seven-year-old body. I would say, "You need to call the police if you need help right this minute, and you can call my Daddy at his office in the morning." I proudly gave them Daddy's office number and proceeded to limit the conversation and hang up the phone.

But the people calling often wanted to talk, and I wanted to listen. Of course, the conversation would go a little longer. These phone experiences taught me a lot about people whom I would otherwise never have known. I was white and privileged in the South in the early 1950s. Most of the people who called were women were being mistreated by their husbands, physically and/or financially. They were desperate, and they wanted the Judge to instantly fix their situation. I encouraged them to call the police immediately if they were in harm's way.

But what was harm's way? I never saw Daddy hit my Mom or even threaten to do so. Many of the women calling were frightened knowing that the men in their lives might hurt them. I had my eyes opened to the dark side of life and saw the power of listening and referring those in need immediately to someone with more power than this seven-year-old girl had.

Often I would run to Daddy after a call and report I had done my best by listening carefully, and then telling them to call the police. Daddy always seemed calm in his reactions to my stories, reassuring me the police would handle the situation. I had listened to darkness but was also very protected from darkness. From these sheltered roots, I listened and learned that I was privileged—and with privilege came responsibility.

The responsibility showed up every Sunday after church. My family would walk the halls of the Methodist Hospital, where Daddy was chairman of the board. Daddy would stop and ask each employee—including nurses, doctors, janitors, and cooks—how they were. We would eat lunch with the employees in the cafeteria. Yes, cafeteria food accompanied by kind inquiry into the lives of each person who made the hospital function.

This memory reminds me of a wise saying: "The service we render others is the rent we pay for our room on earth." These weekly hospital visits created deep gratitude to my family for helping me understand the existential fact that we are simultaneously in the process of living and dying together.

Curiosity

I was an innately curious child. I consistently asked the adults in my life obvious questions. Often these questions were uncomfortable for the adults, but thankfully I was not punished for asking. I would not say I was encouraged, but I kept asking.

We had an African American maid named Vangie who, in addition to cleaning our home, washed and ironed our clothes, often staying late to finish her work. I remember asking my parents at the dinner table, "Why can't Vangie eat with us?" My mother's reply was always the same to many of my questions, "When you are older, I will tell you." This quick dialogue ended with me picking up my plate and saying, "Well, in the meantime, I am going downstairs to eat my dinner with Vangie."

Down the stairs I would go with my dinner plate in hand. No one followed me, but rather let me do my thing. As I settled into a chair next to Vangie, who was ironing, I asked her, "Why can't you come upstairs and eat dinner with us?" Vangie never looked up, but kept on ironing and said, "Child when you are older, I will answer you." Wow, Mom and Vangie have the same boring answer, so I am going to come downstairs and eat my dinner next to Vangie until I get older. Right? Makes sense doesn't it? In a child's world, I did not want to leave Vangie out and actually loved being with her. Some evenings I would eat my dinner next to Vangie while she ironed and other evenings I would eat upstairs with my family. No one stopped me or questioned me. In retrospect, this was grace! At the ironing/dinner sessions I would ask Vangie more obvious questions.

"How come your skin color is different than mine?"

"It just is the way the Lord made us, different in color."

I learned that skin color made a huge difference in our lives. When I would sometimes hop in the car with Mom to take Vangie home, I saw more differences in the neighborhood where Vangie lived. I saw poverty there, but the paradox was the respect Vangie merited from her family for being employed in the Judge's home.

I was in awe of these differences with no answers from the adults regarding the pronounced disparity. I soon came to understand injustice and how it worked, but never why. I made a commitment to do something about this injustice. For me, the color of skin did not matter; Vangie and Grannie modeled for me wisdom through compassion, tolerance, forgiveness, and love.

Martin Luther King, Jr.

In 1966, fifty-four years ago, I had the great honor to hear Martin Luther King, Jr. speak at the Johnson C. Smith University (JCSU) in Charlotte, North Carolina. I, along with my white college roommate, Leigh, were the only white people in the audience. Our connection to get into this event was a friend of ours whose mother was a professor at JCSU. We had unbelievably good seats in the third row from the front. There are moments in life when you know, even as they are happening, that your life will be forever changed. This was such a moment. Dr. King looked directly at Leigh and me and asked in his very strong, clear voice, "What are you doing with your life?" I thought to myself, "I am making good grades in college. Am I supposed to be doing something else?" And again he looked straight at us and asked, "What are you doing with your life?" His talk went on about the precious gift of life and using your limited time well. Then I remembered what Grannie said when I was younger: life doesn't go on forever.

Dr. King talked openly about the fact he would most likely be killed, and said he was willing to die for his commitment to the integration of African American people. My thoughts went a lot deeper to his question, what was I doing with my life? This question became my mantra for many months after that event. I started looking at endings, not beginnings. College would be over soon and what was I going to do? A privileged life of traveling and drinking after college made no sense when I dared to contemplate my own death. Meeting Dr. King woke me up to the importance of using time with intention and commitment.

Two years later when I learned of Dr. King's death, I wept. I marched, sat in the back of public buses, wrote letters, and protested the injustices suffered by African American people in the South. I started living from the inside out, not from the outside in. I began following a much larger guidance from inside to my living with intention and commitment.

I had spent enough time in the South to know I did not belong there. I needed to find my people, my tribe. Eventually I left the South and found my people in northern California, where many doors opened for me.

The Shoe Fits

Existential-humanistic psychotherapy has been the perfect fit with my roots in taking responsibility for my life and my passion for social justice. I was drawn to a psychotherapy career with curiosity and love of listening to people with troubles very early in my life.

I studied many models of psychotherapy in graduate schools, and my resonance came with Carl Rogers's person-centered humanistic work (Rogers, 1965). This model gave me a language for what I had experienced in my childhood: empathy, unconditional positive regard, and congruence. I had the honor of meeting Rogers at a meditation gathering and witnessed him walking his talk with everyone, including me.

I admired his congruence and knew that if I, too, wanted to walk my talk, I would need to experience psychotherapy as a client. I entered psychotherapy with a humanistic psychologist, Eleanor Hamilton. Those years of inner exploration with Eleanor were transformative and would take a very long chapter to share. Individual psychotherapy is essential to becoming a therapist. Who wants to take a car to mechanics who wouldn't work on their own vehicles?

The combining of humanism with existential practice happened at the doctoral level of my studies, under the unexpected supervision of Jim Bugental. The first time I met Jim was in his small office in Santa Rosa, California in the early 1980s. I had no idea who this man was, but my friend and colleague Ann Dreyfus, who had introduced me to Carl Rogers, said Jim was "the best." Jim was very willing to meet with me when I told him I had not read anything he had written. Of course, I remembered his name from textbooks in relation to existential-humanistic psychology, but at that point in my career, I was more interested in how far I had to drive for another leg of supervision for both clients and my doctoral dissertation. Santa Rosa was close to home.

We met, and I promised not to read anything Jim had written for one year while he supervised my cases. He wanted to train someone to follow the subjective life of the client without the use of theory. I liked the idea of no reading very much and was full of curiosity about how Jim followed a client's subjective world. Toward the end of the interview, Jim asked if I had any questions. I had been drawn to a photo of a man with a wonderful smile on the wall behind Jim. So I went for what was "real" for me, which I quickly learned was of great value to Jim.

"Who is the man in the picture?" I asked. Jim reached back to the photo, picked it up, and tears began to moisten his cheeks. "This is Al Lasko, my best friend. He died recently." Jim looked up from the photo and looked into my eyes with a presence rich with the truth of what truly matters in being human—human relationships. I was experiencing authenticity in the moment. This is how he followed everyone's subjective world. He lived it fully with vulnerability and honesty.

Jim taught me through tears, humor, storytelling, silence, intellectual discussions, disagreements, writings, walks, lunches, and any opportunity he could take to question, to explore, and to follow his insatiable curiosity about the subjective world in the actual moment. Case consultation was not "about" the client but rather the lived moment of consultation. Essential to my consultations was what happened inside of me when I brought the client into discussion. For example, Jim invited me to pace in his office when I shared that my client often paced during sessions. This client had been labeled schizophrenic for many years. As I paced in Jim's office, I felt the isolation and fear of this label and tears streamed down my face. Words were not needed.

I returned to seeing this client with a depth of presence to her emotional pain that was what Jim called my *pou sto* for our long work together. Pou sto, a Greek term meaning a place to stand, in psychotherapy is a steady inner stand with the client while exploring the struggles of being human.

This experience of walking in another's shoes happened in so many different forms with Jim. After group consultations we would often go to lunch. Jim liked a certain restaurant that employed a waitress he nicknamed "Giggle Box." She had an infectious laugh and no matter how many struggles we had listened to that morning in consultation, listening to Giggle Box was just as important to us. Balance was always important.

In his later years, Jim lost a lot of his memory but took the loss as an opportunity to live fully what he had valued so deeply all of his life—the actual moment. His last years were spent mostly with his amazing wife, Elizabeth, enjoying the beautiful blue heron in their backyard, softly petting his beloved dog, Dickens, and sharing so many other wonderful moments of love and joy.

I struck a deal with Jim toward the end of his life. If there was a life after death, he would send me a message that I could not mistake. About a week after he died, I was waiting in my office for a client when a framed picture suddenly fell off the wall and landed at my feet. It was a poster from an International Transpersonal conference with the words "Individual Choice and Universal Responsibility." I found tears welling up in my eyes. I was not sure, but it seemed to be the promised message. Being a stubborn student, I had to get one more message. Later that day, there was a letter in my mailbox from a local mortuary with the following message: "You too will die one day! Today and only today you can purchase your cremation for 50 percent off."

Okay, I got it. These words reminded me of one of Jim's frequent phrases, "pointing with your elbow," which he used to emphasize the necessity, yet limitation, of words in attempting to describe one's subjective experience. Thank you, Jim, for gently and humorously "pointing with your elbow" to the truth. Jim's teachings are alive in me, and I dearly miss calling him to hear, "Hi, just a minute; let me turn the music down" (Heery, 2011b).

The Written Word

It was very important to Jim to get the written word published about existential-humanistic psychotherapy. On that topic, I and many of his other students published frequently. To motivate me to write and publish, he worked avidly with my writing and encouraged me to read a variety of literature about the existential, including classics by formative thinkers such as Frankl (1984), May (1958), Tillich (1952), and Yalom (1980,1985). I encourage and often require my students to read and absorb these invaluable resources.

Jim's encouragement included asking me to critique his last book, *Psychotherapy Isn't What You Think* (1999) prior to publication. He fine-tuned my writing by co-authoring three articles with me, starting with "Unearthing the Moment" (Heery & Bugental, 1999), then "Listening to the Listener: An Existential–Humanistic Approach to Psychotherapy with Psychotherapists" (Heery & Bugental, 2005a), and "Meaning and Transformation" (Heery & Bugental, 2005b).

In the meantime, I published on my own and with other colleagues. I took on a deeper responsibility in 2013 when I started my own publishing company, Tonglen Press. I have published three books and more than 10 articles and chapters in psychology textbooks with other publishers. And adding spice to my menu, I have interviewed Albert Ellis on his method of cognitive behavior therapy, bringing to light similarities and differences with the existential-humanistic model (Heery, 2000).

To support my lifelong commitment to social justice, in 2002 I founded a non-profit organization, the International Institute for Humanistic Studies (IIHS). The Institute offers trainings for students, interns, and professionals in existential–humanistic psychotherapy. IIHS also provides scholarships for minority students who are and will be serving underprivileged populations after they complete the trainings. The seven-year-old Myrtle who answered the Judge's phone and heard frightening stories, created, as an adult, a means to help address the darkness through empowering minorities to help minorities.

A book grew out of the trainings with a collection of writings from a number of students applying the existential-humanistic model to a variety of populations (Heery, 2014). I carried on Jim's passion for writing and publishing with my own students, using the Tonglen Press platform. The publishing work progressed further when in 2009 I compiled *Awakening to Aging* with my neuropsychologist colleague Gregg Richardson, followed by a second edition (Heery & Richardson, 2015). Both editions reached many readers on the challenges of aging—exploring death and dying and making meaning from loss and grief (Heery, 2014, 2015). The subject that called to me as a child at my Grannie's feet follows me to this day.

In 2017, I followed in Jim's footsteps and was honored as the first woman to receive the Rollo May Award for Independent and Outstanding Pursuit of New Frontiers in Humanistic Psychology—given by Division 32 of the American Psychological Association. My nomination for this award was submitted by my former student and now colleague, Louis Hoffman. The rippling out of work inspired by Jim continues with great authenticity as we serve those in need with compassion, courage, hope, resilience, and tolerance.

Authenticity Remembered

As I look over my shoulder at my international teaching experiences, I see faces, stories, tears, laughter, and so much more all weaving together the givens of the human condition. I feel humbled by the depth of each individual's story, by their reaching deep inside themselves in front of primarily strangers to make meaning of their lives (Heery, 2012, 2019).

I remember a tall, well-dressed Russian woman who attended a training I led in Russia. The suit she wore every day was the same and in perfect order. I noticed her physical appearance each day and wondered about her. I recall her certainty and her quiet manner. I trusted she would speak in time, which she did, and there was the surprise.

On the second day of the training, I had begun speaking to the given of finitude and how each of us carry the fact of our death. She raised her hand and said with certainty that she had cancer and might be dead in a few months. She continued to share that she was making the best of each moment, which included looking her best and being as honest as possible in all relationships. She actually felt grateful to her cancer for her present depth of appreciation in living each moment.

I shared through my translator how deeply moved I was by her honesty and courage. Since I do not speak Russian, I relied on my intuitive sense to connect with her and the participants at this vulnerable moment. I was sensitive to the depth of her sharing, looking closely into her eyes and gently moving my eyes to each participant. The caring from participants was palpable in the room. Some eyes were moistened and all were obviously moved. I invited the participants to share their feelings with her if they felt moved to do so. One of the participants who knew her and her health crisis spoke with great depth of appreciation. First, she thanked her for her honesty with the group about her health. Then with great emotion she shared how important she was to her in deciding to stop complaining about her life and begin appreciating her life. By watching her friend face her cancer with dignity, she had gained a new life. Others followed with stories that were moving, and the group drew closer.

The experience of sharing a life-threatening illness with a group is powerful no matter what country or circumstance. In this teaching situation, the students immediately experienced the connection of sharing the possibility of an individual death. In teaching, there is "talk about" a subject and a "lived experience" of a teaching. This experience took place many years ago, and I do not know if this participant lived or died. I do know that her vulnerability brought the group into an immediate depth of authenticity that I had seen in many other groups in many other locations. The fact of her possible death and what she chose in facing her death was a huge piece of global authenticity. The possibility of her death brought us each into the reality of death. Even now, eight years later, I can still see her in my mind and hold this experience close to my being. The courage to share her confrontation with her own death with me, whom she did not know, and with others who were mostly strangers to her, has been engraved on my heart.

Teaching in different countries can be enriched by being a part of different students' and therapists' journeys in learning. When I complete a training and wave good-bye to my colleagues at the airport, I turn to myself. I am surrounded by other travelers, but I sit alone. I look out the airplane window remembering all the shared moments of honesty, vulnerability, and courage. I may or may not ever see these individuals again. There is a sharp aloneness to these moments, which I recognize.

I, along with everyone else, ultimately arrive in this world alone and leave alone. Life is with others, yet each of us is ultimately alone. This paradox of being *a part of* and a*part from* follows each of us no matter where we live (Bugental, 1987; Heery, 2001).

Humpty Dumpty and Time Out

> Humpty Dumpty sat on a wall,
> Humpty Dumpty had a great fall.
> All the king's horses and all the king's men
> Couldn't put Humpty together again.
> *Classic Nursery Rhyme*

Mother Nature has given the world COVID-19 and put us in time-out through required social distancing. Isolation and loneliness are rampant. In this process we are seeing many Humpty Dumpties falling off walls with no king or king's horses or king's men putting Humpty together again.

We are seeing countless physical and financial deaths. The world is in an existential crisis with the main resource for help being ourselves. There is no need to turn to a king anywhere, but rather to ourselves to search closely the behaviors that impact the lives of others. By choosing to wear a mask, we can actually protect someone from possible death. How amazing to know we can do this! Perhaps the broken Humpty Dumpty can be put back together by our conscious caring.

Many years ago in my private practice, I saw a mother whose daughter had been murdered. What can any therapist say or do in such a tragedy? I gave her my heart full of care, compassion, and love. Yes, I say love in psychotherapy. The love I had for this woman's suffering infused her with hope. Once she asked me:

"Do you have a child?"

"Yes, I do."

"I could feel you did by the way you look at me with, what shall I say, love?"

"Yes, it is love."

"I hope this never happens to you."

"If it does, I will come see you."

Tears moved slowly down our cheeks as we gazed with love deep into each other's motherly eyes.

Tomorrow is Mother's Day 2020. I will remember this mother and how much our loving, therapeutic relationship supported her in becoming more than she or I ever expected. She later started a non-profit for children from the inner city and organized many acts of service. Humpty Dumpty did get broken, but the parts were put back together through acts of service and kindness to others.

I say to present and becoming existential-humanistic therapists, do not underestimate the healing power of love and compassion.

And to Mother Nature I say, I am listening with my heart. I will come out of this sheltering to a new normal, knowing my actions remain true to the complete wellness of the earth and all beings who dwell upon it.

References

Bugental, J. F. T. (1987). *The art of the psychotherapist.* W.W. Norton & Co.
Bugental, J. F. T. (1999). *Psychotherapy isn't what you think.* Zeig Tucker & Co.
Frankl, V. E. (1984). *Man's search for meaning: An introduction to Logotherapy.* Simon & Schuster.
Heery, M. (2000). Interview with Albert Ellis, MD, on REBT [Video]. https://www.psychotherapy.net/video/albert-ellis-rebt
Heery, M. (2001). Inside the soul of Russian and American psychotherapy trainings. *Journal of Humanistic Psychology, 42* (2), 89–101.
Heery, M. (2002). Food for the soul. *Journal of Humanistic Psychology, 42* (3), 89–101.
Heery, M. (2009). Global authenticity. In L. Hoffman & M. Yang (Eds.), *Existential psychology East-West* (pp. 215-228). University Professors Press.
Heery, M. (2011a). Baby boomers on conscious aging. *Journal of Transpersonal Psychology, 43* (2), 256–259.
Heery, M. (2011b). Pointing with my elbow: Remembering James F.T. Bugental, 1916–2008. *Journal of Transpersonal Psychology, 43* (2), 124–127.
Heery, M. (2014). *Unearthing the moment: Mindful applications of existential-humanistic and transpersonal psychotherapy.* Tonglen Press.
Heery, M. (2015). A humanistic perspective on bereavement (2nd ed). In K. J. Schneider, J. F. T. Bugental, & J. Fraser Pierson (Eds.), *The handbook of humanistic psychology* (pp. 535–548). Sage.
Heery, M., & Bugental, J. F. T. (1999). Unearthing the moment. *Self & Society, 27* (2), 25-27.
Heery, M., & Bugental, J. F. T. (2005a). Listening to the listener: An existential-humanistic approach to psychotherapy with psychotherapists. In J. D. Geller, J. C. Norcross, & D. E. Orlinsky (Eds.), *The psychotherapist's own psychotherapy* (pp. 282–296). Oxford University Press.
Heery, M., & Bugental, J. F. T. (2005b). Meaning and transformation. In E. van Deurzen & C. Arnold-Baker (Eds.), *Existential perspectives on human issues* (pp. 253–264). Palgrave Macmillan.
Heery, M., & Richardson, G. (Eds.) (2015). *Awakening to aging: Glimpsing the gifts of aging* (2nd ed.). Tonglen Press.
Martel, Y. (2001). *Life of Pi.* Harcourt, Inc.
May, R. (1958). *Existence: A new dimension in psychiatry and psychology.* Basic Books.
Rogers, C. R. (1965). *Client-centered therapy.* Houghton Mifflin.
Tillich, P. (1952). *The courage to be.* Yale University Press.
Yalom, I. D. (1980). *Existential psychotherapy.* Basic Books.
Yalom, I. D. (1995). *The theory and practice of group psychotherapy* (4th ed.). Basic Books.

Chapter 8

Fifty Years of Evolution: Becoming an Existential Therapist on the Journey to Becoming My Authentic Self

Nathaniel Granger Jr.

Many of us are drawn to the paths of least resistance, never questioning the meanings of life's pitfalls, potholes, detours, and accidents along its proverbial highway. Often finding oneself at an impasse when confronted with a fork in the road, we would rather turn back to less optimal conditions and contend with the knife at our backs that had been intensely nudging us all along than to venture blindly down any of the less-traveled roads afforded by the fork. Although some will contemplate going left or right, the road leading to becoming an existential psychotherapist is the road, most often, not chosen at all. It is not the road on which one sets out to travel, in that there are no signs, no painted lines, no apparent lights, and, for the most part, no rules. This road is not smoothed with the pavement of absolutes and indisputable theorems, and instead of asphalt, you will find dirt, gravel, mud, and many hard rocks. Nevertheless, this road, though mostly unassuming, is not far from one's chosen path. In fact, it runs parallel to the road we're already on much like the service road next to the interstate highway. We rarely notice this road, let alone choose it; but, rather, when the paved road with its directional signs and its painted straight lines dividing the lanes no longer serves us, the road to *Existentialism* chooses us— beckoning a search for meaning in the meaningless. Albeit most will stay on the current road, infinitely stuck in traffic, but the service road, as it were, calls out only to those less fearful of taking it.

Finding the Inner Rebel

"I rebel; therefore I exist." (Camus, 1984, p. 81)

When considering my journey to becoming an existential psychotherapist, I must surmise that a great deal of the decision-making (tongue-in-cheek) process was out of a desire to resist authority, control, and/or convention. I would speculate that rebelliousness coerced me to jump off the interstate onto the service road. From the time I was born, I rebelled! Not in an amoral or anarchic sense, but rather one of not wholly ascribing to the beliefs of others about the world, human behavior in general, me specifically, and, notwithstanding, the manifestation of God. I was born several weeks early into this world as we know it, to teenage parents and weighing only 2 pounds, 13 ounces. The obstetrician looked at my parents, and with a pitiful grimace, shook his head to indicate the inevitability of my demise. I was placed in the neonatal intensive care and would spend the first three months of life in the hospital. Back in the '60s, preemies did not survive. The experts said "No"; however, something in my nature would rebel against that notion. Something inside of me said "Yes." Despite having to do it against insurmountable odds, I would survive. *Something*... something beyond my infantile reasoning and yet always, even primordially, in my psyche.[1] Afterwards, I came home equipped to face poverty, alcoholism, drug addictions, molestation at the hand of babysitters, and many other perils associated with "Ghetto USA." The wine put in my baby bottle so I could go to sleep would predispose me to a self-destructive life. At age three, I was given shots of whisky to "put hair on my chest and to make me a man." My father would later give marijuana and cocaine to me as a young teen. Nevertheless, the yearning to procure a life outside of the ghetto, not the physical one but the mental one, persisted. At age 8, my parents had hung two large psychedelic posters on the wall downstairs in our new house. These posters caused some embarrassment, as one, titled *Black Magic* was a ripped, provocative Black man with a huge Afro. The other, *Black Magic Woman*, was a beautiful, shapely Black woman with a too large Afro and exposed breasts accentuated by the black light in the incense-perfumed room. I became obsessed with neither him nor her but, rather, with another psychedelic poster my dad had hanging between the two. I would commit the words of that poster to memory.

---

[1] Psyche (*Psyché* in French) is the Greek term for "soul" or "spirit" (ψυχή).

Besides the *Color Me Brown* (Giles, 1963) coloring book my parents bought, depicting the beauty of Blackness, to offset the whitewashed curriculum of the Chicago Public School system, it was perhaps the first lyrical expression to elucidate my existence.

Being Myself

> "I do my thing and you do your thing. I am not in this world to live up to your expectations and you are not in this world to live up to mine. You are you and I am I. And if by chance we find each other, it's beautiful." (Perls, 1969, p. 4)

It wasn't until I was in graduate school decades later that I realized the penman of those words. Nevertheless, the goal of understanding my existence and realizing my purpose burned with an insatiable desire to be the best me possible for not only myself but humankind. I wanted to be like *God*, a god, or something in the realm of god-ness, not to flaunt my leadership skills or my supernatural gifts (being facetious), but to make this world a better place. In all of my Blackness, of which I was very much aware, the quest for self-actualization continued, facilitated by that same dad, as he would often come in from a long day's work and upon entering the house, shout "Say it loud," to which my brothers and I would in unison reply from the lyrics of James Brown's 1968 song, "I'm Black and I'm Proud!" My sense of self was intricately woven into my sense of being Black. In a strange sense, my consciousness of Blackness was more discernable than that of even my self. Momma called me "Nookie." My dad called me "Nate." My teachers called me "Nathaniel." When I wasn't sure of who I was, two things I was sure of: I was in America and I was Black. With that alone, an inherited drive was passed down generationally to rebel against a system designed to strip me of my personage just as my ancestors were stripped of their being and packed on ships to be forever shackled by chains of discrimination upon landing in Jamestown, Virginia in the year of 1619.

The Fear Within

> "There is no illusion greater than fear." (Lao Tzu, 2006, ch. 46)

One of the twelve themes revealed by Richards (2007) in *Everyday Creativity and New Views of Human Nature* is androgyny. As a child, I remember having much angst about conforming to predetermined gender roles. I found just as much enjoyment in playing "house" as I did with racing my cars on the Hot Wheels track. I especially enjoyed making brownies on a cousin's Easy-Bake Oven. I didn't have any sisters, so I was very excited at the chance to visit female relatives and friends—it was a welcome break from everyday "boy" norms, as one might expect in a house with two other brothers and a homophobic, Afrocentric dad. At home, I could express my creative personality through drawing muscle men, cars, and superheroes or building robots and skyscrapers with Legos. However, for girls, the possibilities seemed endless; creativity could freely flow without judgment. The courage to create was nurtured. I could be a fashion designer and design an *en vogue* wardrobe for paper dolls; I could paint the night sky with different color stars streaming from a Lite Brite; I could pretend to be a world-renowned chef as I baked cookies or mixed various syrups to come up with the most extraordinary flavored snow cones. I could even vacillate between being a hair dresser and make-up artist for Barbie and being a barber to my G.I. Joe, with the life-like hair—and not be terribly disappointed at the knowledge that Joe's beard would not grow back and the life-like hair was held in place by glue, making for a not-so-debonair haircut. The freedom to create was exhilarating and the process of creating was far more intoxicating than Dad's old whiskey. Within the *flow*[2] of creating, I did not have to be masculine or feminine, a boy or a girl, straight or gay. Realizing this existential freedom allowed me to embark upon a path transcendent to any of these polarizations. I most often felt this freedom at Grandma's house. At Grandma's house, I always felt safe and, most of all, loved. "There is no fear in love," according to the Bible, "but perfect love drives out fear, because fear has to do with punishment" (1 John 4:18). At Grandma's house, I could play, explore, and create without the fear of punishment. At Grandma's house, her unconditional love for me allowed space and freedom to be. In his book *The Polarized Mind: Why It's Killing Us and What We Can Do About It*," Schneider (2013) proposes that "polarization begins with fear, and extreme polarization begins with extreme fear" (p.14). Fear is the impediment of creativity—it precludes *flow*. As a child, my greatest fear was that of not being "boy" enough, or worse, being a "sissy;" but at Grandma's I was free to be either, or better yet, neither. The only time Grandma would be angry at me and I would cause a noticeable

---

[2] Csikszentmihalyi's term for feeling total absorption in a challenging, goal-oriented activity.

dissatisfaction in her countenance was when I, as a result of my own fears and the consequent polarized mindset, in her kitchen exclaimed, "Michael Jackson is gay!" I immediately wanted to retract that statement and winced at the disdain in Grandma's eyes as she struggled to find words to correct me. After a tense pause, she retorted, "Michael Jackson has enough money to be whatever he wants to be; what about you?!" What Grandma was conveying had nothing to with wealth but everything to do with freedom. "Live and let live," she would often instruct. Grandma, of whom it has been told, "had four husbands, one of which was her own," knew that to fully live was to approach life free of the judgments of self and others— a life free of polarizations and filled with wonderment and awe! I learned as a young child (at Grandma's dining room table) to color with ALL the crayons in my crayon box. However, it wasn't until I realized that I could mix blue with pink and get purple that I was awed; this, for me, was worth celebrating.

I was also awestruck by the American recording artist Prince. His androgyny was captivating, and *Controversy*, his fourth studio album, released on October 14, 1981 by Warner Bros. Records, opened with a title track that raised questions that were being asked about Prince at the time, including his race, sexuality, and religious affiliation. The song flirted with blasphemy by including a chant of *The Lord's Prayer* and its lyrics set to verse much of my existential underpinnings. Prince questioned whether we should believe the various things people accept without question: if we must be Black or White, or gay or straight. He inquired into his beliefs. He questioned the rules and longed for a world beyond their limitations.

Prince, his androgyny, his musical gifts, and his courage to be unapologetically himself seemed to cause a visceral reaction in Dad that he struggled to hide. If Dad had no other gifts, he exemplified the gift of gab—but he was uncharacteristically tight-lipped when it came to anything relative to Prince. Apart from being homophobic, I think Dad was jealous of the fact that Prince could be more man than he was and, at the same time, more "woman" than he could possibly handle. Moreover, the fact that I idolized Prince, perhaps more than I idolized my dad, was most problematic; however, that was not my problem, but his.

Making My Own Meaning

> There is something infantile in the presumption that somebody else has a responsibility to give your life

> meaning and point... The truly adult view, by contrast, is that our life is meaningful, as full and as wonderful as we choose to make it. (Dawkins, 2006, p. 403)

At the obscure dawning of emerging adulthood, I decided for a New Year's resolution that I wanted to get closer to God. My brothers, a few neighborhood friends, and I were packed in my bedroom one late December, heavily under the influence of marijuana, philosophizing about life's meanings and making resolutions for the upcoming year. My brother stated that his New Year resolution was that he would quit smoking, to which I exclaimed, "You gonna quit smoking weed?!" He replied, "Naw, man. I'm going to quit smoking cigarettes but I'm going to die with a joint in my mouth." We went around the room. One would lose weight, another would go back to school, and another would get a job. Everyone had a different resolution. Finally, the lot fell on me to come up with a New Year's resolution. Well, of course I would be last; after all I was the host of the party, the promoter of the discussion—the ringleader. I resolved that in the new year, "I want to get closer to God!" By that time in my life, I had smoked enough weed, along with other modalities in pursuit of a higher level of being, that I could see no greater aspiration to have than getting closer to God. Above all, He is the Most High! The room filled with a deafening silence for a span that in that moment felt like an eternity. At last, the silence was broken by a consensual assent, "Yeah, that's a great idea!" Everyone decided that they, too, would get closer to God and on the first Sunday of the new year, we were all going to church in order to fulfill this purpose. Needless to say, everyone's New Year resolution was broken by that Sunday morning with an excuse about why they could not go to church with me. Disappointed, I went anyway. I set out walking on that cold Chicago morn. I was young and poor with no money or car. Nevertheless, with no particular church in mind, I would somehow not so much find the right church as I would find God. I walked, took a few puffs of a joint I had saved from the night before, and walked some more. I thought I was delusional, tripping[3] even, as I "heard" a voice directing me to go back to a particular church I had passed several blocks away. I turned around and went back and found myself standing there in the cold trying to make sense of the "Order of Services" on the Morgan Park Assembly Church bulletin board. It was foreign to me. I went up the stairs and into the church. The smell I will never forget. There was no

---

[3] Experience hallucinations induced by taking a psychedelic drug, especially LSD.

cigarette smoke like at Grandma's house—a smell I had grown to associate with unconditional love. There was no marijuana smell. It didn't smell like stale beer and vomit, a scent reminiscent of the lounge where my mother worked as a bartender. In fact, it was a smell unfamiliar to my senses and yet quite familiar to an unidentifiable part of my being. It smelled clean, but not a Pine-Sol clean like at home when I had to mop the kitchen before Momma came home. The foyer of that church smelled holy—it smelled like God. It felt as if God Himself had not only welcomed me but had enveloped me with His love. I sat in a Sunday school class where the teacher, a jovial looking man whose skin was as black as onyx, with a brilliant smile adorned by snow-white teeth, asked me if I was saved.[4] Humbly I answered, "Yes, I think so," thinking to myself "Saved from what?" The Sunday school teacher simply said, "Stick around and I will be praying for you." I did. I stuck around and was later baptized in the name of the Lord Jesus Christ for the remission of my sins and filled with the Holy Ghost, as evidenced by speaking in tongues[5] as the Spirit gave utterance, as was the belief of this Apostolic Pentecostal Church. That cold Chicago afternoon I would rise and walk in a "new life!" I got rid of the cigarettes, the drinking, the marijuana, and even the fornicating (until later I realized that there was more fornicating inside the church than there was out...but that's another story). Nevertheless, I was exuberantly joyful to be saved! I struggled, however. The rules and regulations seemed to buffet my freedom to simply be. Apart from the abstention of everything pertaining to or characterized by the flesh or body, its passions and appetites, sensual and carnal pleasures, we had to abstain from even the appearance of evil in our attire. We couldn't wear shorts or short sleeve shirts in the summer; certain styles of clothing were considered "worldly" and as a young, good-looking guy, I didn't want to be guilty of causing anyone to lust. We couldn't go certain places or participate in certain activities that were prohibited for *saints*, such as clubs, bars, certain schools and fraternities, secret organizations, etc. After all, we were "bought with price" and that was metaphorically and, as we were led to believe, literally the Blood of Jesus! For the most part, it was tolerable. We were indoctrinated with "obedience is better than

---

[4] In Christianity, it is deliverance by redemption from the power of sin and from the penalties ensuing from it.

[5] Speaking in tongues, also known as glossolalia, is a spiritual gift in which the gifted person speaks words in a language unknown to them, as they are empowered by the Holy Spirit. Some Christians believe they speak in heavenly languages, or languages of angels.

sacrifice" and I so desperately wanted to be obedient, but I just couldn't. I just couldn't follow every rule that oppressed my being what I felt God had created. In complying with the rules, I realized early on that I could not be me. After all, if God made me, why would He be so opposed to my being? Suddenly, my wretchedness became inevitable and, with it, my state of selfhood invalidated. Besides, I had a problem with those little lapel pins the pastor's wife would sell that we all had to wear. The little silver pins that said "Jesus Only" seemed to always cause a visceral reaction that I struggled to conceal, especially when another saint (human) would ask, "Did you buy your Jesus Only pin?" I still, to this day, struggle with the implication of *only* as applied to anything and especially Jesus. I digress.

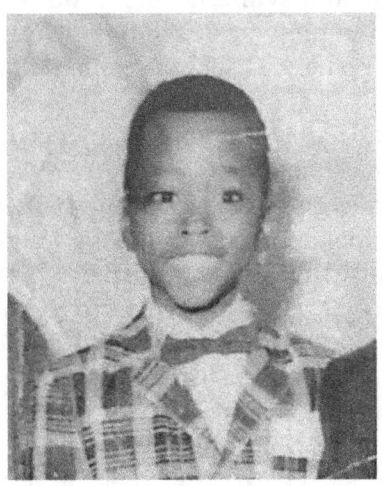

Becoming

Convictions are more dangerous foes of truth than lies.
(Nietzsche, 2009, p. 1)

Although I had not finished high school, donning the label "high school dropout," I enrolled in college. At the time, my maternal uncle was the Dean of Student Affairs at Columbia College in Chicago and was able to enroll me without a high school diploma, with the contingency that I would have my General Equivalency Diploma (GED) prior to graduating. Nevertheless, I joined the Army after two semesters. While at Columbia, having an affinity toward liberal arts, I took a course called "Artists in Apprenticeship" (AIA). This course would stretch my creativity perhaps more than anything ever had. As a child, I loved art. I was able to draw, paint, build, and create. I spent countless hours drawing at Grandma's dining room table, lost in creativity as I basked in her cigarette smoke intermingled with unconditional love. As a youth, I always had some project going on, whether it was making Christmas cards, or building go-carts, or spray painting my bike, or building a tree house. I was responsible for making slingshots for the other neighborhood boys and would charge a quarter to cover the cost of rubber bands. My creativity was evident in many areas, from catching and dissecting frogs to installing ceiling fans and hanging wallpaper at 11152 South Homewood Avenue, one of the several tiny new houses built by developers that my parents bought when Blacks migrated into the once flourishing, predominantly White, neighborhood on Chicago's far South Side. Mrs. Thomas, the prejudiced White lady down the street called them *shanties*. Our home was within a more than two-block radius consisting of Homewood and Esmond Avenues, the street named after my elementary *alma mater,* Esmond Elementary School, where the neighborhood kids nicknamed me *Professor.* It was at that elementary school, where everyone in the neighborhood attended and graduated the 8th grade, that I took my first psychology course. As much as I was intrigued by the study of human behavior, I was even more intrigued by the idea portrayed by Lucy in Charles Schultz's *Charlie Brown* episodes that I could set up a booth with a sign stating "Psychologist" and, for a small fee, could listen to people's problems, help come to a solution, and get paid. I learned early on that my creativity, paired with a rudimentary knowledge of human behavior, could be used compassionately as well as dangerously. One kid in particular became grossly strung out on drugs. He was one of my childhood buds. Upon seeing me years later, completely ravaged by years of addiction, he said, "Professor, I got my first joint from you." I was of course saddened by the fact that I could've been the sole contributor to his less-than-desirable fate—but by this time I was different. I was saved! I told him how sorry I was and offered Jesus to him. This would be the same Jesus who I believed would help me get through college. Now, the major requirement of this AIA course was to examine oneself and allow that existential analysis to culminate in an expressive art piece for a final project. Easy enough, or so I thought! After all, I could draw a picture or paint an acrylic on canvas. Perhaps a sculpture or song would suffice. I pondered through most of the semester about what I would do for a final project—an art piece depicting my existential journey. Others had ideas and most had already started work on their project when the instructor approached me about missing the deadline for submitting a topic for the assignment. I had nothing. I somehow knew to pray, and at Morgan Park Assembly Church I was even taught to fast—so I prayed and fasted. After much prayer, meditation, tears, and inner discourse, I decided on a poetic expression. This would not be simply the writing of a poem about the beauty of nature with all of its serene wonderment or an emulation of "Amazing grace, how sweet the sound that saved a wretch like me," but rather a dirty and rocky drive, drawing from my soul all of what was good, bad, and ugly as I took the courageous leap off the beaten path to the road less traveled: the service road. Suddenly the curtain went up, and I found myself sitting on a stool, center-stage in a darkened, packed auditorium in downtown Chicago, trying to swallow the lump in my throat, trying not to show my nervousness—and hoping that no one in the audience would notice my hands shaking as I made a concerted attempt to steady the paper held in my hands. I had no suspicion that people in the audience would be moved to tears. I had no intimation that my final project would receive an award. I had no idea that students and faculty would want the autograph of this 19-year-old kid. My biggest hope was that I would pass the class. So, with not even the slightest notion that in the end I would receive a standing ovation, I read "Nookie, Nate and Nathaniel, Me Myself and I, (What I've Been Through and How I Survived"; Granger, 1982).

> Born in Chicago
> Raised in a working-class slum
> The most I ever wanted
> Was to find Solidarity, with whom?
> With "Me, Myself and I"
>
> "Myself" never had the courage
> To dig within "I"
> "I" could see my many facets
> "Me" was afraid/"Me" was insecure
> Some things I had to reveal
> Some things that I had to retain
> "I" could see
> "I" wanted to pretend to be blind
> "I" could see right through "Me, Myself"
> Few people knew "Me, Myself"
> "Me, Myself" is real
> "I" is real, but

"I" is covered with a lid
"I" is in love with "I", but
"I" must fall in love with "Me, Myself"
"Me, Myself" must see "eye to "I"
I must find Solidarity, with whom?
With "Me, Myself and I"

Nookie is my nickname
Laugh if you will
You're not the first/You're not the last
You don't like it? So what
"I" don't like it, but that's me
Nookie is really the "Me"
And "I" or "Myself" can do nothing about it
The "I" used to hate "Me"
"I" wanted to kill me
"Myself" wouldn't let him
People that know "I" know that I is happy
They don't know "Me"
"Me is miserable
"Me" loves people
People love "I"
Few know Nookie
I feared to expose Nookie to most

As I go on, you shall discover
That I'm really shy an undercover
Some say that I am extroverted; I tell you I'm not
I'm just trying to find Solidarity
With "Me, Myself and I"

Nate is the fate
Of "Me, Myself and I"
Nate is "Myself/"Myself" is Nate
"Myself" is a conjunction
Connecting "Me" with "I"
Nate has done it all
Hanging on "Me" and leaning on "I"
Jack-of-all-trades
Master of none
Felt the misery of "Me"

Shared the pride when "I"
Nate was Super Cool
Smoking marijuana
Snortin' cocaine and tac
Lying, stealing, cheating,
Just to get a high
What in the hell was wrong?
"Myself" had to get it together.

Friend of Satan's
Doomed for hell, how did I live?
Living in the darkness of a contiguous shell
I desperately needed Solidarity
With "Me, Myself and I"

Nathaniel is the "I"
Of "me, myself and I"
Without Nathaniel
"Me, Myself" would be helpless
Nookie and Nate would be lost
What "I" has seen
"I" has try to forget
"I" is intelligent
And "I" is in love with "I"
I know the flaws of "Me" and "Myself"
"I" has tried to avoid "Me, Myself"
"I" is conceited—He has the right to be
Striving for perfection
"I" very seldom falls
Having very few flaws, if any
All mistakes made by "I"
Can be attributed to "Me, Myself"

"Me" loves people, but it's simply sexual
"Myself" is not as horny, yet somewhat sensual
"I" is smart and quite intellectual
However, there must be solidarity with "Me, Myself and I"

"Myself" was manipulated
Into trying to be cool
Busting out of an L7 Square

I thought was the name of the game
Craps, Blackjack, Pity-Pat
If you play your cards right
Everything's going to be alright
Let's bet
The sky is the limit
Hand me a beer/Pass me a joint
Put it out, here comes Momma
What is she talking about?
She must be drunk
You're the one who brought me here
Now you gotta' deal with it
I didn't ask to be here ya' dig
The hell with you, them, everybody
The only thing I'm concerned with is "Myself"

"Myself" was in a world of darkness
Looking for revenge, yet needed empathy
Trying to be grown, but only a baby
I wish the world had shown some sympathy
If Solidarity was with "Me, Myself and I"

The love I have for people
Caused "Me" much trouble
"I" at times don't like "Me"
"Me" has mostly a sexual love
And "I" knows it
The love "Me" has for people
It's very strong at times
Black, White, Blue, Green
Male, Female, Anything
"Me" has dibbled here
And "Me" has dabbled there
Black, White, Blue, Green
Male, Female, Anything
Few know "Me": I've kept "Me" secluded
Some know "Me": "Me" has been caught dibbling
If you know "Myself and I"
You are among thousands
If you know "Me", you are one in a million

I never thought the day would come
When I'd introduce "Me" to you
For it is easy to know "Myself and I"
But to know "Me" too...?
I am finding Solidarity with "Me, Myself and I"

"I" know the truth
Of "Me, Myself and I"
"I" ain't no fool
"I" is intelligent
And quite intellectual
The truth "I" hid
Because of pride
Why did "I" hide?
Because of pride
It's nobody's business but mine
"I" stood on a pedestal
To supersede my faults
I know this neurotic spontaneity that is found in "Myself"
I know the erotic intensity that is basically "Me"
It's serendipitous to discern and reveal my hidden truths
Because of "Me," I was in a secret Inferno
Because of "Myself," I searched for rightness
Because of "I," you now know "Me"
"Me, myself, and I" is damn close to perfect Solidarity

"Me, Myself and I"
Just wouldn't get along
The intellectual "I"
Hated the sexual "Me"
The sensual "Myself"
A little bit sexual/A little intellectual
What the hell
The house in an uproar
Cocaine on the brain/wine on the mind
Had a good sense going to waste
Going deeper and deeper into darkness
Satan had me bound
Bound and dressed for hell
Suicide I thought, suicide I tried

> God wouldn't let me; I've burned if I'd died
> The light of God has come to me
> I will survive, I now can see
>
> "Me, Myself and I" can now live as one
> For where I was lost, through God I am found
> With faith in God I shall survive
> "Me, Myself and I" is going upward bound
> "Me, Myself and I" can now live in harmony
> For there is now Solidarity within "Me, Myself and I"

Compelled to congruency with Freud's trichotomy of the unconscious, id, ego, and superego; the trichotomy of the human mind, body, and soul; and the trichotomy of the Godhead, Father, Son, and Holy Spirit, "Me, Myself and I" is a personal heuristic view of self that was employed early on to survive this thing called life. Born in Chicago, raised in a working-class slum, the most I ever wanted was to find solidarity... with "Me, Myself and I." A quote from a friend resonates with me in the present: "Life is hard, but living is wonderful!" (D. Herbert, personal conversation, 2011). Life's highway is replete with twists and turns beyond our wildest imaginings. However, without embracing the fact that there are obstacles along life's highways—bumps in the road—we would miss the challenge to create. We would never adapt to life to the extent of declaring, "but living is wonderful." According to Hoffman, Richards, and Pritzker:

> Creativity is essential to the renewal of Humanistic Psychology. Its very nature is change, adaptation, and renewal. It is a vehicle for our higher human possibilities. One becomes a mindful agent of the future, rather than an automaton running through preset routines, habits, and duties. ONE BECOMES ALIVE. (2012, p. 35)

It is also the vehicle by which we travel from the proverbial interstate highway to the service road to *existentialism*.

I was very much on that road, however. As in the song "A Horse with No Name" (Bunnell, 1971/72) by the folk rock band America, my road, like America's horse, had no name, at least in my mind. Furthermore, as in the song, it felt good to be sheltered from the rain of societal injunctions imposed upon me as a young African American man about what it means to be a man; out of the torrential rain of religious dogma comprised of rules and regulations that were impossible to maintain without the complete expenditure of self; and, certainly, out of the oppressive outpouring of structural racism and generational trauma that would render me perpetually enslaved if not entirely by a racist system, by my mind. And yet, paradoxically, *that* one thing that continues to cast a cloud on the purpose of my existence, incarcerating my body, endeavoring to break my spirit, instead of subjugating me becomes the catalyst for creativity.

What I Am

> Man is the only creature who refuses to be what he is.
> (Camus, 1984, p. 12)

One of my clients, a young Black male, recently asked, "How do you know so much about people?! Did you learn that in school?" I can answer that schooling played a major part in my becoming an existential psychotherapist, but not in a traditional sense. Fate may have had its place as well. Nonetheless, although schooling enhanced the *study* of people, the etymology of my skill may be many decades prior. Leaving Columbia College to join the Army, in hindsight, may appear to have been asinine; however, it was more another act of rebellion, like following the beckoning of the service road, and jumping off the Interstate to realize the meaning and purpose of my existence. Initially, I wanted to enlist in the Air Force, but back in the early '80s, the U.S. Army was the only branch of service that would allow one to enlist without a high school diploma. Again, it was a very cold Chicago morn in December when my mother and I walked to the bus stop. I somehow knew, as the tears froze on my cheeks, that once I got on the bus there would be no more tears of fear about leaving the comforts of 11152, which I had come to know as home. Nevertheless, upon landing in Fort Dix, New Jersey and finding myself in a large room with other "newbies" like myself, fear was palpable. For the first time, though, it wasn't my usual fear but the fear of my comrades, as the drill sergeant spewed expletives and threats with the assurance that for the next eight weeks, he would be our mother, father, sister, and brother—our everything. I marveled at the sight of so many grown men crying, their tears evident. Amidst the drill sergeant's pontifications, I heard him say, "At the end of the cycle, one of you Privates will be promoted from E-1 to E-2 for demonstrating both physical and mental mastery. One of you will be promoted for being the *Super-Trooper*." He then said with a boisterous shout, "Now, everybody get the fuck up out of here!" As everyone grabbed their Government Issue of one rucksack and two duffle bags, I watched them rush to the door, jamming the doorway as they all tried to exit simultaneously. After the last troop was out of sight and I was obviously the only one left, I threw one of my duffle bags over my left shoulder and the other over my right, and casually walked up to the Drill Sergeant, who peered at me from behind a desk through pop-bottle-thick lenses that made his eyes appear larger than humanly possible. Clearing my throat as I discreetly, yet boldly, approached, I inquired, "Drill Sergeant, did I hear you say that after Basic Training one person will be promoted from E-1 to E-2 for being the *Super-Trooper*?" "Yes, I did Private," he answered gruffly. "Well," I said matter of factly, "I'm going to be *that* one!" Leaning forward, lifting halfway out of his seat, he simply said, "Get the fuck out of here, Private!" Although I was neither the strongest nor the fastest in my platoon, from the outset, I was the one to courageously and creatively jump off the Interstate onto the service road, declaring, "I'm going to be *that* one!" For the next eight weeks, you may have my body and, in some ways, my mind, but you cannot have *me*—you cannot have my existence, my existential freedom to be. I continued to push to "Be All You Can Be," as the Army's slogan said back then, but, most important, I demonstrated to the drill sergeant and the other troops the existential freedom to choose. This became apparent later when the drill sergeant addressed the platoon and said, "If anybody in here has any problems, don't come to me, but go to Rev" (the nickname given to me by my comrades because of both my willingness to counsel and my unapologetic willingness to pray). In the end, I was that one promoted for being the "Super-Trooper."

After Basic Training, I went to Advance Initial Training (AIT) in Aberdeen Proving Ground, Maryland, not far from Baltimore. I had enlisted in the Illinois Army National Guard as a 44B Metal Worker, and it was during AIT that I learned to create by welding, glass cutting, and auto body repair. This was perhaps the most exacting time of my life. I was able to create glass and metal sculptures. Our Military Occupational Skill (MOS) handle was "Cold Steel," It was also during AIT that I had to learn how to juggle my time between learning my craft, cleaning the barracks, and going to school at night—only to get up and do it again the next morning at "o-dark-thirty." Here, though, no one knew me as the *Super-Trooper*. I was, however, identified as the one person in the entire Company[6] who did not have a high school diploma and was thus given permission to go to school at night if it did not interfere with my military training and other military duties during the day. I was stretched to capacity and, again, on that road less chosen. Once again, "Me, Myself and I" would surprisingly receive an ovation when the Company Commander called the company to attention and me "front and center" to present my high school diploma and military coin, saluting me for a "job well done." In my mid-twenties, the exceptionality of receiving my diploma was far more meaningful than if I had graduated at 18, the traditional way. Unbeknownst to me, at least cognitively, it was all part of my making.

After AIT, I went back to the unit in which I had originally enlisted, the Illinois Army National Guard Armory on 52nd and Cottage Grove. Going back to the South Side of Chicago was uncomfortably regressive. Like a dog returning to its own vomit, going back to my bedroom at 11152 felt dismal. I used to love my room and that hadn't changed, but I had. Going back to Morgan Park Assembly Church was no longer a favorite God-seeking venture but rather a religious duty. Though welcomed, I no longer felt at home. I am happy, however, that this was where I met my wife. I had just come home from AIT and attended a revival where Evangelist Iona Locke was speaking on the topic of lies. I was clean-cut, buff, and wearing my Class A (dress) uniform. When I saw her, I couldn't keep my eyes off that beautiful woman sitting across the aisle, and I knew in that moment that she was going to be my wife.

---

[6] A company has anywhere from a few dozen to 200 soldiers. It's a tactical-sized unit that can perform a battlefield function on its own. A company consists of three or four platoons and is generally commanded by a captain.

She was visiting, and after church we exchanged pleasantries. In fact, she gave me her number. Cell phones were not out yet, and the house phone was disconnected—my mom justifying that with "A phone is a luxury item and we can't afford luxury items." I got her number and called her later from the train station a block away from my home, igniting a courtship that would culminate in many years of marital bliss (and what not). While at Aberdeen, I attended a small church in Havre de Grace, Maryland. This church was a little different than Morgan Park. You really did "come as you are," and the praise and worship seemed to come from a purer place—not one of wearing the right attire or living a life above reproach, but from a place of one's innermost being, from existence itself. It was from a place of freedom and, moreover, love. People were free to worship without losing who they were. Everyone seemed to want to be there with one another and with God. I had never experienced such acceptedness at the all-Black church at home. For the first time in my life, I was in the midst of Koreans, Chinese, Mexicans, Blacks, and Whites brought together with a sole (soul, even) purpose of worshipping their God in addition to, paradoxically, celebrating the beauty of humanity. Mind you, this little church would've been excommunicated from the Pentecostal Assemblies of the World, the governing body of Morgan Park Assembly. This church gave me a greater appreciation of humanity and God. And, no, there were no Jesus Only pins.

Upon returning, I didn't fit in at my National Guard unit either. Where existentialism will lead you to realizing your purpose, at my unit there was nothing that needed welding and there were no vehicle windows to fix. Whatever my purpose in life was, doing nothing or sweeping the motor pool wasn't it. Since there was no job for me, my unit decided to send me back to school, reclassifying me to learn how to repair generators. I would be a generator repairman. They insisted that I must go where they sent me based on the needs of the Army. Generator repair is certainly a needed occupation and is the destiny of some searching individuals, who upon finding it declare, "Aha! This is exactly what I'm supposed to do! This is my purpose!" However, I knew *existentially*—from that deep place in your soul that brings solidarity to your "Me, Myself and I," that place that is the integration of all your parts including the genetic material that holds the very cries of your ancestors—being a generator repairman was not a part of my story! I rebelled. I decided to go back on active duty status and to do so as a 91A Combat Medic. As a matter of fact, I enlisted with the idea that one day

I would be a doctor. My ASFAB[7] test scores were relatively high and the cunning recruiter, knowing that my dream was to one day become a doctor, led me to believe that joining the Army as a medic would give me an educational and financial advantage and would be the first rung on the ladder to becoming a doctor. As a youth, I wanted to be a medical doctor. Later, however, I didn't care if it was a Doctorate in Basket Weaving; I just wanted "Dr." in front of my name. Priding myself for being a Jack-of-all-trades-and-master-of-none was never sufficient. The "Jack-of-all-trades" was befitting but the "Master-of-none" was unacceptable. And, so, I would spend the next decade or so on active duty. As a medic, once you became a Specialist/Corporal (E-4), you could apply for the 91C nurse course. My dad was not happy when I told him that I wanted to be a nurse. Out of his homophobia he exclaimed, "Nurses don't make any money! Why don't you become an engineer or something?" Although he would've prided himself on being a socialite, he did not understand prosocial behavior (Belsky, p. 178) of sharing, helping others and caring, and I, inversely, was never moved by the notion of making money for the sake of money apart from helping others. As a youth, I would bring home anything from a stray pigeon with a broken wing, trying to help mend its wing with a popsicle stick and masking tape, to a dejected baby rat. I once even caught a bat and tried to nurse it back to health with fruit slices and drops of milk. I used a tiny baby bottle from a cousin's baby doll. Whenever any of the kids had a cut covered with a bandage, I was quick to say, "Let me see." Dad would say to me quite often, "Nate, you can't save the world." I had finally grown to figure as such, but reasoned that if I could just save one, and that one saves one, together we can all eventually save the world. So, I rebelled against my dad's wishes and became a nurse; not only a nurse, but also a teacher, a preacher, and eventually, a "doctor." Learning has always been paramount for me. Once I started the work on getting my GED, I never ceased to take classes, even if it was a correspondence course, or EMT course, courses in general studies at the University of Colorado at Colorado Springs (UCCS), where I would receive a Bachelor's degree in psychology, to a Master's degree in counseling and human services. Yet unbeknownst to me cognitively, it was all towards my becoming an existential psychotherapist.

After graduating from UCCS, a few options were before me, but the one that was "calling" me was the Colorado School of Professional

---

[7] The Armed Services Vocational Aptitude Battery (ASVAB) measures developed abilities and helps predict future academic and occupational success in the military.

Psychology (COSPP). I met with the school's founder, Emory Cowan, who took me on a tour of the school that occupied the Old Colorado Springs Train Station in downtown Colorado Springs. Emory, as I know him now, was warm, genuine, and proud as he described to me the PsyD program offered by the school. I was enthralled by Emory, as well as the intimate, family-like setting offered by the Colorado School of Professional Psychology. Well into my 40s, I put out to the universe that I would earn my doctorate before age 50. At the new-student orientation, through various confidence-building activities, I bonded with individuals who would become friends for life. The camaraderie was almost like that of Basic Training many years prior. The first class I took was a 7100 class, meaning it was an upper-level course generally taught toward the end of the program and closer to graduation. However, due to the "roll-of-the-dice" method of scheduling, I took my very first class in the doctoral program on January 8, 2007, Theories of Personality. This class allowed me to not only study various theories but also coerced me to consider my own personal theoretical orientation. Excited about COSPP, the PsyD program, and my first course, along with the instructor, I figured, based on what I had learned from the first lyrical expression to elucidate my existence at age 8 (Fritz Perl's "I do my thing...") and the Master's program in counseling and human services at UCCS, that my theoretical orientation would be well grounded in Gestalt therapy. It was, however, the heartfelt conversations after class with my professor, Louis Hoffman, that would facilitate freedom to broaden my horizon, particularly as it pertains to human beings. Louis, as I now call him, in addition to "friend," never pushed any particular orientation at me but rather walked alongside me, allowing me to explore my truths, as it were, while he knew intuitively that I was already on the road to existentialism and that I had perhaps been on that road for a very long time. Louis would not be my instructor again until almost three years later with my very last class in the program, History and Systems. Needless to say, my course work at COSPP was bookended by Louis Hoffman. During the span of time in between, I would make appointments to meet with Louis every chance I could, often fearing I was wearing out my welcome. He had become my academic advisor, confidante, and most of all, my friend. I remember him taking students to China. This sparked a sort of resentment in me, which I justified with the fact that I could not afford to go. Nor did I particularly want to go, as I was dealing with chronic pain issues, adding to my disinterest in traveling to China for fear of an 18-hour flight. This internalized resentment forced me to look deeper into self, to conclude that I was actually jealous. I wanted my friend exclusively. It was about this time that my clinical supervisor, Dick Gee, advised me right before I was to see a client, "Today, Nathaniel, I want you to forget about everything you've learned as far as treatment modalities. Today, I just want you to be yourself." This was again validated when Louis, my chosen dissertation chair, responded to my topic deliberations with, "Nathaniel, you don't have to conform." I had taken the plunge onto that existential service road with a proposal for *Perceptions of Racial Microaggressions*[8] *Among African American Males: A Heuristic Inquiry* (Granger, 2011) and was feeling a desire to retreat to the path of least resistance. Nothing is more liberating than being yourself, and, ultimately, I was being given permission to be myself—to realize my existential purpose and to freely embrace it.

Me, Myself, and My Foundation

> Knowing yourself is the beginning of all wisdom.
> (Aristotle)

I joined the American Psychological Association's (APA) Division 32, Society for Humanistic Psychology (SHP) as a student affiliate. At one of the earlier SHP conferences I attended, the question arose, "Where are all the Black humanistic psychologists?" To which I replied, "You're looking at him." Although appreciation for diversity has been a part of the paradigm from its inception, Hoffman, Cleare-Hoffman, and Jackson (2015) noted in *The Handbook of Humanistic Psychology: Theory, Research, and Practice* that, until recently, humanistic psychology has had a long, uncomfortable history of not attracting diverse individuals from varied cultural contexts. They emphasized that if humanistic psychology is to fully demonstrate its commitment to inclusion of diversity it must: a) attract individuals representing various forms of diversity, b) encompass a range of ideas and epistemologies (ways of knowing), and c) incorporate approaches that authentically challenge and transform humanistic psychology. It was apparent that not only was I the only person of color to be a member of the Society for Humanistic

---

[8] Microaggressions are the brief and commonplace daily verbal, behavioral, and environmental indignities, whether intentional or unintentional, that communicate hostile, derogatory, or negative racial, gender, sexual-orientation, and religious slights and insults to target persons or groups (Sue, 2008; Sue, Capodilupo et al., 2007).

Psychology, but that the environment was unwelcoming to marginalized groups, particularly people of color. "Diversity" was neither paramount nor operationalized in the Society's functioning. Although diversity and inclusion were core values of APA, the Society for Humanistic Psychology was rigid in maintaining its status quo consisting of old White men. "Diversity," I would often say, "is not what is written on a plaque on the wall but rather, when you see me, you are looking at diversity." Committed to transforming the face of existential-humanistic psychology, I felt that the division needed change. As a young member, I helped formulate the Diversity Task Force, with the intention of making the Society for Humanistic Psychology a "home" for all. As a result, SHP was finally becoming more diversified. This, however, was not without incidents. I was later elected to the board and became secretary, during which time insensitivities to the idea of diversity and inclusion would often cause tension in the executive board meetings. This led to some off-putting, microaggressive comments from some of our patriarchs. As secretary, and the only African American on the board, I silenced one particular meeting that had become prejudicial in behavior by granting, "Lest we forget, if there is anyone privy to what goes on in the proverbial White House, it's the Black butler." I don't think I had ever seen such a ghostly sight as the color drained from the White faces around the table and the conference roomed filled with silence—something uncharacteristic for a group of existential-humanistic psychotherapists. Being part of this group required courage, but most of all, it demanded heeding the *call* to becoming an existential psychotherapist. Asked by a board member at the SHP conference in Hawaii some years back if I had loved being there, I retorted, "I can't say I love it. It's more of a calling." This calling would in the end position me to become president of APA Division 32, Society for Humanistic Psychology with the presidential theme of *Embracing our Fear, Courage, and Love in Pursuit of a Just Community*. That theme was not just exclusive to my presidential year but to my whole existence: to ultimately reach that day with no regrets—knowing that every experience—be it good, bad, or ugly—worked together to get me to the place where I lived a generative, purpose-driven life (not self-seeking). I aimed to actualize the meanings of my existence and influence others along this journey as an existential psychotherapist, embracing life with optimism, vigor, and above all, gratitude for all humanity.

References

Belsky, J. (2019). *Experiencing the lifespan* (5th ed.). Worth Publishers.
Brown, J. (1968). Say it loud: I'm black and I'm proud [Song]. Vox Studios.
Bunnell, D. (1971/72). A horse with no name [Song recorded by America]. On *America*. Warner Bros.
Camus, A. C. (1984). *The rebel: An essay on man in revolt* (A. Bower, Trans.). Vintage Books. (Original work published 1956)
Dawkins, R. (2006). *The God delusion*. Houghton Mifflin Co.
Giles, L. H. (1963). *Color me brown*. Johnson Publishing Co.
Granger, N. (1982). *Nookie, Nate and Nathaniel, Me Myself and I: What I've been through and how I survived* [Unpublished manuscript]. Columbia College.
Granger, N. (2011). Perceptions of racial microaggressions among African American males in higher education: A heuristic inquiry (Publication No. 249044820) [Doctoral dissertation, Colorado School of Professional Psychology]. Proquest Dissertations and Theses Global.
Hoffman L., Cleare-Hoffman, H., & Jackson T. (2015). Humanistic psychology and multiculturalism: History, current status, and advancements. In K. J. Schneider, J. F. Pierson & J. T. Bugental (Eds.), *The handbook of humanistic psychology: Theory, research, and practice* (2nd ed., pp. 41–55). Sage.
Hoffman, L., Richards, R., & Pritzker, S. (2012). Creativity in the evolution of humanistic psychology. *Self & Society, 40* (1), 10–15. https://doi.org/10.1080/03060497.2012.11084238
Lao Tzu. (2006). *Tao te ching* (S. Mitchell, Trans.). Perennial Classics. (Original work published around 4th century BCE)
Nietzsche, F. (2009). *Man alone with himself*. Penguin Books. (Original work published in 1878)
Perls, F. (1969). *Gestalt therapy verbatim*. Real People Press.
Prince. (1981). Controversy [Song]. Warner Bros. Records.
Richards, R. (2007). *Everyday creativity and new views of human nature: Psychological, social, and spiritual perspectives*. American Psychological Association.
Schneider, K. J. (2013). *The polarized mind: Why it's killing us and what we can do about it*. University Professors Press.
Sue, D.W. (2008). *Microaggressions in everyday life: Race, gender, and sexual orientation*. John Wiley & Sons.
Sue, D., Capodilupo, C., Torino, G., Bucceri, J.M., Esquilin, M.E., Holder, A., & Nadal, K. (2007). Racial microaggressions: Barriers to the counseling/therapy process. *The American Psychologist, 62*, 271–286.

Chapter 9

Standing on the Shoulders of Giants: Becoming an Existential–Humanistic Therapist

Orah T. Krug

It happened when I was 25, sitting one summer afternoon at my kitchen table. I'd just finished a difficult phone conversation with my father, who, insisting he knew better than I, had declared my future plans to move to California to be a dreadful mistake. Authoritative yet loving, my father had always been a force to be reckoned with. Even though I dearly loved him and greatly admired his intellect, I frequently bristled under his controlling manner. Hanging up the phone, I felt the familiar feeling of anxiety in the pit of my stomach that often accompanied his disapproval.

Then it happened. In a flash my anxiety disappeared and was replaced with an overwhelming feeling of well-being, accompanied by a thought, simple and clear: "This is *my* life to live." At that moment, for the very first time, I consciously experienced a sense of ownership of my life, becoming conscious of being the "author of my life" (Yalom, 1980, p. 218). I understand to many, this "epiphany" may seem mundane; yet for me, in its simplicity and clarity, it was extraordinary and life changing.

Links to my epiphany reach back to a book I'd read in college—*Escape from Freedom* by Erich Fromm (1965). As a history major, I was intrigued by Fromm's explanation of the rise of totalitarian governments in Germany, Italy, and Russia, but it was his ontological argument that spoke to me on a personal level. Fromm tells us that individuals have a conflicted relationship with freedom. Even though they strenuously battle for freedom, they relinquish it to a totalitarian government that promises to remove the responsibility of freedom from them.

Why *are* people so willing to relinquish their freedom? Why *does* accepting responsibility for one's life feel like a burden? Fromm's answer to these questions intrigued me. For me, his answer was not merely an abstract theory. His answer resonated within me. One statement I made repeatedly as a child was, "You can't force me." As a child, I felt controlled and believed I needed to fight, constantly, for my freedom. Consequently, this belief, which often meant hiding my private life from my parents, diverted my attention from any conscious desire to be taken care of or any wish to relinquish my freedom.

As I learned later, through personal therapy and life experiences, this desire to be taken care of was strongly, albeit latently, present. I also came to understand why Fromm's explanation of our ambivalent relationship with freedom and responsibility was personally relevant. I didn't know then that Fromm was articulating a central theme of existential thought. What I *did* know was that he spoke to my *lived experience*. As it turns out, the relationship with my parents and the impact of reading *Escape from Freedom* set me on a path to becoming an existential-humanistic therapist.

A Brief Overview of Existential-Humanistic Therapy

A brief overview of existential-humanistic therapy will set the stage for my therapeutic journey. Existential-humanistic therapy focuses on *how* the person who comes for therapy is coming into being and coping with this ontological awareness. It asks: "How is *this* person, in this present moment, coping with his or her awareness of being alive?" It is *ahistorical*; that is, the past is important only insofar as it is alive within the person in the present moment. It seeks to understand a person as a *human-being-in-the-world*—related to their physical, personal, and social worlds; the person is not simply a collection of drives and behavior patterns within an encapsulated self. It assumes that each person is more than the sum of his or her parts. *Each person constructs a particular world from unique perceptions of the world.* This process results in the creation of oneself and one's world construct and self-protections. Finally, existential therapy assumes that "the person and his [sic] world are a unitary, structural whole ... the two poles, self and world, are always dialectically related" (May, 1983, p. 122).

Consequently, existential therapy takes a step back from examining a person's drives and specific behavior patterns; with a wider scope, it understands these in the *context of the structures of that person's existence* (May, 1958, p. 37). Furthermore, this therapy assumes that a person's self and world constructs and self-protections are not abstract but actual, and, though they may be hidden from conscious awareness, nevertheless are evident (though perhaps implied) in the present moment. These structures of existence express themselves through words spoken and not spoken, through bodily gestures, through voice tones, dreams, and behavior patterns.

The existential therapist aims to know the person who comes for therapy at this "structural" level. To accomplish this, the existential-humanistic therapist enters their client's self-constructed personal world, using their own personal contexts to bring a full and genuine presence to the therapeutic encounter. The Latin root for *presence* is *prae* (before) + *esse* (to be)—*presence* means "to be before." Consequently, presence in a therapeutic setting can be understood as the capacity "to be before" one's own being and "to be before" another human being.

Presence involves aspects of awareness, acceptance, availability, and expressiveness in both therapist and client. Presence implies that the encounter is real. For Martin Buber (1958), it means that the person who is before me has ceased being an "it" and has become a "thou"; it means that we are humans who include each other in each other's recognition. Indeed, as Marcel (1951) suggests, intersubjective presence is the starting point where *we are* exists, as opposed to *I think*. If one can be truly present with another, then a genuine encounter has occurred.

A genuine encounter is what the existential therapist seeks. In a genuine encounter, the therapist is not objectively detached but rather is deeply attuned to and engaged with a client, participating in the client's world in order to illuminate and help the client illuminate what is alive in the living moment. The purpose of this endeavor is to have the person "grasp their being." Why is this "grasping of being" so critical? Recognition of being makes conscious the reality that, according to May and Yalom (1995), *I am* the one who actively responds to my environment; *I am* the one who is choosing. A recognition of being—in other words, a recognition of *personal agency*—is at the core of existential psychotherapy. Without it there is no sense of responsibility for creating one's world. With this recognition comes an awareness of and responsibility for choosing and creating. If one does not recognize one's being in this sense, no change can occur. It is important to note that this recognition "is not in itself a solution to an individual's problem. It is, *rather, the precondition for the solution*" (May & Yalom, 1995, p. 263).

To facilitate this "grasping of being," the existential therapist needs to cultivate presence on several levels. They need to cultivate presence with self and with the other and presence to the "in-between," or relational space. As mentioned earlier, the cultivation of presence is a way of being, an intention, and an activity. This way of being in the here-and-now is characterized by openness, engagement, and deep attunement to the unfolding processes of both participants that allows the therapist to substantially grasp the client's structures of conscious and unconscious existence and illuminate them as they are manifesting in the here-and-now. To illustrate, I was working with a client who refused to take another tissue even though the one she was using was torn and tattered. Being an existential therapist, I commented on my client's refusal to take another tissue. Her client's eyes welled up with tears as she realized that this behavior was a familiar way of being and she said, "I always just make do with what I have."

By engaging with the client in this way, the existential therapist is cultivating *intra*personal presence by illuminating what is implicitly present but unacknowledged by the client. The existential therapist can then cultivate *inter*personal presence by asking, "How was it for you to tell me that you always just make do?" Notice that now the focus is on the in-between, or the interpersonal processes between client and therapist. By working in this way, the client becomes more sensitive to their own subjective processes as well as to the interpersonal or relational processes existing between them. With this expanded awareness a client begins not only to experience the freedom of and responsibility for their life choices, but also begins to struggle with the heretofore unknown self-protections—those attitudes, beliefs, and ways of being that have constricted their life and relationships, such as "I always make do."

My Journey of Becoming an Existential–Humanistic Therapist

I have been working from an existential-humanistic perspective for over 40 years. In that time, I've published numerous books, chapters, and articles articulating my existential-humanistic approach to its theory, practice, and education of therapists. As I reflect upon my long career, I sense how I've "grown down into myself," James Hillman's (1996) phrase from *The Soul's Code*. Hillman posits that our life's challenge is to "grow down into ourselves," by facing our fate (i.e., working with our wounds) and becoming the person we were meant to be. That seems to accurately describe my journey of becoming a therapist and a teacher. I've encountered many personal and professional challenges along the way but engaging in them has been worth the effort. I have become a better person, bolder, kinder, and more sensitive to the needs of others as well as to my own. I have become more intimate with friends and family as I risked sharing my more vulnerable, hidden parts. Professionally, I'm delighted to say that after 40 years, I still look forward to working with clients or students. Practicing, teaching, and training consistently stimulate my curiosity and challenge me to find greater depths of presence and creativity. I'm certain my continued enjoyment comes from being able to cultivate personal and relational intimacy with those I work with. Working in the "here-and-now" allows me to be truly present, caring, and alive in the moment. When I'm able to help clients and students experience a way of being that has protected but also constricted them, I feel an extraordinary joy and satisfaction. How many of us have the privilege to help another reclaim a disowned part, thereby healing a long-standing trauma? These moments are nothing less than moments of awe.

Although numerous theorists and therapists including Rollo May, Eric Fromm, Paul Tillich, and Alfred North Whitehead, have influenced me, two masters of existential-humanistic therapy, James Bugental and Irvin Yalom, were most prominent in shaping my therapeutic values, attitudes, and style. I have never regretted learning therapy primarily from these two mentors. I trained with Jim Bugental for over twenty years, by participating in a weekly consultation group and for six of those years attending his *Art of the Psychotherapist* series. When "Arts" ended, most of the participants wanted to continue, so we formed our own retreat-training group. For the first few years, we invited Jim to work with us, and when he retired, we invited a series of prominent therapists to join us for a portion of the retreat. Our group is called "Arts Omega," and over a span of 20 plus years we've invited new participants to join our core "Arts" members. We continue to meet each spring at a beautiful retreat center in Sonoma, California.

My training with Irvin Yalom began in 1994 when five experienced therapists and I asked Dr. Yalom to be our consultant. Our little consultation group composed of the same six people met for almost 25 years. We eagerly showed up each month at Irv's apartment in San Francisco until a few years ago, when Irv needed to lessen his work schedule. Our group still meets regularly but, regretfully, without our esteemed leader.

Before describing my training experiences with Bugental and Yalom (for an in-depth description see Krug, 2007), I'll share my first encounter with each of them. I often think how monumental those encounters were for me because the choices that followed shaped my professional and personal destiny.

First Encounter with Jim Bugental

I first met James Bugental one Friday morning in 1976 at his home office in Marin County. I was with a group of "wet behind the ears" graduate students who were interning at a family service agency in the San Francisco Bay Area. Our supervisors, who had worked with Bugental, arranged for us to spend the day with him. Knowing Bugental only by reputation as the distinguished psychotherapist and author James F. T. Bugental, I was impressed even before I sat down.

Bugental started the day by reading a chapter from his soon-to-be-published book, *The Search for Existential Identity* (1976). In his cozy office, Bugental read to the six of us about "Lawrence," whom he described as "this competent machine, which is so unaware it is a man" (p. 21). Listening to Bugental, I was impressed with his sensitivity, perceptiveness, and the immediacy of his approach. I was deeply moved as I listened to how he worked with his client's rising panic when Lawrence told him of an article about red ants that devoured a man alive. Bugental's sensitivity to Lawrence's embodied emotions and his skill in helping Lawrence express his fear, while simultaneously mirroring back to him his struggle to contain it, resonated deeply with me, even though at that time I could not have described what Bugental was doing.

After the reading, Bugental did an experiential exercise that I have never forgotten. First, each of us picked an object out of a paper bag without looking at it. Bugental told us to simply feel it, resisting the temptation to name it, and then allow whatever associations about it to surface in our consciousness. I was fascinated with the experience. Bugental had managed to create a context for us to have a unique encounter with an everyday object by not immediately labeling it (mine happened to be an eraser!). In this simple exercise, I experienced my desire to label something quickly and avoid the discomfort of not knowing. I began to realize that the immediate identifying or labeling hindered my ability to be present in the moment, thereby diminishing the richness of my experience. Of course, on that day I had no idea how this concept was a pillar of his therapeutic approach. I would understand that later.

After lunch, he asked for volunteers to work with him. Throwing my usual caution to the wind, I raised my hand, an act for which I have been always grateful. Sitting opposite Bugental, I was immediately struck by his presence. A mixture of sensitive attunement, presence, and compassion emanated from his twinkling eyes. His presence to my words, body language, and voice was simultaneously surprising and a bit unnerving, but ultimately it felt deeply supportive. Without explicitly saying anything, he invited me to become curious about these aspects of myself, and as I did, I found myself going deeper, connecting to feelings I had not been aware of. After our work together, sitting quietly in my chair, I very clearly heard myself say, "I want to learn how to do this work."

For several months prior to this day with Bugental, I had been questioning whether a career in clinical psychology was right for me and had been considering a return to my position as a high school history teacher. But after the day with Bugental, being a teacher was no longer an option. My path was clear, there was no more confusion. I knew I wanted to be a psychotherapist and learn how to work with the immediacy and presence that Bugental brought to his work. It never occurred to me that I could actually have the opportunity to learn from Bugental himself. That opportunity serendipitously presented itself about 10 years later at a pool party.

On that hot summer day, I was chatting with my good friend and colleague Karin Kleiner as we twirled our toddlers in the shallow end of the pool. Karin described a workshop she and husband Richard had just attended at Esalen, given by "this wonderful therapist, James Bugental." Her words stopped my twirling. I had not forgotten the memorable encounter 10 years earlier with Bugental and the promise I had made. My excitement increased upon learning that Bugental was offering a 10-week *Art of the Psychotherapist* training course at the Humanistic Psychology Institute in San Francisco. I enrolled in the course the next week. My long and life-changing association with James Bugental had begun.

First Encounter with Irv Yalom
One day in the fall of 1998, Richard Kleiner told me about a talk that Irvin Yalom was giving at Saybrook Graduate School the next day. I immediately cleared my schedule to attend. At that time, I only knew of Yalom through his books, two of which had affected me greatly. The first was *Love's Executioner* (1989), a series of case studies that offered an intimate and personal portrait of Yalom practicing the art of existential psychotherapy.

I noticed halfway through the first chapter that he practiced existential therapy quite differently than did James Bugental, my current teacher. Although they both worked experientially with a focus on the here-and-now, each tended to focus their client's attention on different dimensions of the here-and-now. Yalom's focus was quite often on the *inter*personal dimension whereas Bugental's was typically on the *intra*personal. Having trained with Bugental, I was familiar with illuminating my client's intrapersonal processes but less familiar with illuminating what was happening between me and my client. I was not only intrigued by Yalom's interpersonal approach, which seemed to cultivate a different kind of intimacy, but was also moved by his evident care and attention to the relationship.

I also liked *When Nietzsche Wept* (Yalom,1992). It is a delightfully readable work of historical fiction that explores "the conception and birth of existential therapy" (Yalom, 1998b, p. 374). Yalom weaves a tale that engages Friedrich Nietzsche, the eccentric and brilliant existential philosopher, in a paradoxical therapeutic relationship with Josef Breuer, Freud's friend and mentor. The relationship is paradoxical because both believe themselves to be the healer for the other; because of this belief, each man is "healed" by the other. It is through this plot device that Yalom not only explores the tenets of existential therapy but also challenges the assumption that it is only the patient who is "changed" or "healed" by a therapeutic relationship. Yalom's account of the deeply personal and genuine relationship between Nietzsche and Breuer added to my growing curiosity about how he practiced existential psychotherapy.

At the talk, thirty of us made a semi-circle around Dr. Yalom, who was seated at one end of the cozy Rollo May Library. A small, compact man, I noted that his face looked kinder than it appeared on the book jacket of his numerous books. Wearing a leather vest with a long medallion hanging from his neck, he looked more like a writer than a therapist. Yalom was paradoxically engaging and shy. After explaining the premise for his new book, *Lying on the Couch* (1998), he quickly launched us into his world as he shared two of his dreams.

He dreamt the first, he told us, soon after his mother had died. In the dream, his Jewish family, all now dead, lined the stairway of his home. One of his aunts was moving so fast that she made a buzzing sound. Immediately drawn into his dream story, I realized how much he reminded me of my father, who, like Yalom, was Jewish by religion, a professor by trade, and a gifted storyteller by nature. My father always relished telling a good tale to his students, knowing how much learning could be had from it. I sensed Yalom felt the same way.

Yalom shared another dream he had had just before his friend, mentor, and former therapist Rollo May died. In the dream, May was wearing a T-shirt that said "Smokey the Bear" on it. Yalom told us that when he visited May, he told him about the dream, and together they explored its meaning. As Yalom spoke of this conversation, his tender tone conveyed the intimacy of his relationship with Rollo May and of the time they had shared together. The gathering gave me a chance to "know" Yalom more personally. I was intrigued with his use of dreams to access unconscious material, but I was even more intrigued by his apparent intention to reveal himself to us in the telling. This well-known therapist did not present a client's dream, but instead chose to share two of his own dreams. I now know that his willingness to be transparent at the gathering came from one of his core beliefs—the value of self-disclosure.

By self-disclosing, Yalom embodied a key existential attitude—that of being a "fellow traveler" (Yalom, 2002). Yalom believes we are all "fellow travelers," and that each of us, no matter who we are, struggles to bear the existential givens of life. "We are, all of us," as he says, "in this together" (p. 14). After working with Yalom for many years, I have come to appreciate the importance of incorporating this attitude into my life and work. I knew that morning that I wanted to learn from him but I did not think it possible. How was I to know that I would be invited, a year later, to join his consultation group and begin a fascinating journey, learning about life and psychotherapy from this wise and caring man?

Learning from Bugental and Yalom: Similarities and Differences
As teachers, Bugental and Yalom shared many similar attributes. One was their belief in the ability to facilitate growth and change. They managed to instill this belief in me; in part, through their skillful attunement to the client's process. For example, Bugental might say: "I notice you say you're fine, but your eyes are welling up with tears." By attending to the here-and-now, that is, to the implicit intra and interpersonal processes underlying the content, they showed us how to be present to clients' *ways of being*. Yalom would often remind us that we need to spend less time "talking about" life *outside* the therapy room and more time "being in life" *in* the therapy room. My mentors offered powerful lessons on how to effect healing and change.

Additionally, Bugental and Yalom demonstrated the art of relationship building and the value they had for it. They also conveyed their belief that therapeutic training needs to develop the "person" of the therapist as much as teaching skills and techniques. They both believed only emotionally mature therapists can engage in life-changing therapy. Both were dedicated to teaching and skillful in conveying these lessons. Finally, both created opportunities for community building. Each in their own way demonstrated the value of close-knit groups—groups in which permanent bonds of friendship and professional collaboration could be established.

There were, however, significant differences between them as teachers, not unlike their differences as therapists. Bugental focused almost exclusively on how to cultivate *intra*personal or subjective presence, that is, illuminate what is *actual but unregarded* within the individual. He brilliantly reformatted the traditional consultation experience to include exercises, demonstrations, and role-play techniques that provided experiential learning about our clients' and, most important, our own lived experiences and self-protections. Bugental's approach facilitated explorations of my own protective patterns, worldviews, and biases that were impeding my work. His approach helped me become a more empathic, less defended therapist, and ultimately a more effective one. But probably even more significant was how his approach helped me develop my emotional maturity. Working with Jim opened my eyes to how my distancing stance both protected me from being controlled or judged, but also how it prevented me from becoming more intimate with others. I learned how the stance served to guard my wound—a sense of not being good enough. Bugental brilliantly understood our protections as *spacesuits*: we constructed them at a young age to *protect* us from anticipated shame, pain, and hurt. Paradoxically, they also *constrict* our capacity to be truly free and truly intimate with others. As I began to understand my self/world construct, protections, and wound, I became more willing to risk greater intimacy with others. I found unexpected support, care, and love. Slowly, my fear that I wasn't good enough began to dissolve as my confidence grew.

Certainly, the high value that I place on developing the *person* of the therapist in my own trainings and consultation groups comes directly from my experiences participating in Jim Bugental's trainings and consultation group. This was one gift he gave me. The other was an exceptionally effective model of training: his five-day, yearly intensive training retreats, my inspiration for the residential training program that I developed as Clinical Director of the Existential–Humanistic Institute (see Krug & Schneider, *Supervision Essentials for Existential–Humanistic Therapy,* 2016).

Yalom's significantly more relational and eclectic therapeutic approach differentiated his existential perspective from Bugental's. Like Bugental, Yalom focused us on *intra*personal process. However, even more prominent was his focus on *inter*personal process. He provided us, in a traditionally structured consultation meeting, with unexpected experiences of group process and interpersonal learning. For example, if he sensed some interpersonal issue was present in the group, he might ask one of us: "How are you feeling in the group right now and who would you like to speak to?" Yalom also encouraged us to work with clients' dreams, often sharing his own clients' dreams with us. Finally, he always pointed out the implicit and explicit existential issues that might be manifesting in our work with a client.

Not only did Bugental and Yalom attend to different aspects of the "here-and-now" as teachers; they also differed significantly in their style of teaching. Bugental's teaching style was at times less supportive than his therapeutic style, though no less present. Although his personality played a part, his occasional critical feedback seemed a reflection of his passionate desire to have his students truly understand his approach. Unfortunately, Bugental's kind and supportive therapeutic "coach" sometimes became a tough drill sergeant-like" teacher. His style created a hierarchical, less collegial learning environment.

Yalom created a no less challenging learning environment than Bugental, but Yalom's way of teaching was always supportive and accepting, resulting in a more collegial, less hierarchical consultative atmosphere. Yalom's teaching style brilliantly modeled how to be a compassionate "fellow traveler." I have tried to follow in his footsteps by embodying a "fellow traveler" attitude with my clients and supervisees. Their feedback tells me I've succeeded; they report feeling sufficiently safe and accepted, thus allowing them to work with whatever self-protections may be impeding their therapeutic effectiveness.

The Creation of Existential–Humanistic Institute (EHI)
In 1997, Kirk Schneider and I, along with our colleagues Nader Shabahangi and Sonja Saltman, founded the Existential–Humanistic Institute (EHI) in San Francisco, California. Inspired by our mentor, James Bugental, and with his support, we envisioned EHI primarily as a teaching institute with a mission to educate the next generation of therapists interested in practicing from an existential-humanistic perspective. EHI held its teachers to a high level of academic achievement and clinical experience. We required of them extensive personal therapy and training with an existentially oriented master therapist. The curriculum I developed emphasized what we valued: We expected participants to master our learning objectives that supported existential-humanistic clinical competency. Specifically, students needed to demonstrate an ability to put the principles of existential-humanistic therapy, such as cultivating personal and relational presence, into practice. An equally important objective was to develop the *person* of the therapist. We seem to have created an effective curriculum mix, based on the positive feedback from students (see Krug & Schneider, 2017 for testimonials) and from our colleagues. In 2016, the Society for Humanistic Psychology (Division 32 of the American Psychological Association) awarded EHI the Charlotte and Karl Buhler Award for outstanding organizational contributions to humanistic psychology in recognition of its educational and training programs.

Homage to Victor and My Sons: Getting My Doctoral Degree
After forming EHI in 1997, I left Bugental's consultation group and began teaching my own students as EHI's Clinical Training Director. In 1999, I met Victor Goulet when Kirk brought him to an EHI party at my house. We started dating and soon fell in love. We've been together for twenty-one wonderful years. Victor played a crucial role in my decision to begin a PhD program at Saybrook University in 2001. At that time, I had been practicing my craft for 20 years and was the training director of EHI, in addition to raising two teenage boys on my own. I had a full plate and consequently had no interest in adding any more challenges to my life! But Victor urged me to get my doctoral degree. He was certain that having a PhD would elevate my credibility as a teacher, clinician, and researcher. I resisted his suggestion for some time but Victor, being the determined man that he is, persisted. Even though I knew I wanted to make a contribution to the field of psychotherapy beyond my consulting room, I'd always avoided this challenge, not wanting to be an academic like my father. My career as a psychotherapist had been predicated on the desire to take a different path than my father. He was an extremely successful history professor at the University of Chicago, to whom I never wanted to be compared. Victor convinced me that I could forge my own academic path. He was unwavering in his belief that I could make an even more significant contribution to the field if I had a PhD. I have never regretted my decision and am forever grateful for his presence in my life.

I also could not have graduated without the support and encouragement of my two sons, David and Daniel Bracke. They willingly relinquished carefully prepared meals in favor of an enthusiastic support for my studies. They admired my dedication to the goal and appreciated that I "stayed the course," demonstrating that one should never give up even though the road is long and challenging. I cherish the memories of when they'd come into my study, seeking me out to talk about something important in their lives. Our talks were a welcome break from my writing or reading and I know they kept us close. Victor and "my boys" (mature men now) are the heart and soul of my life.

My doctoral studies exposed me to the likes of Rollo May, Paul Tillich, Martin Buber, Friedrich Nietzsche, Soren Kierkegaard, and Alfred N. Whitehead. Their perspectives on the underlying structure of human experience and the nature of being deepened my understanding of existential philosophy and provided me with a more solid foundation from which I practice existential psychotherapy. My doctoral dissertation was a theoretical and clinical comparison of my two mentors: exploring how the cultivation of presence by Bugental and Yalom contributes to our understanding of what constitutes existential therapeutic theory, practice, and education.

Standing on the Shoulders of Giants

Contributions to Existential–Humanistic Therapeutic Theory and Practice

I had the opportunity to put my research to good use after graduating in June 2007. Immediately after graduation, Kirk invited me to be his co-author on a text for the American Psychological Association, *Existential–Humanistic Therapy* (Schneider & Krug, 2010, 2017). We organized existential-humanistic therapeutic theory around the central theme of cultivating presence, a term I first used in my dissertation (Krug, 2007). The term not only implies the here-and-now, but also describes the therapeutic attitude or style, that of *cultivating*, as well as the therapeutic intention or aim, that of *expanded presence*. My lengthy associations with Bugental and Yalom resulted in an effective integration of their different approaches. As a result, in the first text with Kirk, we redefined existential-humanistic therapy as a therapy with both a *subjective and relational focus* (Krug, 2009; Krug & Schneider 2016; Schneider & Krug, 2010, 2017). I argued that this type of integrated presence gives existential-humanistic therapists a wider lens from which to see and illuminate varied patterns of being, be they intrapsychic or interpersonal. I engaged in further research, as Clinical Director of EHI, with an efficacy study of EHI's training program. Examining our experiential trainings with students over a five-year period, we reviewed the efficacy of the curriculum and the teaching approach. We included the findings in *Supervision Essentials for Existential–Humanistic Therapy* (Krug & Schneider, 2016). In addition to the aforementioned research, I've continued to investigate how *existential meaning-making* is at the heart of therapeutic change. My focus on the *meaning-making process* has brought new attention to the influence of personal context on perception, contact, and change (Krug, 2010, 2016; Krug & Schneider, 2016; Schneider & Krug 2017).

As two of the current leaders of existential-humanistic therapy, Kirk Schneider and I have encouraged its evolution as an integrative methodology. Kirk began this evolution with the advent of "existential-integrative" (EI) therapy (Schneider & May, 1995; Schneider, 2008). Schneider and May developed a framework for engaging a variety of therapeutic modalities within an overall existential or experiential context. In our textbook, *Existential–Humanistic Therapy* (Schneider & Krug, 2010, 2017), we expanded on this innovative perspective by offering a phenomenological method for understanding human beings, not through a lens of abstract theory but through a direct encounter with their experiential worlds. With this method of cultivating therapeutic presence as a foundation, existential-humanistic therapy became an effective approach for a strikingly wide range of both client populations and additional therapeutic modalities. As a result, today's existential-humanistic therapy has become for many an increasingly integrative therapy by being a bridge to both mainstream and existentially oriented therapies (see support of this view in Wampold, 2008).

Contributions to the Clinical Training of Existential–Humanistic Therapists

My years of learning from Bugental and Yalom keenly shaped my vision of what constitutes effective therapy and how to teach it. My years of working with them most certainly influenced my desire to follow in their footsteps as a teacher of my craft. This was the impetus for creating EHI. I became fascinated by the therapy process and pondered two questions: "What constitutes effective therapy?" and "What constitutes effective therapeutic training?" Indeed, my dissertation was a first attempt to answer those questions (Krug 2007).

As mentioned previously, I argued for a new conceptualization of existential-humanistic therapy and for an innovative teaching approach that integrates a relational focus with an intrapsychic focus, with the cultivation of presence as the therapy's foundation (for an in-depth understanding, see Krug & Schneider, 2016). In my trainings and consultation groups, participants learn how to work in the here-and-now to cultivate personal and relational presence with clients. This helps them develop deep empathy and appropriate responsiveness to their clients' lived experiences. Often students will role-play their clients to experience their clients' personal worlds—worlds constructed through the meaning-making process.

A core focus of my trainings and consultation groups is experiential learning related to the meaning-making process. Students learn *how* the meaning-making process is responsible for the creation of one's self/world constructs and self-protections. I believe it is crucial that therapists learn not only about their clients' self/world constructs and self-protections but learn about their own, as well. In order to experientially grasp the meaning-making process, participants engage in exercises illustrating how they construct their own personal worlds—from which they "see the world they make!" One's personal world or context includes a view of self, others, and the world, and the protections constructed to guard against overwhelming shame, hurt, or pain. By inviting the students to engage with their own contexts (an exercise not to be confused with therapy), they develop *experiential* understanding and empathy for their clients' personal contexts and self-protections. Moreover, engaging with their own contexts helps them understand why a client's anger or overcompliance might trigger them. All my students want to learn about their triggers and self-protections, and all agree that this focus is one of the most valuable aspects of their therapeutic training.

I also focus students on the existential or ontological realm in their work with clients. They learn about the existential givens by exploring their own reactions and feelings related to death, separateness, contingency, or meaninglessness. They learn to recognize how their clients might be avoiding an existential given such as death, contingency, or separateness by being excessively risky, or excessively rigid, or by merging with their partner. They come to understand how a symptom like a panic attack or insomnia could be a manifestation of an existential given. They learn how to work with these self-protections and symptoms so their clients can face and gradually accept the previously avoided given, ultimately finding strength in their courage to be.

Bugental and Yalom's differing styles of teaching greatly influenced my understanding of how to support students' learning and competency. The literature suggests that a heavy focus on teaching techniques may hinder the development of therapist competence and relationship-building skills, two elements predictive of successful therapeutic outcome (Elkins, 2007; Norcross & Lambert, 2011; Wampold, 2007). I wholeheartedly support an emphasis on the art of relationship building and the development of the whole person (Bugental, 1987; Duncan, 2015; Elkins, 2015; Gendlin, 1994; Norcross & Wampold, 2011). My mentors certainly downplayed teaching techniques and modeled skills that fostered my therapeutic competency and ability to build relationships. Bugental and Yalom were in the "people-building business" as each, in his own way, conveyed an existential attitude towards life and education.

Bugental's riveting presence and attention to the subjective realm implicitly shouts, "Wake up, be conscious, venture forth and become who you are!" As my teacher and mentor, he provided a soil rich in experiential nutrients, which fed my capacity for personal reflection and self-understanding (Krug, 2007). Yalom whole-heartedly attends to building the therapeutic relationship, whether he is suggesting how to cultivate intimacy and safety with clients or actually engaging in this process with one of his consultees. Yalom's relationship-building encounters with me over the course of many years substantially increased my sense of safety, trust, and attachment with him and the group (Krug, 2007).

The existential therapy teacher faces the dilemma of not being able to teach about lived experience. As Tillich (1959) suggests, the existential teacher "can only create in his pupil by indirect communication that 'Existential state' or personal experience out of which the pupil may think or act" (p. 90). I deeply believe in the need to create those personal experiences, recognizing that *abstract ideas do not transform, but lived experiences do*. Lived experience, such as presence, can't be taught; rather the existential teacher must embody an authentic and congruent presence, thus indirectly communicating the "Existential state" to their students.

From my training experiences, I concluded that existential-humanistic therapeutic education needs to cultivate a belief in the potential for change, provide a model for the process of change, and germinate a belief in the trainee's ability to "midwife" change. Another crucial element of therapeutic training, not often explored, is the need for a safe and accepting learning environment. Such an environment develops, in part, when a therapist remains with one master therapist, in a constructive and supportive supervisory relationship, for a significant number of years. The familiarity of the same teacher in and of itself lays the groundwork for a sense of safety and acceptance. What also matters is the teacher's style. My inclination to cultivate a more collegial, less hierarchical learning context with my students was clearly influenced not only by my personal values but also by the difference in how I was treated by Bugental and Yalom. It certainly is true that who we are as therapists and supervisors can be significantly influenced by how we were treated by our therapists and supervisors.

An often unrecognized, yet crucial, element of therapeutic

education is developing a sense of *community* for students. Specifically, teachers and supervisors need to value and develop close, supportive therapeutic communities in which their students can feel held, accepted, and loved. Being part of a "therapeutic family" can significantly reduce the isolation of private practice and enhance one's competency, satisfaction, and enjoyment of the work. The value of creating a therapeutic family is unfortunately an underappreciated and underdeveloped aspect of therapeutic education that should be addressed. My creation of communities in training programs and consultation groups certainly was inspired by my mentors' intentions to build community.

Always Becoming, Never Arriving
In May 2015, I interviewed Irv Yalom at the opening ceremony of the First World Congress of Existential Therapy in London. After an hour of lively conversation, I asked Irv if he had any closing thoughts to share with the international audience. To my surprise, he pointed to me as an example of a master therapist who continues to hone her craft in an ongoing consultation group. He went on to say how important this ongoing learning was if one is fortunate to have a "therapist–colleague–friend group" with whom one can risk sharing therapeutic and life missteps, confusions, and dreads as well as joys, successes, and awe. As I reflected later on his words, I realized that both Jim and Irv had modeled ongoing learning, as they both participated in leaderless consult groups as master therapists. I have had the good fortune to participate in three forums of ongoing learning: my monthly consult group with Yalom, now a peer group; my yearly retreat with colleagues and friends from the Bugental "Arts" series; and my past participation as a teacher/consultant and curriculum developer of EHI's training programs. The value of each cannot be underestimated; each afforded me different learning experiences as a therapist and as a supervisor; each invigorates and stimulates me, challenging me to reflect, change, and grow in different creative ways.

The consult group with Irv offered a forum in which to bring a case about a client or a supervisee with whom I feel "stuck" or disempowered. My group never disappoints, as they invite me to explore some aspect of myself, the client/supervisee, or the relational field that I've missed. Sometimes we share our personal challenges, a process that Irv participated in as well, and occasionally Irv raised a group process issue that has been running unseen in our background process. Our over twenty-year connection has cemented our bonds of friendship, germinated a joyful camaraderie, and forged mutual respect and trust for one another. Even though Irv is no longer our leader, our group continues to meet regularly, engaging in the same lively work we did with Irv.

My "Arts" group affords five days in which to relax, engage in deep personal work, and share my newest projects with my friends and colleagues in beautiful and nurturing Sonoma Valley, California. The opportunity to work on personal issues in our large and small groups, which meet daily, is always a possibility. If I have a pressing personal, relational, or professional issue that requires attention, I know that my skilled colleagues and the invited consultants will engage with me to explore it. Some of my deepest psychological work has been done at these retreats. I've learned a great deal about group process, and also how the group can be useful in facilitating the illumination or resolution of a personal or relational challenge. And of course, if conflict arises between members, the group has become a safe container in which the conflict can be resolved. This learning has contributed enormously to my competency as a group leader of workshops and consultation groups.

In addition, my EHI affiliation supported my learning about leadership, curriculum development, and teaching. We offered each other support and feedback on the effectiveness of our various teaching modules, and on our overall teaching and relationship-building skills as we facilitated our experiential retreats. At each experiential, we always had at least two teachers present in addition to three teachers-in-training. The "village of teachers" supported teaching transparency, which allowed for immediate feedback and self-correction when necessary. Because we taught in front of our colleagues, there was always the opportunity to give and receive feedback on our teaching style, content value, and teaching competency. It was, therefore, an excellent learning environment in which to cultivate one's teaching and supervisory skills.

In 2019, I made the difficult decision to leave EHI and form Krug Counseling, Inc. My goal was to carry on my teaching and consulting on my own. In addition to my own clients, I have four therapists associated with my practice who see Krug Counseling clients and consult with me. Also, I teach existential-humanistic therapy, leading five consultation groups and offering training workshops for therapists. Leading numerous consultation groups and trainings has refined my understanding of what constitutes an effective group in content and style. It has helped me hone my group leadership skills as well as create effective experiential learning to teach the principles of existential-humanistic practice and develop the "person" who is the "therapist." My students strongly support these unique aspects of the group. They appreciate how I invite them to role-play their clients and to experientially grasp how their personal context might be stalling the therapy process. All the while, I strive to embody a "fellow traveler" attitude, implicitly saying: "We are all in this together, and we all get triggered because of our contexts. Take a risk because there's always something to learn."

My ongoing journey of "becoming" keeps me curious about the mystery of being and the myriad ways that humans can construct their personal worlds. It fills me with awe and wonder for the therapy process. How is it possible for two people to affect one another so profoundly—so that healing and change occur not only for the client but often for the therapist, as well? Likewise, how is it possible that teaching and supervising from this perspective can transform not only a participant's professional life but personal life as well? I am immensely grateful to my mentors, Jim and Irv, whose shoulders I stand on, who instilled in me a deep love for this work and who helped me grow into the therapist and teacher that I am today. Working as an existential-humanistic therapist and teacher is a fascinating and stimulating enterprise and for me remains a perpetual recipe for engagement, awe, and wonder. If past patterns are accurate predictors of future ones, then I'm certain that I'll never stop growing and becoming.

References

Buber, M. (1958). *I and Thou.* (R.G. Smith, Trans.). Charles Scribner's Sons.
Bugental, J. F. T. (1976). *The search for existential identity: Patient-therapist dialogues in humanistic psychotherapy.* Jossey-Bass.
Bugental, J. F. T. (1987). *The art of the psychotherapist.* Norton.
Bugental, J. F. T. (1999). *Psychotherapy isn't what you think.* Zeig, Tucker.
Duncan, B. L. (2015). The person of the therapist: One therapist's journey to relationship. In K. Schneider, J. Pierson, & J. Bugental (Eds.), *The handbook of humanistic psychology: Theory, research, and practice* (2nd ed.). Sage.
Elkins, D.N. (2007). Empirically supported treatments: The deconstruction of a myth. *Journal of Humanistic Psychology, 47,* 474–500.
Elkins, D. N. (2015). *The human elements of psychotherapy: A nonmedical model of emotional healing.* APA publications.

Fromm, E. (1965). *Escape from freedom.* Avon Books.
Gendlin, E. T. (1994). Celebrations and problems of humanistic psychology. In F. Wertz (Ed.), *The humanistic movement: Recovering the person in psychology* (pp. 330–343). Gardner Press.
Hillman, J. (1996). *The soul's code.* Random House.
Kierkegaard, S. (1985). *Fear and trembling* (A. Hannay, Trans.). Penguin.
Krug, O.T. (2007). A comparative study of James Bugental and Irvin Yalom: Two masters of existential psychotherapy. *Dissertations Abstracts International.* (University Microforms International No. 3288752).
Krug, O. T. (2009). James Bugental and Irvin Yalom: Two masters of existential therapy cultivate presence in the therapeutic encounter. *Journal of Humanistic Psychology, 49* (3), 27–39.
Krug, O. T. (2010, August) Is existential meaning making at the heart of therapeutic change? In K. J. Schneider (Chair), *Is there an existential-humanistic foundation to effective psychotherapy?* Symposium conducted at the meeting of the American Psychological Association, San Diego, CA.
Krug, O. T. (2016) Existential, humanistic, experiential therapies in historical perspective. In A. Consoli. L. Liebert, (Eds.), *Comprehensive textbook of psychotherapy: Theory and practice* (2nd ed.). Oxford University Press.
Krug, O. T. & Schneider, K. J. (2016). Supervision essentials for existential-humanistic therapy. American Psychological Associaton.
Marcel, G. (1951). *Mystery of being—faith and reality.* Gateway Edition.
May, R., Angel, E., & Ellenberger, H. (Eds.). (1958). *Existence: A new dimension in psychiatry and psychology.* Basic Books.
May, R. (1983). *The discovery of being.* Norton.
May, R., & Yalom, I. (1995). Existential psychotherapy. In R. Corsini & D. Wedding (Eds.), *Current psychotherapies* (5th ed., pp. 262–292). Peacock.
Norcross, J. C., & Lambert, M. J. (2011). Psychotherapy relationships that work. *Psychotherapy, 48,* 4–8. doi:10.1037/a0022180
Norcross, J. C., & Wampold, B. E. (2011). Evidence-based relationships: Research conclusions and clinical practices. *Psychotherapy, 48,* 98–102. doi: 10.1037/a0022161
Schneider, K. J. (2008). *Existential-integrative psychotherapy: Guideposts to the core of practice.* Routledge.
Schneider, K. J., & May, R. (Eds.). (1995). *The psychology of existence: An integrative, clinical perspective.* McGraw-Hill.
Schneider, K. J., & Krug, O. T. (2010). *Existential-humanistic therapy.* American Psychological Association.
Schneider, K. J., & Krug, O. T. (2017). *Existential-humanistic therapy* (2nd edition). American Psychological Association.
Schneider, K. J., Pierson, J., & Bugental, J. (Eds.), *The handbook of humanistic psychology: Theory, research and practice* (2nd ed., pp. 457–472). Sage.
Tillich, P. (1959). *Theology of culture.* Oxford University Press.
Wampold, B. E. (2007). Psychotherapy: The humanistic (and effective)

treatment. *American Psychologist, 62*, 857–873.

Wampold, B. E. (2008, February 6). Existential-integrative psychotherapy comes of age[Review of the book *Existential-integrative psychotherapy: Guideposts to the core of practice*]. *PsycCritiques* I, Release 6, Article 1. (Published by the American Psychological Association, Washington, DC)

Yalom, I. (1980). *Existential psychotherapy.* Basic Books.

Yalom, I. (1989). *Love's executioner.* Harper Perennial.

Yalom, I. (1992). *When Nietzsche wept.* Harper Collins.

Yalom, I. (1998). *Lying on the couch.* Harper Perennial.

Yalom, I. (2002). *The gift of therapy.* Harper Collins.

Chapter 10

My Journey to Existential Psychology: A Dialogue with Colleagues at the Zhi Mian Institute

Xuefu Wang

Upon receiving an invitation to write a chapter for this book of narratives, I brought some of my students and colleagues together to listen and reflect upon my stories about the path I followed as I became an existential-humanistic therapist. Throughout this conversation, their questions led me to many memories as I tried to answer them accordingly. This chapter, then, is nearly a transcription of that valuable dialogue.[1]

How and when did you first encounter existentialism and existential psychology? Why did you choose to become a psychotherapist, and then an existential therapist? Is there anything in relation to your educational background and life experience?

In 2007, I found myself at a Sino-American forum on religious psychology at Zhejiang Normal University. It was break time. Three men came out of the meeting room and sat on the sofa in the lobby, starting a random conversation. They were Louis Hoffman, Mark Yang, and me. Louis and Mark raised a question to me: "Xuefu, what is the situation of existential psychology in China?" That question was like a key that opened the subsequent years of our friendship and collaboration. It was right at that moment that my journey to existential psychology set sail. As the conversation moved on, we became increasingly excited. As one Chinese saying goes, "It is much to be

---

[1] My deep appreciation goes to my friend Louis Hoffman and Julia Falk for their editing effort to accurately represent my writing in the English language.

regretted that we could not have met earlier, but how fortunate that we met then rather than later or not at all." (相见恨晚). We found that the three of us have a deep, strong feeling for existentialism, and, specifically, existential psychology. We have a similar educational background, along with shared personal interests. We all received psychological education in a theological context. Our psychological training has been integrated or enriched with resources from existential theologians and philosophers such as Soren Kierkegaard, Paul Tillich, and existential psychologists such as Rollo May, Victor Frankl, James Bugental, and others.

People of my generation in China were fortunate to encounter the outside world on the occasion of China's opening. When the so-called Cultural Revolution in China, which was a political movement that caused immense devastation to our cultural heritage and blocked communication with the world outside our nation, came to an end, China resumed its college entrance examination system. I was enrolled in college education with many fellow students of my age. It was a time when various schools of Western thought were given access to China, including, among others, philosophy, literature, and psychology under the name of existentialism. Hence my education ranged beyond Chinese literature and culture to include Western existential scholarship (though very limited) such as the thoughts of Nietzsche, Kierkegaard, Pascal, Camus, and Kafka, as well as Freud and Jung.

In 1979, I was admitted to a teacher's school to study courses in English, Chinese, and educational psychology. After graduation, I was assigned to teach English at a primary school in a mountainous area of northwest Hubei province. Like the situation in my own village, the local people had labored, lived, and multiplied on this land for generation after generation. Their life was so poverty stricken that they attached hope to their kids for a turn of fortune's wheel through education— but opportunities were slight, if we could not bear to say none. I joined the endeavor with other fellow teachers but saw not a single student admitted to schools beyond the mountains. A sense grew in me that this was not the place where I would spend the rest of my life. My life journey would go on, but I did not know how to go further or even where to go. Around then, I happened to read a book by Victor Hugo (1866), *The Toilers of the Sea*, borrowed from a young man who strove so hard to become a novelist. The book sparked a passion in me to strive for a life different from the status quo. A path of uncertainty awaits an explorative soul like me, and likely the young man who lent me the book.

The day I left, I heard voices calling to me from the hilly slope alongside the road: "Good-bye, Teacher!" It was the child cowherds who were once my students. Like them, I, too, was a drop-out teacher! I had a sense of regret and guilt as I thought of them.

I entered Nanjing Union Theological Seminary in 1983. This experience served to equip me with more knowledge about existentialism, as I learned a little about Kierkegaard, Tillich, Nietzsche, and Pascal, to name a few. But I was most influenced by Jesus Christ, whose life to me seemed quite existential in terms of his authenticity, his embodiment of full humanity, his emphasis on love and relationship, and his discernment of human nature. His incarnation demonstrated the fullest sense of empathy, and his confrontation (in the sense of *zhi mian*[2], facing life with courage and authenticity) with the Pharisees illuminated the hypocritical personality. My theological education did not, as it normally should, lead me to pastoral ministry, but it did take me to a deeper understanding of human beings in a humane, existential way—living out our human lives toward the fullest sense of love and the deepest level of awareness.

I pursued literature in Nanjing University, where I majored in modern Chinese literature. Lu Xun, who emerged as the most acute

---

[2] Zhi mian is a term from the Chinese literary figure Lu Xun that served as the basis for a form of therapy I developed, Zhi Mian Therapy. For more information, see Wang (2011, 2019); Dueck and Wei (2019); and Yang (2019).

thinker as well as the most talented writer in 20th century China, was my area of study. Lu Xun lived at the turning point when China transitioned itself from tradition to modernity. The May 4th New Culture Movement strongly advocated for re-evaluation of China's traditions. Though short-lived (only two to three years and soon replaced by the national independence movement, war against Japanese invasion, and the subsequent civil war between the communists and nationalists), its significance is widely recognized. Hu Shi (2001), a leading figure of the May 4th New Culture Movement, likened it to the Renaissance in Europe, calling it the Renaissance of China. As one of the sincerest reform-minded intellectuals of the time, Lu Xun advocated the new culture while relentlessly exposing and criticizing the cruelty of the old traditional culture. That culture aligned with a long history of feudalism, under which, in Lu Xun's scrutiny, the Chinese character was thoroughly poisoned and ruined. He devoted himself to the search for a new character or personality that could help reform or transform Chinese character or the national psyche. The ideal personality he advertently pursued was what he called "the warrior of the kingdom of spirit" (Lu Xun, 1998a, p. 84). He investigated and examined a group of Western reform-minded thinkers and writers, such as Nietzsche, Kierkegaard, Dostoevsky, Tolstoy, Byron, and Shelley. He hoped that these visionaries would be cultivated and grow on the land of China, shouting out in the wilderness like the prophet Jeremiah or John the Baptist and Jesus, to wake up Chinese people whose spirit had fallen into a slumber in an iron house (Lu Xun, 1998a, p. 419). These visionaries were revolutionaries, reformers, rebels, and fighters who stood against all sorts of stereotypes, such as hypocrites, and escapists from human society. They were independent individuals who, in contrast to "the subjects of the tyrants" (Lu Xun, 1998a, p. 366), had passion for reform, who made choices based on their own judgment, and took responsibilities. They discerned right from false, were authentic and courageous, and stood in opposition to what Lu Xun depicted as the *Ah Q* mentality,[3] the prototype of escaping personality. The Ah Q mentality was reluctant to take a step toward reform, painted reality for self-comfort rather than to make a difference, flattered those

---

[3] The Ah Q mentality is derived from Lu Xun's story, *The True Story of Ah Q* (2002), which has been translated into English. It was originally published in China in several segments from 1921 to 1922, and subsequently published in Lu Xun's book, *A Call to Arms*.

in power, and eulogized the delusional grandiosity of a dynasty that tread on the powerless.

As we all know, you were teaching at Xiamen University, which was an admirable position that many people would eagerly want. How did you come to make the decision to give up teaching at the university and pursue psychology studies in the United States?

When I ponder how and why I became an existentialist or an existential therapist, or in a broader sense, an existentially informed individual, I recall many choices that I have made all along my life's road. The given situation since my early childhood provided me choices that I could naturally have made. For instance, I could likely have become a peasant because my parents farmed on the land. I could have become a carpenter because my grandfather was accomplished in carpentry. I could have become an owner of a snack stand because my father made fried dough sticks for a living, which sustained the whole family. I could have become a novelist as I pursued that during my high school years. I could have continued teaching as my lifelong career at a primary–middle school after I graduated from Zaoyang Teacher's School, but I moved on for a theological education at Nanjing Union Theological Seminary. I could have become a pastor after graduation from seminary, but I furthered my pursuit in literature in Nanjing University. Again, I could have maintained my rostrum at Xiamen University where I taught Chinese literature and Chinese culture. Life, however, does not necessarily take the path that is expected. It was during this period that I happened to get involved in a counseling center called Xiamen Care Corner, which was established and sustained by a group of professionals from Singapore. That was in the early 1990s, when the Care Corner was an early pioneer in this emerging field in China, which proved to be the entryway for me to step into this service profession of counseling. The initial experience was so impactful on me that I was completely amazed. How could I imagine that there would be this way of influencing people—by talking with them! And it worked wonderfully! It suited me so well, just as though it were tailored for a person like me!

The flow of time brought me to that spot, many years later, where Louis, Mark, and I were sitting together talking about existential psychology. With that question raised by Louis and Mark, I began to reflect on how I have embarked on this journey. Things always happen in their own way before you realize it.

Counseling or therapy, however you may understand it, is a job, an enterprise, a vocation, and a way of being that embodies who you are. You have private conversations with people, and through this you influence people to change for the better—to live a better life, to be a better person. Sometimes, though, it is not always known how or why, that change happens. I still remember one moment when I was so excited that I could hear the voice of my heart beating in a rapid rhythm. I received a phone call from a college student who had been my client for a time, his voice quivering in excitement: "Before I came to see you, I had thought of quitting my study or killing that guy whom I feared so much and hated so much. But, unbelievably, I reconciled with him. I thought of making a phone call just to let you know how relieved I am now."

When I recall my experience of getting along with people, even from my very early life, I have been one who likes relating to people and forming intimate relationships. I may not be well suited to public performance, but I do like communicating with people in a personal way and enhancing our mutuality. I do not relate to judging them as less conforming, less pretending, less calculating, and often less successful in normal people's eyes. Rather, I see in them a retained quality of humanity that our culture does succeed in dissolving and diminishing rather than in reserving and restoring. Such qualities include uniqueness, openness, generosity, authenticity, and kindness, though they may look rough or unshaped. General culture may shun them, but people like me greet them.

Ever since I started my counseling career, though insufficiently trained as I was in that circumstance, I could work with people in a natural way, assuming an equal, respectful manner and an experiential, cultural sensitivity. I understood them because my life experience and amicable personality have prepared me for an easier accessibility into them and acceptance of who they are. Before working with clients as a professional, I had accumulated considerable amateur experience at helping people through their difficulties—or to be more exact, I was a friend to each of them. Perhaps this was a natural readiness for the choice of counseling that I made later when I happened to encounter it. Existential-humanistic psychology continues to attract me more than other approaches because I, growing in a bottom-up process in our society, could touch base with people in terms of understanding their dilemma and their experience of striving for a better living. Counseling, as I understand it, is life encountering life, while not so much a strategic, structural, or scientific undergoing. It is more about experiential relationship, explorative process, understanding, empathy, and trust that gradually forms between two human individuals. The encounter, rather than staying on the surface, goes deeper than any forms of common human relations. That's the psychology I pursue as an existential therapist, or as I often think of myself, a zhi mian healer.

In 1999, I resigned from my teaching at Xiamen University and went to study at Andover Newton Seminary in the United States. My area of study was psychology, religion, and pastoral counseling. I learned from courses about Carl Jung's analytical psychology, relational psychology, family systems theory, marriage and family, child development, and others. My graduation thesis, *Beyond Fear-Escape Mechanism* (Wang, 2002), touched upon fear, anxiety, and awe, which exemplifies how I was influenced by the existential theology, philosophy, and psychology propounded by Soren Kierkegaard, Paul Tillich, Victor Frankl, Rollo May, and others.

I was invited to Fuller Seminary Graduate School of Psychology as a visiting scholar in 2008. I studied and did research with Alvin Dueck, the Evelyn and Frank Freed Professor of the Integration of Psychology and Theology. He received his PhD in clinical psychology at Stanford University but told me in conversation that he would rather replace its scientific substance with philosophy. He received eight years of analysis and training at a Jungian institute and demonstrated an unquenchable passion for cultural psychology, or psychology and culture. For many years he traveled around the world to become informed about people of different countries who are endeavoring to develop indigenous psychologies, making himself available to them for encouragement and support. I am one of those cared for, encouraged, and supported by him. I got to know him in person in 2004. In the following years, he put me in connection with existential-humanistic psychologists from the United States, among them Louis Hoffman and Mark Yang, who became my "fellow travelers" on the way to existential psychology.

I did not fully realize my existential legacy until 2007 when I met with Louis and Mark, who kindled a light that beckoned me to step further into the existential journey. Existentialism, in whatever forms, had encroached into my life before I got to know its undeclared presence and incubated influence. When studying at Fuller's School of Psychology as a visiting research scholar, I participated in an existential meeting at University of the Rockies, organized by Louis Hoffman. I met

Kirk Schneider, David Elkins, and other leading figures in the field of American existential-humanistic psychology. From that moment on, Louis, Mark, and I began to talk about how we could initiate a troika journey to promote East–West dialogues in existential psychology. To the best of my knowledge, existential psychology, in its intellectual form, was introduced in China in the 1980s. Books by Ludwig Binswanger, Medard Boss, R. D. Laing, Rollo May, James Bugental, Victor Frankl, and Irvin Yalom were translated by scholars such as Yang Shaogang and Guo Benyu. Gradually, more translations appeared of newer works by Kirk Schneider, Emmy van Deurzen, and others. The Zhi Mian Institute has also joined this endeavor and is planning to organize a team of translators for existential psychology. When it comes to the practice of existential therapy in China, I am a pioneer, along with a group of people at the Zhi Mian Institute who identify themselves as practitioners of existential or existentially informed therapies.

You have been collaborating with Western existential psychologists. How did that happen?

In 2009, while living at Fuller Graduate School of Psychology as a visiting scholar, I worked with Louis, Mark, and a group of university professors and doctoral students (mostly from the University of the Rockies) to organize an existential psychology forum in China.[4] It was the fruit of collaboration with Nanjing Population and Management College through Yan Fengming. Most important, in 2010, the First International Conference of Existential Psychology was held in Nanjing. It was an East–West dialogue in existential psychology between Chinese existential experts and American existential psychologists. The conference was initiated by Louis Hoffman, Mark Yang and me in collaboration with Tao Laiheng, professor at Nanjing Xiao Zhuang College, and Sun Lizhe, founder of the China Institute of Psychology. The conference greeted a galaxy of American existential-humanistic psychologists, including Kirk Schneider, Erik Craig, Ed Mendelowitz, and Ilene Serlin. At the First International Conference on Existential psychology, Kirk Schneider gave an opening keynote speech about awe-based psychology, while Erik Craig spoke on existence, Louis Hoffman on existential psychology, Ed Mendelowitz on Rollo May's legacy, and

---

[4] For more information on the development of existential-humanistic psychology in China, see Thrash et al. (2019) and Hsu et al. (2019).

Ilene Serlin on whole-person healthcare. Chinese experts also participated and presented, including Guo Bengyu, Zheng Richang, Jia Xiaoming, Shen Heyong, Wang Jie, Fuhong, Ren Qiping, and Zheng Shiyan. The event in 2010 was acclaimed by Guo Benyu of Nanjing Normal University as a milestone in the development of existential psychology in China. I presented on the theme of "Zhi Mian and Existence" at the first conference, claiming zhi mian therapy and its existential connection and quality. The term of *zhi mian* impressed Western colleagues such as Louis Hoffman, Mark Yang, Ed Mendelowitz, and Erik Craig, and they have since helped to introduce zhi mian by publishing my articles in United States psychology journals and books. Such kindness and generosity!

Subsequently in 2012, in collaboration with Sun Shijin, professor at Fudan University (host institution of the conference), the Second International Conference of Existential Psychology was held in Shanghai. Then in 2014, the Third International Conference took place in Guangzhou, in collaboration with Yang Shaogang of Guangdong University of Foreign Studies (host institution of the conference). In 2016, the Fourth Conference in Hong Kong, hosted by Hong Kong University was facilitated by Mark Yang. Through conferences, forums, training courses, and publications, zhi mian has been given a voice of its own as an indigenous existential psychotherapy. At the Second Conference in Shanghai, Louis and Mark advised the conference committee to use zhi mian as the conference theme. I was excited to see that many presenters from outside of China presented about zhi mian in relation to their area of study. One paper given by Al Dueck (2012) was titled *The Cultural Psychology of Lu Xun and Wang Xuefu*, which later became a chapter in *Existential Psychology East–West* (Volume 2). Many Chinese participants were surprised to see that zhi mian, representing a Chinese cultural concept and a fledgling psychological approach, was raised up, promoted, recognized, and emphasized by a group of Western psychologists. What open minds and humble spirits in terms of promoting East–West psychological dialogue and cultural exchange!

To my surprise, my existential journey contained a special event in 2013, when the Society for Humanistic Psychology (Division 32 of the American Psychological Association) gave the Charlotte and Karl Bühler Award to the Zhi Mian Institute and me, awarded "For an Institution and an Individual Associated with an Institution that has made an Outstanding and Lasting Contribution to Humanistic Psychology." People may ask: Why Zhi Mian, an unfamiliar institution? Why Wang

Xuefu, a plain person? Although I can't answer that question fully, I suspect the answer lies in my collaboration with American existential-humanistic psychologists toward promoting East–West dialogue in this field, and in my effort to develop the indigenous psychology of zhi mian, with its existential-humanistic concerns and qualities.

Moving another step forward on the journey, I attended the World Congress of Existential Therapy in London in 2015, presenting "Zhi Mian, a Chinese Existential Approach to Psychotherapy." My presentation was published in *Existential Analysis*, further confirming me as a Chinese therapist joining the world community of existential therapy. Recommended by Kirk Schneider and Erik Craig, I also joined the Scientific Committee of the World Congress and witnessed the process and discussion for defining existential therapy. I was invited to contribute a chapter to the *World Handbook of Existential Therapy* on the development of existential therapy in China and other Asian countries. With my presentation, I introduced Lu Xun to a worldwide audience at the Congress.

Before you shifted to psychology, you were in literature. We know that you are deeply influenced by Lu Xun. What does Lu Xun mean to you in terms of your choice of psychology, and in relation to an indigenous zhi mian psychology and existential psychology?

When I scan the panorama of influences that brought me to existentialism, Lu Xun stands salient. I see him as not only the most brilliant writer of 20th century China, but also as a thinker discerning the Chinese psyche and cultural collective unconscious. Lu Xun's thinking, which I call zhi mian thinking, lays the cultural foundation for my zhi mian approach to psychotherapy and for my actual therapeutic practice. My psychological exploration has benefited from, and been enriched by, the legacy of Lu Xun's literary creation and cultural insight. Similar to Nietzsche, Lu Xun called for a re-evaluation of Chinese tradition and values. Living in a transitional period between China's ancient and modern times, he examined and introduced Western thinkers, poets, scientists, and novelists into China. Standing on his rich heritage of Chinese intellectual accomplishments, Lu Xun also received influences from Western learning. He admired the revolutionary minds of the West who acted as positive forces to advance human history but were misunderstood and mocked as mora poets (almost monosyllabic). But in the land of China, Lu Xun stood up to give them full admiration. It is said that the young man Lu Xun was once called the Nietzsche of China. Here I must clarify that instead of copying Nietzsche Lu Xun is a genuine Chinese thinker, echoing the same existential voice as his Western counterparts. Zhi mian, literally meaning to face reality, is a word coined by Lu Xun, imbued with rich Chinese historical, cultural, social, and psychological implications—along with ingredients of Western existentialism.

Ah Q, the character Lu Xun (2002) created in his novel *The True Story of Ah Q*, was so engaged in seeking mental comfort that he was far away from reality and lost his real self. He represented a personality or psychology called the Ah Q mentality, a drive toward escape. Ah Q never admitted any defeat in his life. What he did was disguise his defeat in false triumph or false psychological bliss. The illusory escapism only left a trail of obvious defeats, making his life comical and sad. He sacrificed his real self and pretended he was always a triumphant hero. According to Lu Xun's interpretation of Chinese culture and history, China had been walking the way of escape, one of whose forms was self-deceit. Lu Xun uncovered the shadowy part of the Chinese psyche and depicted it as mental escapism, while I, in observing and thinking about the present reality of Chinese society, conceptualize it as "survivalism." Contrary to existentialism, survivalism appears as living for the sake of self-survival while caring little or nothing for the life and death of others; suffering without reflection on the cause of suffering, and so supporting the repetition of suffering; coveting material goods out of insecurity, but never secure and satiated, so tending toward hedonism. Mental escapism or survivalism, according to Lu Xun, grew and flourished out of the long history of feudalistic oppression and deprivation in China, and took deep root in the Chinese character or personality. As an antidote to it, Lu Xun (1998b) proposed a new character called "the warrior of the world of mind" (p. 84). He says, "The real warrior dares to face life directly as it is, no matter how gloomy it might be; and to look unflinchingly at one's circumstances, no matter how blood drenched it might be" (p. 274).

In my therapeutic work with my fellow Chinese people, based on my life experience and the heritage of thought from Lu Xun, I have been exploring and developing an approach called zhi mian psychology or zhi mian therapy. It genuinely represents an effort to understand Chinese people from past and present generations: their living conditions, the challenges they meet, the attitude and strategy or style they employ to survive, and, in general, the culture they create in their lives. I strive to understand how I, as an existential therapist or a zhi mian healer, can discern and differentiate in this culture the elements that are supportive, cultivating, and nurturing from those that are hurting, damaging, or impeding. Following in the footsteps of Lu Xun, I also advocate for cultural renewal and personal transformation. At the Zhi Mian Institute, we work with each individual in therapy by encouraging them to have the courage of zhi mian (facing reality), rather than escaping from reality. We do so in the spirit of zhi mian, which shares the courage and authenticity that existential psychology values so highly.

You lived in an enclosed, backward village in your early life, with few probabilities of contact with new thought. How did a person from your circumstances grow yourself into an individual with independent thinking?

When I claim to be an existentialist or existential therapist, I cannot ignore how I have grown into the person I am now. I was born in a village, enclosed and backward in terms of culture as viewed from a modern, urban mind. My childhood reflected the living conditions of many Chinese striving for minimum survival. I experienced how my fellow villagers lived, how they understood things, how they related to others, how they exposed their stark nature when deprived of living resources, and how they were driven to a reduced state of humanity. It is a culture close to nature, presenting with a full range of human qualities and experiences: feeling and emotions; a life attitude of resilience; intimacy in relationships; the bearing of hardships and dilemmas; the want of and eagerness for opportunities and fullness of life; material poverty and even coarseness in lifestyle and manner of expression; close-minded, lacking spiritual nourishment; demonstrating an unawareness of ugliness, jealousy, or hatred; and holding poisonous concepts such as prejudices, misunderstanding, and mistreatment of women and girls. All these obstructive, impeding, hurtful elements surrounded me like air, but they were also intermingled with kindness and common sense.

Being both aware and unaware, I started my existential journey from that village. All along the way, I have met with others and interacted with them. They have been significant to me to various degrees. When I reflect on my journey to existentialism, I remember many people who provided me with a stream of resources that nurtured my soul. My grandmother, for example, received an old-style private school education and, for reasons I did not know, became a Christian. Her life was a combination of Chinese tradition and Christian teaching. Her understanding of life and interpretation of the Bible, along with her special affection for me, brought much comfort and satisfaction and offered me a perspective beyond material lack and spiritual scarcity. It is beyond my ability to express the importance to me of so many stories about my grandfather, my parents, my wife and kids, my relatives, my teachers, my schoolmates, my friends, my colleagues, and my clients (whom I call visitors)—all of whom I have encountered in person or in other ways, from the past until the present, from China and from other nations. They contributed the materials that, bit by bit, have built my existentialism. Together, they form a "being-in-the-world" around me. They are individuals, but at the same time, they have become part of me. We are independent from one another, yet we are not separated. We are fellow human beings. It is in this sense that I call myself an existentialist.

We are all situated in certain circumstances, surrounded by the elements we interact with, which I call culture. We are basically influenced and shaped by our given culture. People living in the same situation may share something in common, but gradually live a different life from others. When I assume that it is culture that makes the differences between people, I don't mean that we are passively influenced or determined by the natural culture that is given to us. We, at the same time, can gradually become conscious of how we understand the given culture, how we respond to it, and how we make choices based on our consciousness of it. Our life can become constantly enriched, because we are not only chosen by our culture but we are also culture choosers. We can choose to become gradually aware of our culture and broadened by our culture. My existential journey is composed of an experience, an event, the people I met and got along with, a book I read, and so forth. They are not just natural givens that I have accepted but are choices that I have made.

In a certain given situation, people maintain or potentially hold certain kinds of possibilities and hope. We live now in a situation with cultural elements that we choose to touch upon and interact with. A lot of the outcome depends on which elements you touch upon and interact with. Some elements may block you, leaving you no way out, like a dead end. But other elements you touch upon and interact with may open a door or pave a way out, giving you space and leading you to certain possibilities or opportunities. In my own life conditions, I happened to touch upon some elements that gave me a way forward. These elements seemed to be promising some things ahead and encouraging me, whispering: "There is something beautiful prepared for you in the route ahead. Just go get it!" Sometimes we may call this luck or fortune. Sometimes it seems that we have that motivation, that desire, that sense, that hunch, that instinct. You hope for something to happen, and then you touch it, and something does happen as you expected. When I look back at the path that I've been walking alone, I see many helpful elements that I happened or chose to touch upon, and they opened one door after another, inviting me to strike out one way after another. What do I call this? It's a consciousness, which means you are aware of it. I don't know how a child like me grows to have such a consciousness or awareness. I do remember sessions in which I worked with young people. I generally asked them a few questions: "What is your current situation?" Or, put another way, "Do you see the elements of which your reality is composed?" Additionally, "What elements do you have within yourself and around you that you find supportive, or that might be called resources?" I sat with people and explored these elements, examining each so that people could get to know their meaning or implication. I wanted to see my clients become conscious through this exercise, discerning their reality and making decisions based on those elements that were discerned.

When we find ourselves in a stark reality that is given to (not chosen by) us, we need to face that reality and discern opportunities in it and try by all means to find a way out for self-development or self-actualization. We can collect resources that support us to move forward. We place ourselves into relationship with others so that they can become "significant others" to us.

Zhi mian therapy is concerned a lot with culture. How do you explain this? How does this aspect of it relate to existential psychology or therapy?

Existential-humanistic therapy has a fundamental concern: "What does it mean to be human?" This is the universal question that every human must face and reflect upon in response to certain situations in life. It concerns essential issues (or we say existential concerns) that all human beings can never avoid or live without. It is in that sense that we call ourselves existentialists. We reflect on who we are, where we are from, why and for what purpose we live, what our destiny is, and even more. The themes that concern us in our existential search are things like meaning, choice, freedom, anxiety, death, relationship, responsibility, and so forth. By asking this question about the meaning of being human, we probe for a better understanding of ourselves and a deeper awareness of our reality and the elements that compose it.

Zhi mian psychology is deeply concerned with how people interact with culture and how culture influences and shapes people. The central question we help people to explore in our therapeutic fellowship is: "What does my culture mean to me?" or, "How has my culture been working to shape me into the being that I am?" A person has to be conscious of themselves, of the cultural elements that influenced them, and of the choices they have made based on this consciousness. Our destiny may be composed of two things: one is the cultural elements that influence us; another is the choices that we make in response to the cultural elements. A conscious person may also be called an existentialist. Or an existentialist may be well-conscious of themselves and their situation. They take the zhi mian attitude as they face life: to examine it, to be aware of it, and to make choices based on their awareness of life. In that sense, they themselves can form their own destiny. Thus, they would live fully as an existential figure. There is influence from culture, and there is choice making that comes from being aware of the culture and its influence.

When we talk about the similarities and differences between human beings, we observe the same shared humanity, but different cultures maintain different languages that speak to each of us. Therefore, we respectively are shaped differently by our own culture. At the same time, different cultures can meet and exchange in terms of values and styles of life. Hence, different cultures interact with and influence each other. Being an existential therapist, I do find resonance between Chinese culture and Western existentialism, in the sense of understanding and responding to the human condition. Through the channel of existentialism, I draw healing resources not only from Lu Xun of modern times, but also from Zhuangzi, Confucius, and Lao Tzu of the Chinese traditional ages.

You relate the many influences on you from Lu Xun and Western thought. Are there any other sources of influence that have shaped you into a psychotherapist informed by existentialism?

I also have been influenced by my intellectual heritage, mostly literature. The middle school years of my education mostly occurred during the so-called Cultural Revolution. However, unlike many other youngsters in the village, I happened to be fond of reading. The books I read most were novels, which paved the way for me to turn to literature as well as psychology in later life. It also is possible that the Chinese classical novels provided me with a discerning perspective on Chinese culture and the Chinese psyche, as they depicted the living situation of Chinese people. They demonstrated their attitudes toward living, how they understand themselves, how they correspond with others, and how they get stuck and transcend their own limited experience. Additionally, they show how people are alienated from humanity or eventually live out their own potentiality, how they prepare themselves in ways that others may not understand, and how they choose this path and part with other paths. Everyone has their own path—me, too.

Traditional Chinese thought has also influenced me, more than I can elaborate here. Chinese culture, in the form of its thought system, is mainly composed of three streams or schools: Confucianism, Taoism, and Buddhism. Each contains ingredients that resonate with existentialism. Perhaps we might say that humans of different cultures would naturally reflect on their own existence and touch on themes in common. This may be called a general existentialism, by which I mean that people share the same existential view while their thoughts may not be specifically categorized into the Western school of existentialism. When I view Chinese thought from an existential perspective, I realize how I have been influenced by this stream. I recognize the influence of ancient philosophies, such as the concept of yin and yang (阴阳). It is such a paradoxical wisdom that it helps me to view humanity and human life. In my view of humanity, I propose a healthy state of integration that is like light being intermingled with darkness. In contrast, in human mental problems, I often see a state where one of these elements has been isolated in the rejection of the other. My healing effort is to facilitate reconciliation or harmony of natural light with natural darkness, so that humans are relieved from an unnecessary fight with the natural things in them. I especially admire Chuang Tzu in terms of his creative thinking and imagination. He left a rich legacy of metaphors that can inspire us to pursue awareness and freedom. His reflection on death is in deep resonance with existentialism—in this sense, Chuang Tzu is a genuine existentialist. I see it also in Lao Tzu's (1963) idea of *Wu Wei* (无为), meaning non-coercion or following the way of nature. I fathom its meaning in discerning and bringing healing to human obsession and compulsion, which can present in an extreme way in certain psychological conditions. Additionally, in Lao Tzu I find the concept of "extends himself but not at the expense of others" (直而不肆) (p. 65) very much like the existential quality called authenticity (本真). Likewise, Confucius (2014) shares a similar notion of "recompense for injury with justice" (以直报怨) (p. 154). In Confucianism we see some resonance with existentialism in terms of an emphasis on personality cultivation and the life actualization of existential-humanistic psychology: becoming who you are, or actualizing your potential. Confucianism also stresses the extension of *xiao wo* (小我), the smaller self, to *da wo* (大我), the greater self. This reminds me of how Maslow proposed the actualized self. Buddhism, in reflection on the human condition of suffering, endeavors to seek self-liberation or self-disengagement by practicing meditation for insight or awakening. Chinese medicine, with its holistic understanding and concern for human health, along with a systematic dredging approach to treatment, also influenced my approach to psychotherapy. All these—and still more yet to be named—have helped to prepare me to embark on my journey to existential psychology.

How do you look at yourself and the Zhi Mian Institute from the existential point of view?

Now my narrative arrives at the place where I stand, the Institute for Zhi Mian Psychotherapy. It is an existential institution rooted in Chinese culture, developing an indigenous model integrated with existential ingredients, and offering professional service to my fellow Chinese people. We are a private counseling center. However, we also have training and research programs. We have courses on existential therapy and a center for existential studies. We intend to initiate a systematic training program of educational courses, inviting existential therapists from around the world to come for existential training and education.

Becoming an existential therapist has been a gradual formation of my being—that role is part of who I am. All these years later, I have become more informed about myself (and at the same time, recognized by others) as an existential-humanistic therapist. I have found a new perspective from which to view myself, my fellow human beings, the culture that has shaped me (and is still shaping me in its evolving ways), and the world that I am living in with my fellow human beings. In the general sense, all human beings, to a certain degree, can be viewed as existentialists. But to be specific, there is a group of people who have special concerns and expressions about these existential themes, and they call themselves existential philosophers, writers, artists, and therapists. I am honored to be in this existential flow.

Returning now to that scene in 2007 where I met Louis Hoffman and Mark Yang, I know that I am still on the way to answering that question they raised. Our years of collaboration are part of the answer, in terms of promoting East–West dialogue in the field of existential psychology. But, looking around, I find that I am also on the journey with many other Chinese colleagues, not just in my community at the Zhi Mian Institute, but also with an emerging group of existential scholars, therapists, and students. We have Mark, Louis, and other American existential psychologists on a Chinese training platform. We have a group of existential followers from across the whole of China. We are gradually seeing more therapists who claim to be humanistically oriented and existentially informed, such as Ye Bing in Shanghai and Fei Xiaoyi in Beijing. I also see scholars and therapists of younger generations working in the field, such as Zheng Shiyan, Sun Ping, Zhang Xin, and others. A group of students trained at the Zhi Mian Institute are growing existentially informed, such as Zhang Guoxian, Zheng Lei, Zhu Yixun, and Cheng Jiaojiao, with still more in training—Jiang Mingfang, Zhao Hongyu, Shu Xiaoyun, Gan Lingling, Guo Xiaosong, Xia Yuhan, and Mai Jinli. I am not alone.

References

Confucius. (2014). *Confucian analects: The great learning: The doctrine of the mean* (J. Legge, Trans.). Shanghai Joint Publishing Press.

Dueck, A., & Wei, G. Q. (2019). The indigenous psychology of Lu Xun and Xuefu Wang. In L. Hoffman, M. Yang, M. Mansilla, J. Dias, M. Moats, & T. Claypool (Eds.), *Existential psychology East–West* (Vol. 2, pp. 17–46). University Professors Press.

Hsu, A., Broomé, A., Mansilla, M., Phoo, E., Dias, J., Moats, M., Hoffman, L., & Yang, M. (2019). Further development of existential-humanistic dialogues in Southeast Asia. In L. Hoffman, M. Yang, F. J. Kaklauskas, A. Chan, & M. Mansilla (Eds.), *Existential psychology East–West* (Vol. 2, pp. 111–131). University Professors Press.

Hugo, V. (2002). *The toilers of the sea* (J. Hogarth, Trans). Modern Library. (Original work published 1866)

Hu Shi. (2001). *The Chinese renaissance*. Foreign Language Teaching and Research Press.

Lao Tzu. (1963). *Tao Te Ching*. Penguin Group.

Lu Xun. (1998). *Complete works of Lu Xun* (Vol. 1). People's Literature Publishing House.

Lu Xun. (1998). *Complete works of Lu Xun* (Vol. 3). People's Literature Publishing House.

Lu Xun. (2002). *The true story of Ah Q* (Y. Xianyi & G. Yang, Trans.). The Chinese University Press.

Thrash, J. C., Kaklauskas, F. J., Dow, M. M., Saxon, E., Chan, A., Yang, M., & Hoffman, L. (2019). Existential-humanistic psychology dialogues in China: Beginning the conversation. In L. Hoffman, M. Yang, F. J. Kaklauskas, A. Chan, & M. Mansilla (Eds.), *Existential psychology East–West* (Vol. 2). University Professors Press.

Wang, X. (2002). *Beyond fear-escape mechanism* [Unpublished graduation thesis]. Andover Newton Theological School.

Wang, X. (2011). Zhi mian and existential therapy. *The Humanistic Psychologist, 39*, 240–246. https://doi.org/10.1080/08873267.2011.592465

Wang, X. (2019). The symbol of the iron house: From survivalism to existentialism. In L. Hoffman, M. Yang, F. J. Kaklauskas, A. Chan, & M. Mansilla (Eds.), *Existential psychology East–West* (Vol. 2, pp. 3–15). University Professors Press.

Yang, M. (2019). The beauty of zhi mian. In L. Hoffman, M. Yang, F. J. Kaklauskas, A. Chan, & M. Mansilla (Eds.), *Existential psychology East–West* (Vol. 2, pp. 47–55). University Professors Press.

Chapter 11

It Began in My Father's Library: On Becoming an Existential Therapist

Kathleen Galvin

Becoming an Existential-Humanistic Therapist

Awakening to Existence
What follows is not intended to be logical and rational. An individual's life is an affair full of intended and contingent events. Follow my narrative as you will and entertain your own thoughts and feelings as they come.

My Awakening
My awakening to my existence, the beginning of my journey to embracing an existential-humanistic point of view to psychology and therapy, began when I was fifteen years old. It started in my father's library.

My Father's Library
With eyes closed, I can picture the large room that was the center of our family home. At one end, separated by a counter, was the kitchen. There was a stand with a TV, a couch, and my father's recliner. At the other end of the room was a wall of bookshelves. My father had a wonderful library. Most of the older books were heavy hardback books, the newer ones more affordable paper backs. There were books of history, literature, and politics. A good number were books that Harold Bloom (1996), the literary critic, included in his canon of Western literature; books that "were good, and great, and true" (Thring, 1957, #127). There were the sonnets and plays of Shakespeare; an anthology of English verse; Charles Dickens, of course; and Melville's *Moby Dick*. There were Joseph Conrad's *Heart of Darkness* and *Lord Jim*; Thomas Carlyle's *The French Revolution*; Gibbon's *The History of the Decline and Fall of the*

Roman Empire; a few books on Greek and Roman philosophers; several volumes on the Russian Revolution; and William Shirer's *The Rise and Fall of the Third Reich*. He had American history, including *The Federalist Papers*, Bruce Catton's history of the civil war, and books on Abraham Lincoln. Also included were Mark Twain's *Huckleberry Finn* and his travel log, *Innocents Abroad*, and novels by Steinbeck, Kurt Vonnegut, Graham Green, John le Carré, Thomas Wolf, and Gore Vidal.

In my father's library, I learned to read, to dig deep, and to look at life from different perspectives: literature, philosophy, theology, history, anthropology, political science, sociology, and psychology. I developed a reading style I describe as polymorphously perverse, that is, getting pleasure from many, varied books on different issues. My reading habit intensified in college and graduate school. I read widely, read often, and consulted the great minds and hearts of the ages. While not fully aware in younger times, I was struggling to understand human beings. No other subject seemed as fascinating and perplexing as that of the human being. I didn't know it then, but I was taking my first steps toward being an existential-humanistic psychologist.

What Does It Mean to Be a Human Being?

Knowing is a Process of Unknowing

The more I learned, the more tenuous was my hold on knowledge. Much that I learned at school needed to be unlearned. Much was so superficial as to be of very little value. Some was pure propaganda intended to prepare students to be good, docile citizens for the ruling elite.

My reading saved me. Like Mark Twain, I didn't let my schooling get in the way of my learning. I learned that human beings were always attempting to improve themselves and their societies; yet, despite all the effort, we human beings didn't eliminate many of our vices. The human pursuit of power and greed was brutal and bloody but, perhaps, not as bloody as when human beings defended "the Truth." The French Revolution taught me that good intentions often ended badly. Liberty, fraternity, and equality produced the Reign of Terror and Napoleon. The Bolshevik Revolution produced the Gulags. American exceptionalism justified American expansionism and endless wars to ensure corporate profits. The high priests of the great religions were great hypocrites, and no good deed went unpunished. Mark Twain (as cited in Devota, 1962), with his great sense of sarcasm, wrote, "There is one true religion, several of them" (p. 180). A human being, as the

British historian Thomas Macaulay (1872) observed, "was so inconsistent a creature that it is impossible to reason from his belief to his conduct, or from one part of his belief to another" (p. 124).

Disoriented and Confused, Spiritual but Not Religious

I knew enough Shakespeare to recall Macbeth's cry of despair: "Life's but a walking shadow, a poor player that struts and frets his hour upon the stage and then is heard no more. It is a tale told by an idiot, full of sound and fury, signifying nothing" (Act V, Scene V). Was life merely a dream rounded with a sleep?

Human beings need creative illusions that protect them from the harsh reality of their existence and provide meaning, purpose, and a connection to something greater than themselves. I understood that the Age of Reason gave us science but took away the religious illusions that kept human beings sane in a world that made them feel puny and vulnerable. God was dead, or only lost, and a lot of people were out looking for him. Meanwhile, traditions, beliefs in universal, timeless truths, moral imperatives—all that was solid—faded into air (Berman, 1996). We human beings were on our own to create meaning and purpose.

Existential-humanistic thinkers are drawn to experiences of disorientation and confusion. These are existential crises. Everybody else seems to dislike existential crises, but existentialists are drawn to them as moths are drawn to light.

During university, I began questioning my traditional Catholic upbringing. I valued spirituality but had doubts about religion. I was a serious Christian in the sense that the life of Christ represented love, compassion, solidarity with the poor, and a passion for social justice. "God is love and who abides in God abides in love" summarized my faith.

The Vietnam war, CIA-backed death squads in Central America, and the civil rights movement set the tone for skepticism toward pretty much every belief system dear to middle class America. A God who permitted so much suffering in the world, a God out there hidden and unconcerned about the here-and-now struggles for social, economic, and racial justice was a God that invited skepticism. My growing skepticism in the God of my Irish Catholic school indoctrination did not extinguish a spiritual thirst. God might be dead, but mystery, a sense of connectedness to something greater than myself, and feelings of compassion toward the people and the world were still very much alive for me. How to be spiritual in a secular world was a philosophical, theological, and spiritual question that I began to contemplate. Around this time, I became interested in the spirituality that supported social action. I practiced meditation and retreated for short periods of meditation and communion with nature.

We are conditioned during our early years, but as we grow we have the opportunity to become increasingly centered in our own sensibilities of life. Authenticity is a growing into oneself; being the person I want to be. A person is authentic if their behavior, beliefs, and values are the result of personal experience rather than merely from automatic, unreflected conformity to circumstances of their birth.

I know now, but did not know then, that I had just passed a critical point in my development as an authentic human being. I overcame childhood conditioning and began taking responsibility for what I believed.

In the shadows of my mind, I was questioning: What does it mean to be a human being? Human beings seemed so full of contradictions, so misguided, so eager to be the masters of their own fate and so inclined to follow the crowd. I could see that human beings could be kind and generous, but they were also cruel and selfish.

Erich Maria Remarque's (1929/2011) anti-war novel, *All Quiet on the Western Front*, made a huge impression on me. I was disturbed by the transition of the jubilant, young students marching off to war with nationalistic fervor, oblivious to what lay ahead and convinced of their invincibility. They marched onward ever fewer through the slaughter and realities of the trenches, then on to the despair of the hardened veteran unable to return home; and, finally, to the relief of death. When I first read this book, I did not know that years later I would work with Vietnam war veterans who mirrored the attitudes and experiences of those who fought the "Great War."

See with New Eyes
Proust and colleagues (2005) noted that a voyage of discovery involves seeing with new eyes more than it does seeking out new landscapes. Ten years living in Asia, working in a dozen different cultures, speaking another language, and building relationships with people for whom I was the strange foreigner—these were experiences that certainly tested my willingness and ability to "see with new eyes." My life and work in Asia, aimed at helping people in their struggle for justice and a decent life, left me with doubts about how to better people's lives; changing people or changing the society—or perhaps both. On

returning to the United States, I observed that, having failed to change society in the '60s and '70s, efforts shifted to changing people. The human potential movement and hundreds of therapies flourished. Both neoliberal economics and positive psychology thrived.

After a decade working in Asia, I decided to pursue a doctoral degree in psychology. I looked at programs at well-known universities to assess the fit between the academic program and my academic and life experience. I had degrees in philosophy and theology and was reading about existentialism. I did a month at Esalen, leaving early because it was too unreal—ah, so beautiful, and too little social awareness. It is so easy to get lost in the labyrinth of the ego. Then, I found the Humanistic Psychology Institute, soon to be Saybrook Institute. I had found a home.

My Brother Gerard: Death and the Affirmation of Life

My brother Gerard died just after he finished high school. He was eighteen. A few years earlier he was a star football player, a gregarious youngster, and full of life. People liked to have him around. He had a big appetite for food and for life. A pain in his thigh that lingered sent him to see a doctor who quickly returned a diagnosis: bone cancer. Within a week, he lost his leg. During the rest of his high school days, he went through two more operations and chemotherapy. Two times he fought to rejoin his friends at school but, shortly after his graduation, he lost the fight and died.

On the day of his funeral, I lingered at his grave while all the others, one-by-one, walked away. I felt a powerful bond of love with him and a terrible pain at his leaving. He suffered so much with such great courage. He deserved a longer life. I felt guilty to be living on. I made a promise to him that day that I would, when my time came, open my heart to death. Until that day, I would say yes to life in its totality, with all its joy and sorrow, gains and losses, hope and disappointments. The bond of love with my brother would not be broken.

Existential Paradoxes
Our creative energies and ability to live vibrant, authentic lives flow out of the experience of contradiction, of paradox, of irreconcilable opposites. Sadly, 21st century people want consistent, predictable, logical outcomes and uncomplicated happiness—not the emotional ambiguity of a struggle with unsettling contradictions.

By the time of my graduation from college, I had a strong feeling that life was a mixed-up affair with many contradictions and paradoxes. Over the years, I have become more convinced that this is so but with the added insight that affirming and living through these contradictions and paradoxes enriches our lives.

We need to be aware of and confront the temptation to define our problems as personal and ignore their social dynamics, to seek pleasure but not pain, to desire a solid identity but fear creative fluidity, to be forever youthful and never grow old. Likewise, to pursue freedom and avoid commitment, or to believe without doubt. Pick your paradox, your polarities; learn to live with wrenching tensions and contradictions.

Soren Kierkegaard (2008) saw the human being as a synthesis of opposing elements: the infinite and the finite, the temporal and the eternal, freedom and necessity, connected and separate. So many of our problems are the result of efforts to resolve and eliminate the paradoxes of human existence. As Morse Peckham (1962) wrote in *Beyond the Tragic Vision*, "not the reconciliation of opposites and antinomies but the full exposure to them and acceptance of them in all their irreducible polarity, this is the task of the (existential) thinker and artist" (page 252). The loss of the contradictions of paradox blocks vital, dynamic irrational forces that energize our creative imaginations to bring forth new possibilities for living.

On New Possibilities

How Many Roads Diverged in a Yellow Wood? Hell, At Least a Half Dozen...

I hate filling out applications that require me to produce a chronology of my life. A good analogy for my life is a circus juggling act. The 70s saw me juggling a half dozen or more intense, overlapping experiences that ended in 1980 when I knowingly entered into the unknown world of academia. As the saying goes, I was following my path. The '80s proved to be just another juggling act. I did what I wanted to do and, as often, what I had to do to survive.

I'll share a few details. During the '70s, I completed a program in counseling at Boston City Hospital, started working on a master's degree, and went to Hong Kong to study Chinese for a year. I returned to the United States to finish my master's degree (philosophy) in a highly innovative, multidisciplinary program that integrated philosophy, sociology, theology, literature, and anthropology in an examination of modern perspectives on living and dying. Then I returned to Hong Kong for another six months of language study and began working with a Young Christian Labor movement. I worked with a wonderful group of Catholic nuns who hailed from a half dozen countries and cultures. Cultural diversity was the norm, not the exception.

With local social workers and young volunteers, we ran a Worker's Center that offered a range of services and spearheaded labor reforms. The work with the Worker's Center kept me busy in the afternoons and nights. On my day off, with a free evening, I taught an innovative experiential learning course at the Adult Education Center of the Chinese University. Most adult education programs started off with 20 students and ended with 10. This class seemed to meet a felt need. Participants brought their friends. The course started off with 20 and ended with 30 or more.

Looking back from the perspective of my current age, I can't imagine how I was able to take on more, but the head nun at the Good Shepard Home for homeless girls took advantage of my youthful energy and idealism to get me to accept responsibility for educating (well, keeping out of trouble) a group of 15 or so adolescent girls three mornings each week—who, in today's diagnostic jargon, all exhibited serious ADHD. This was not my first experience with disadvantaged youth, so I had a little understanding of the challenge at hand. These girls came from broken homes: Some were abandoned as children, some had parents in jail, some were abused, and all faced doubtful futures. To my surprise, the class went well. I broke all the established rules and took the approach that these girls would never benefit from an education that insisted on them adapting to society's needs. I offered a learning experience that adapted to their needs and that was designed to give them an experience of personal success and group agency.[1]

During this time, I shared the lifestyle of the people I served. I lived in a worker's dormitory, in temporary refugee housing and shared a small apartment (400 sq. ft.) with a family. Looking back, this was a great time in my life—many friends, challenging work, always learning, and the Hong Kong street food was cheap and wonderful. (How much Hong Kong has changed.)

Christian *agape*, not Christian dogma, guided me. I was a contemplative activist. At least once a month, I visited a Christian/Buddhist monk who cultivated a vegetable farm and provided a place of meditative solitude. I needed to balance my engagement with people and the unsolvable predicaments of life with an inner life that enabled me to be in the world but not of the world.

Coming out of an Irish Catholic family, having attended Catholic schools, and even having considered entering the religious life, my spiritual sensitivities and intellectual interests struggled to find a harmony, but seemed doomed to fail in this task. I felt that contemporary society was defined by both a profound sense of the rights, dignity, and inherent worth of every individual and a kind of oppressive depersonalization of human life that promotes an indifference, hostility, and varieties of physical and emotional violence. I had no well-defined, logical ideology or scientific explanation for the mess that is existence. Tom Joad's speech at the end of the film *The Grapes of Wrath* (Steinback, 2004) captures what I felt and what purpose defined my life throughout these years.

Well, maybe like Casy[2] says,

---

[1] This program lasted two years and served 30 or more girls. During my years living in and traveling to Hong Kong, I met some of these girls on several occasions by strange chance. A few were mothers with families and others caught up in Hong Kong's night life, but all seemed pleased to see me and I them.

[2] In the *Grapes of Wrath*, ex-preacher Jim Casy is a Christ-like figure who redefines the concept of holiness, suggesting that the most divine aspect of human experience is to be found on earth, among one's fellow humans, rather than amid the clouds. Casy is Tom Joad's teacher and inspiration.

a fella ain't got a soul of his own, but on'y a piece of a big soul—an' then...

Then what, Tom?

Then it don't matter. Then I'll be all aroun' in the dark. I'll be ever'where—wherever you look. Wherever they's a fight so hungry people can eat, I'll be there. Wherever they's a cop beatin' up a guy, I'll be there. If Casy knowed, why, I'll be in the way guys yell when they're mad an'—I'll be in the way kids laugh when they're hungry an' they know supper's ready. An' when our folks eat the stuff they raise an' live in the houses they build—why, I'll be there.[3]

The Siren's Song: Saybrook (Aka Humanistic Psychology Institute)

In 1978, I began looking for PhD programs in psychology. I looked at this graduate school, "nope," and that graduate school, "nope." I felt like a round peg trying to fit in a square hole. A rational, analytic, behavioral, and medical approach to the human being dominated these programs. My life experience and multi-disciplinary education left me believing that this approach narrowed and flattened the human being. I was looking for a psychology program that was fully accredited, that understood human beings to be complex, paradoxical, creative, individual and social, physical and spiritual beings.

I don't remember how I learned about the Humanistic Psychology Institute, soon to be renamed Saybrook Institute. I had an address and a brief description of the Institute. The information available to me seemed too good to be true: staffed by leaders of the "Third Force" in psychology. Rollo May was an associate. I knew his work. The program eagerly supported and promoted qualitative research methods. The Institute utilized an adult educational format of independent learning supported by a demanding curriculum. My master's degree was in philosophy. I was familiar with the philosophical foundations of humanistic thought and had training in clinical pastoral counseling that addressed the psychological and social problems that appeared to be addressed by the faculty and students at the Institute. Instead of feeling like a stranger to psychology, Saybrook (the Humanistic Psychology Institute) made me feel like a lost soul who suddenly found a home.

I wrote (no email in those days) asking for application requirements and, in the meantime, I signed up for a month of workshops at the

---

[3] Retrieved from https://www.youtube.com/watch?reload=9&v=i2JR3FmvVAw

Esalen Institute at Big Sur. I planned to visit Saybrook in San Francisco before returning to Hong Kong.

I flew into San Francisco and took a bus south to Carmel. How I got the rest of the way to the Esalen Institute at Big Sur, I don't remember. I do remember the beauty of Esalen. It was, and still is, an idyllic spot overlooking the Pacific Ocean. Less than a day before, I was on the other side of this ocean in the crowded streets of Hong Kong—hot, humid, noisy, air-polluted, with hawker food stalls selling pig skin, fish balls, and little squids on a stick. I was still thinking in Chinese. I signed in at the Administration building, registered for my courses, and got my work assignments that paid half my tuition. On the way to my shared cabin, I walked past a woman and a man lying naked in the sun. I immediately went into culture shock.

I was signed up to spend four weeks at Esalen but left a week early. I could not relate to the dreamy world of Big Sur. This was too big a dose of the free-wheeling human potential movement for me to handle at that time. I'd had so many years outside the United States, and travel around Asia in the early years of globalization, with electronic and garment sweat shops. These harsh realities left me doubtful that anything that one desired could be obtained. I observed and felt somewhat guilty myself, as most who attended Esalen workshops were seeking escape from society's super ego. Self-indulgence was the source of well-being.

I wasn't completely disillusioned. I met some good people, a husband and wife from Australia, a psychologist from Chile who'd just escaped arrest and fled her country, a German banker oppressed by his success.

The Australian couple and I hitch-hiked back to San Francisco. The following day, I went in search of the Humanistic Psychology Institute (soon to have a name change, Saybrook). I found the Institute in a two-story, wooden commercial building that had seen better days. Up a steep flight of stairs and through a door, and I was in the administration offices. Administration staff and some faculty were busy at one task or another. Here it was, the vibrant center of the third force in psychology. I wondered, "Have I arrived?" I was greeted with kind efficiency, and the individual responsible for student enrollment explained the application process to me, giving me more literature and copies of a recent *Humanistic Psychology Journal*—and handed over the bad news of how much a PhD would cost me.

A Biblical theory of economics graced me with hope: "Look at the birds of the air; they do not sow or reap or store away in barns, and yet your heavenly Father feeds them: (Matthew, 6: 26).

A year or more later, in January of 1980, I was in San Francisco with first-quarter tuition paid, close to broke, living on a couch in a friend's apartment in Chinatown, lost and anxious, looking at a long list of courses, three pre-dissertation essays, and the final hurdle, an original dissertation. How did I feel? God help the person who dared quote to me Frederick Nietzsche (1982): "What doesn't kill me makes me stronger" (p. 464). I wasn't in the mood.

My Saybrook Experience
Four years later, I sat in a small studio apartment in the Richmond district of San Francisco typing on a chunky, early-generation word processor. It was late at night, around midnight. My radio was tuned to a classical station. I typed, read what I typed, typed a bit more, stopped, pulled my hands away from the keyboard, then suddenly realized *it was done.* The dissertation, give or take some editing, was complete. Hard to believe, but I swear it is the truth. Just at that moment, the radio played forth the chorus of Beethoven's Ninth symphony, *Ode to Joy.* My spirit soared.

So ended another stage of my life. It was a difficult, rewarding stage, sometimes lonely, and at other times blessed with the companionship of good people who shared my passion for understanding the wonders and horrors of human existence.

Saybrook was more than an institute of learning. It was a community. Life-long friendships were forged. Alone and together, we plodded through all the work. Saybrook used a distance learning method but not all lived at a distance. Students met often with other students who lived nearby and, when we could, we met with faculty for face-to-face exchanges.

Course work was demanding, often made more demanding because each student was free to adjust courses to their interests. Since many of us had to work as well as study, our work frequently was integrated into our courses. Saybrook students wrote papers and produced dissertations that addressed real life concerns. This integration of academic work with real-world work enriched the Saybrook experience.

There was a lot of writing. For one course, as I recall, I wrote a 50-page paper, then another 75-page paper. The course professor, Stanley Krippner, then requested another 25 pages about a topic my paper only mentioned in passing. I think all this writing prepared Saybrook students to contribute to professional journals and to publish books. I have my differences with our digital world but thank God for word processors.

Yearly conferences were held when the entire Saybrook community of students and faculty gathered together for work and for play. These were times to renew one's resolve to keep moving toward that holy grail of a doctoral degree and to celebrate with those who finally grasped the cup. With each graduate, came the thought: "If he or she could do it, so could I." I've no recollection of meeting someone who would like to do it all over again. Yet, having done it, I, for one, am glad I started the journey and finished, exalted and humbled by the experience.

Those who have reviewed Saybrook graduates' collective contributions discovered that Saybrook graduates are very active in the field of psychology and psychotherapy. Their contributions are significant. The academic training and standards at Saybrook prepared students to go head and toe with students from renowned institutions of learning. My work at Saybrook enabled me along the way to work as an equal with people from Oxford, Cambridge, Yale, and other esteemed institutions of learning.

Since my days at Saybrook (how fast the years have passed), the Institute's reputation has grown and it attracts students from around the world. I am confident that because of Saybrook humanistic psychology stands firm against powerful cultural forces that seek to make psychology other than the source of insight into the fullness of human existence. Psychological knowledge can free people to live rich human lives, but that same knowledge can enslave people, molding them into mere shadows of human beings. We are not reducible to a material substance; though we are physical, we are also spiritual. We adapt to the world and also create a world that allows us to transcend the limits the world sets upon us. When science declares it has nothing to say about fundamental ethical concerns, humanistic psychology insists that to be human is to be ethical and that, problematic as it may be, we need to include our ethical concerns in our psychology. As creatures conscious of our mortality, we are called to ask and answer, "What kind of person do I intend to be?" How will I live my brief existence in the face of all life's unresolvable predicaments? The quality of my life influences others as others have influenced the quality of my life.

What is Existential–Humanistic Therapy?

So, Where Are We Now?

In existential-humanistic psychology, the individual's experience and personal grasp of reality is the primary subject of concern. In contrast to a view of psychotherapy as a rational science that is normative and adaptive to existing cultural and social conditions, existential-humanistic psychotherapy is a dynamic non-rational process that invites the client to become aware of, and take responsibility for, their way of being-in-the-world *with nature, with others, and with society*. Help for the individual is not a planned method of psychotherapeutic techniques, rationally applied and aimed at molding the client to the desired outcome of therapy and the norms of society (Rank, 1958).[4]

What does the above actually mean? One cannot understand existential-humanistic psychotherapy through studying a theory and from an objective, detached perspective. One must participate in the therapeutic experience. I shared the above seemingly random reflections of experiences to illustrate how one explores one's way of being-in-the-world.

My father's library is an actual place. I was 15 years old. I did come to highly value reading, and the dialogues with these great writers formed who I am. My experience of confusion or loss and how I transcended childhood conditioning and took responsibility for my spiritual life actually happened. When I wrote about my feeling of loss at the death of my brother, and my affirmation of my own death, I cried. I still mourn my brother and death is a tragedy I have vowed to embrace when it comes. As such, I gain the power of my existence that flows from an ability to affirm life in its totality. And when I fail to do so, I am humbled; I experience my nothingness.

Existential-humanistic psychotherapy is a way-of-being-in-the-world-*with* a person that facilitates the client's ability to generate new possibilities for living. Other writers and experienced therapists have written powerful descriptive accounts of their relationships with

---

[4] Zweig (1969) questions the issue of either changing society or the person. The "modern" world had, in the eyes of many, become a virtual anti-society; instead of forming the individual, it oppressed them. The problem then became whether to change society—that was the role of Rousseau, the social critics, and revolutionaries—or to "teach the individual how he might resist a society whose inhumanity threatened to overwhelm him" (p. 251). I think our failure to change society has driven us more and more inward to find authenticity in our private lives. Can we be authentic in an increasingly inauthentic society?

clients. Descriptive case studies and recordings of actual therapy are invaluable aids for understanding existential-humanistic therapy. In my experience, the good therapists keep the focus on the client's inner searching; yet, when helpful or unavoidable, the therapist is able to engage the client in an honest, open encounter.

I believe a distinctive and valuable resource that existential-humanistic therapists bring to their work is their grasp of the structures of existence that existential-humanistic thinkers such as Kierkegaard, Nietzsche, Dostoevsky, Sartre, Heidegger, and others, have uncovered. For example, Kierkegaard's (2013) *Fear and Trembling* and *Sickness unto Death* provides powerful descriptions of existential anxiety. He throws light on existential dynamics of personal truth, of passionate commitment. The novelist Dostoevsky (1960, 2008) masterfully describes the psychological, existential conflicts and tensions arising out of life's revolt against an overly rationalized world. Heidegger's (2011) *Daseinanalysis*, with its ontological and phenomenological view of the human being, is a rich source of understanding that helps the therapist recognize the client's unique engagement with the structures of existence.

To summarize, in contrast to a view of psychotherapy as a rational science that is normative and adaptive to existing cultural and social conditions, existential-humanistic psychotherapy is a dynamic non-rational process of personal development, interpersonal encounter, and community engagement. "A final characteristic of man's existence (Dasein)… is the capacity to transcend the immediate situation" (May, 1958, p. 71).

What Lies Ahead?
Drawing on Heidegger's (2011) *Being and Time*, Charles Guignon (2010) offers us a relevant insight on the future and who we are in the "now."

> We can understand who a person *is* only in terms of where that person is coming from and where he or she is going. From a narrativist perspective, actions in the present are fully intelligible only in terms of their place within the narrative unfolding of the person's life—in terms of what has happened up to this point and *where things are headed in general.* (p. 221)

I have talked about where I am coming from, so let me now say a little about where I see humanistic psychologists going, and where I hope to march along.

Filling the Vacuum Left by the Death of God: Disenchantment and Secularization

The death of God has left many people unable to satisfy their basic existential needs. A key question is what, if anything, is filling the vacuum left by the disenchantment of the world? Positivistic, rational science deconstructs the grand metanarratives that enchanted the world. A psychology that is rational, analytic, objective, and amoral cannot fill the vacuum (Rank, 1958). So, what of the problems formally addressed by traditions, family and community life, and orthodox religions? They still remain. In the search for a sense of cosmic unity and significance; answers to suffering and death; the absurdity of a seemingly purposeless and meaningless life;, the dark, anxious feelings, the irrational will struggling against our human fate; life's unresolvable paradoxes and contradictions—how will these existential predicaments be confronted and lived? Are drugs and distractions, and an unending stream of evidence-based therapies able to address the needs of the human soul?

> empirical and metaphysical
> reductionistic and profound
> pessimistic and optimistic
> hard and soft
> intellectual and emotional
> boring and inspirational
> obvious and ambiguous
> conservative and liberating
> public and private
> similar and different
> rational and irrational
> physical and spiritual
> objective and subjective
> self and no-self
> mundane and sacred
> pedestrian and mysterious
> logical and dialectical
> normative and evolutionary
> adaptive and generative
> bureaucratic and poetic

Figure 1. A sample of life's unresolvable paradoxes and contradictions

Humanistic psychology's great task is to create a psychology that is dialectical. By dialectical I mean that the duality (multiplicity) of things—love and justice, freedom and order, good and evil—does not seek a harmonious middle way between them or a Hegelian-like synthesis. It does not seek a step to a higher state of consciousness; nor are they logically separated and treated as contraries.

According to the logical conception of truth, only one of two contraries can be true, but in the reality of life as one lives it, they are inseparable. We understand this experientially, and it is therefore best studied phenomenologically. Philosophy, psychology, and therapy, as I have come to understand and live them, expose life in its totality with an openness to all its contradictions, tensions, and paradoxes. Here is an example that concretizes what I am attempting to explain. It is relevant here and later in my discussion of individualism.

Eros and Agape: "Eroagape"
The dialectical principle replaces liberalism's assumption of ontological individualism and the primacy of self-interest with principles of mutuality and reciprocity, love and will, power and justice. We are always confronting the tension of willfully asserting one's own needs (Eros) and softening our will to acknowledge and affirm the needs of others (Agape). Eros speaks of the will to live, grow, realize one's powers. Agape is the recognition that Eros is a quality of the other's existence. Eros affirms the self. Agape affirms the other. Eros and Agape address our need for a union with others that realizes their singularity as well as our own. This is the courage to be *a self* and the courage to be *a part of*, spoken about by Tillich (1952) in his book *The Courage to Be*. Tillich's lesser-known book, *Love, Power, and Justice: Ontological Analyses and Ethical Applications* (1976), examines these insights in more depth.

God is Dead, Let Ourselves Become Gods

> If God does not show himself on earth, we ourselves have to become gods. From *Wintereise* [Recording] (Schubert, 1989)

In one of the most memorable quotes from Nietzsche's (1982) *Gay Science*, the old hermit Zarathustra leaves his cave and runs into the city, announcing:

> God is dead. God remains dead. And we have killed him. How shall we comfort ourselves, the murderers of all murderers? What was holiest and mightiest of all that the world has yet owned has bled to death under our knives: who will wipe this blood off us? What water is there for us to clean ourselves? What festivals of atonement, what sacred games shall we have to invent? Is not the greatness of this deed too great for us? *Must we ourselves not become gods simply to appear worthy of it?* [emphasis added] (p. 130)

How often is the concluding line in this quote referenced? "Must we ourselves not become gods...?" The Greek myths speak about humans seeking to be gods. In our modern times, human beings are acting as if they *are* gods. Such hubris has brought us to the edge of doom. Any psychology (or psychologist) envisioning the future must consider the consequences of humanity's divine aspirations. "We are living in the Anthropocene age in which human influence on the planet is so profound—and terrifying—it will leave its legacy for millennia" (Macfarlane, 2016, p. 1). The phenomena of the age of humans, the Anthropocene, push every professional and academic discipline into a quagmire of scientific data, popular beliefs, and compelling predictions.

See Where Acting Like Gods Has Got Us

Here is what we face: environmental collapse with the planet no longer able to sustain human life; a nuclear apocalypse, again human extinction the likely outcome; the emergence of social, economic, and political systems that intensify all that is unjust and stifle all that serves a common good. Science, the most overt demonstration of humanity's power to transform the earth and the lives of human beings, is seen as the cause of all our problems and, simultaneously, the source of hope that we can resolve them all. In the age of the Anthropocene (Kolbert, 2014), progress is both bane and boon. In the age of the Anthropocene, we entertain the most conflicting of visions: All is completely interrelated and we are all completely alone. Reason runs wild, encapsulating the planet and human beings in an iron cage of technology, digital data, surveillance, and artificial intelligence. In response, human behavior and thinking are becoming insanely irrational (Ellul, 1967; Marcuse, 1968). In days ahead, humanistic psychologists must dare to think the unthinkable and respond.

Existential Imagination

If we understand that the multiple crises bearing down upon humanity demand radical changes in the individual, relationships, society, politics, and economics—creating new models of human experience—we then understand the importance of cultivating existential imagination. By this, I mean that existential imagination is the power to construct possible models of human experiences. It is the ability to entertain a vision of what is, to imagine what one wants and, more important, what one needs. The great novelists such as Dostoevsky (1950) are able to portray competing worlds and differing models of human experience.

People of great individual and social imagination experience within themselves the failure of existing symbols and understand that new symbols need to be created. The artists, those who by character are exposed more intensely to anxiety, those who struggle with the unresolvable predicaments of life, those who are lost, who are strangers among us, who are a little "crazy," who are like children able to play, and even psychotherapists—these can be the people who create new symbolic expressions, as in *The Cry for Myth* (May,1991). This process of symbolic creation begins with individuals but succeeds only if the process of creation is able to engage communities. Engaging communities is particularly challenging.

Escaping the Labyrinth of Individualism:
Humanistic Psychology as a Psychology of Dialogue

A psychology that is dialectical needs to clarify its understanding of individualism as a belief system and its influence on humanistic psychology. Behavioral and body-based psychologies have addressed individualism by simply discarding the individual self altogether. The individual self is an epiphenomenon. Humanistic psychology, in contrast, puts the self at the center of our understanding of human psychology.

To make a long and complex story short, lacking an external authority (god is dead) that would meet the deep spiritual and psychological need for purpose and meaning, as well as moral guidance and motivation to seek and realize a virtuous life, thinkers of the eighteenth, nineteenth, and twentieth centuries turned inward to find in the depths of the human psyche all that which was previously provided by traditions, family, social roles, and orthodox religions. In theology, economics, political and social sciences, the self-evolved to be increasingly powerful and increasingly isolated and alienated.

This turning inward also reflected the failure of our attempts to reform society. This is Otto Rank's (1958) conclusion: "In light of the sweeping social movements of our time, modern psychology appears as a desperate attempt to achieve internally, in the individual self, what those extreme political ideologies are trying to bring about by a change of social system" (p. 59).

But here is the problem. Individualism tends to portray human beings as much more distinct and autonomous than they really are (Schilpp & Friedman, 1967; Shanahan, 1992; Zweig, 1968). This is certainly true of Romanticism's take on individualism, which has had considerable influence on the development of existential and humanistic thinking.

> ...the aspect of Romanticism that most clearly and fully resonates with the individualistic heritage that preceded it is the emphasis on the powers of the individual in the formation of the self...the Romantics saw the individual as virtually self originated; self-discovery amounted to a process of self-creation. (Shanahan, 1992, p. 91)

In our "be whatever you want to be" human potential culture, the authentic individual is believed to be the last arbiter of truth and goodness. Individuals defend against any outside influences that define who they are and that limit their ability to define themselves. The philosopher Charles Taylor (1992) argues that the concept of authenticity locating moral authority in the individual, to the exclusion of a principle of dialogue, ends in a form of relativism that debases the moral authority of authenticity. Taylor insists that a general feature of human life is its fundamental dialogical character. We do not obtain the language of self-definition on our own, and we are born into and exist within a horizon of meanings that cannot be ignored. Taylor warns us that if we define our problems as simply personal we claim the authority and power to resolve them without reference to others and the social, economic, and political order. In the abstract, we can argue that individuals can evade existential realities and contemplate universal principles or meditate themselves into oblivion. However, if we want to address the outrageous fortunes and the slings and arrows of everyday existence, we need to work through relationships, communities, and international institutions.

The heightened individualism of the twentieth century finds the individual believing they are empowered to define themself and be all that they can be. But those who uncritically embrace this form of individualism find themselves isolated, anxious, alienated, inhabiting a cold, competitive world, and desperate for friendship and community. Shanahan (1992) describes the price the individual pays for the assumed benefits of a self-defining individuality:

> At first the individual felt alienated only from society, as was the case with Romantics. But eventually that sense of alienation linked up with the burden of loneliness imposed on the self by the subjective legacy of its odyssey of self-discovery, so that in the end the self felt alienated, not only from society, but from itself. (p. 121)

An equally penetrating and disturbing insight into the consequence of an unqualified individualism reveals the paradoxical character of individualism. An unqualified individualism that fails to recognize the important role others and society play in the development of the individual prepares the person for the influences of neoliberalism, authoritarianism, and collectivism (Harvey, 2005; Wolin, 1960, 2008).

One of the most astute yet under-appreciated political scientists of our times, Sheldon Wolin (2001), observes that "to get the modern citizen to engage in 'common action' requires a great deal of art…Individualism encourages a general indifference to civic life and mutual suspicion and isolation; it is a major factor in disposing society toward nepotism" (p. 344).

This, I shall call it hyper-individualism, also infests our social media technology. We are alone together, as Sherry Turkle (2012) so poignantly points out in her exposé of how our cell phones leave us lonely and isolated and unable to distinguish between genuine relationship and the digital communication hive.

Once we are cognizant of the insidious influences of an ideology of hyper-individualism, we can begin to counter the constant social conditioning that reinforces this ideology. I envision humanistic psychology contributing to the creation of a psychology of dialogue that enables us to escape the labyrinth of individualism.

Illusions vs. Delusions

Human beings do not live in nature like the animals. We are conscious creatures able to contemplate the infinity of time and space but who struggle with an awareness of our fate as finite creatures. To live, we create what Ernst Becker (1975) termed "vital lies or illusions." Owen Barfield (1988) used the term collective representations. The world we accept as real is, in fact, a system of collective representations. Morse Peckham (1962) preferred the term *orientations*, the thousands of elements, patterns of the mind, cognitive habits, neural paths, and all those elements that grace us with a purposeful and meaningful world. Here I choose to use the term *illusions*, something experienced as real but not real. An illusion gives order to a chaotic reality. The few quotes below capture the meaning of our creative, symbolic ordering of a formless reality.

> If the doors of perception were cleansed every thing would appear to man as it is, Infinite. For man has closed himself up, till he sees all things thro' narrow chinks of his cavern. (William Blake, *The Marriage of Heaven and Hell*, 1960)

> Man needs a second world, a world of humanly created meaning, a new reality that he can live, dramatize, nourish himself in. (Becker, 1975, p. 189)

> ...I do not perceive any thing with my sense-organs alone, but with a great part of my whole human being. (Barfield, 1988, p. 20)

> The great boon of repression is that it makes it possible to live decisively in an overwhelmingly miraculous and incomprehensible world, a world so full of beauty, majesty and terror that if animals perceived it all, they would be paralyzed to act. (Becker, 1973, pp. 50–51)

And finally:

> Only he who has freed himself from the illusions of man and at the same time has seen them as necessary to man, is genuinely redeemed. (Peckham, 1962, p. 262)

Pertaining to Reality and Illusions

Reality and our illusions are not antagonists. Reality is the raw material out of which human beings create the illusions that enable us to live. It is the character of an illusion to restrict, repress, allow, inspire, make meaningful, provide purpose, and order life *so that more life can be lived*.

An illusion becomes delusional when it denies life more than it affirms life. Our task is to create illusions that limit life at a minimum and free up life to a maximum. Illusions are not written in stone; they evolve and, at times, go through great upheaval. I believe we are in such a period now.

Humanistic psychotherapists work to cultivate illusions that enable people to live richer, more vibrant, purposeful, and meaningful lives.

The Task Ahead: The Future That is Me

The diagram I have sketched below captures many of the ideas expressed in these pages. It is not complete. It helps me to envision much that I have learned over the years and what I believe an existentially oriented humanistic psychology should be.

I see the task of humanistic psychology as that of supporting human beings to freely and openly engage with others and with communities of people to discover, develop, and express the fullness of their powers—and to use these powers, individually and collectively, for the betterment of all.

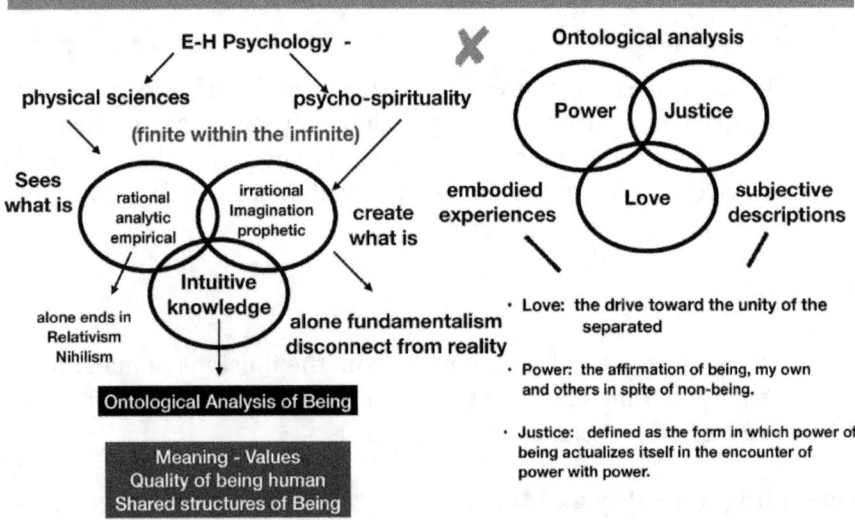

References

Barfield, O. (1965). *Saving the appearances: A study in idolatry.* Harcourt, Brace & World.
Becker, E. (1973). *The denial of death.* Free Press.
Becker, E. (1975). *Escape from evil.* Free Press.
Berman, M. (1996). *All that is solid melts into air: The experience of modernity.* Penguin Books.
Blake, W. (1960). *The marriage of Heaven and Hell.* Trianon Press.
Bloom, H. (1996). *The Western canon: The books and school of the ages.* Papermac.
Devoto, B. (1962). *Mark Twain: Letters from the earth.* Harper & Row.
Dostoevsky, F. M. (1950). *The brothers Karamazov.* Modern Library.
Dostoevsky, F. M. (1960). *Notes from underground and The grand inquisitor.* Dutton.
Dostoevsky, F. M. (2008). *Crime and punishment* (R. Peace, Ed., J. Coulson, Trans.). Oxford University Press.
Ellul, J. (1967). *The technological society.* Vintage Books.
Guignon, C. B. (2010). *On being authentic.* Routledge.
Harvey, D. (2005). *A brief history of neoliberalism.* Oxford University Press.
Heidegger, M. (2011). *Being and time.* Blackwell.
Kierkegaard, S. (2008). *The sickness unto death.* Penguin.
Kierkegaard, S. (2013) *Fear and trembling and The sickness unto death* (G. Marino, Ed., W. Lowrie, Trans.). Princeton University Press.
Kolbert, E. (2014). *The sixth extinction: An unnatural history.* Henry Holt and Company.
Macaulay, T. B. (1872). *Critical and historical essays, contributed to the Edinburgh review.* Longmans, Green, and Company.
Marcuse, H. (1968). *One dimensional man.* Sphere Books.
May, R. (1991). *The cry for myth.* Norton.
May, R. (Eds.) (1958). Contributions of existential psychotherapy. In R. May, E. Angel, & H. F. Ellenberger (Eds.). *Existence: A new dimension in psychiatry and psychology* (pp. 37-91). Basic Books.
Macfarlane, R. (2016, April, 1).Generation Anthropocene: How humans have altered the planet for ever. *The Guardian.* Retrieved from https://www.theguardian.com/books/2016/apr/01/generation-anthropocene-altered-planet-for-ever?platform=hootsuite
Nietzsche, F. W. (1982). *The portable Nietzsche.* (W. Kaufmann, Ed. &Trans.). Penguin.
Peckham, M. (1962). *Beyond the tragic vision: The quest for identity in the nineteenth century.* G. Braziller.
Proust, M., Moncrieff, C. K. S., Kilmartin, T., Enright, D. J., Tadie, J.-Y., & Atget, E. (2005). *In search of lost time.* The Folio Society.
Rank, O. (1958). *Beyond psychology.* Dover Publications.
Remarque, E. M. (2011). *All quiet on the western front.* (B. Murdoch, Ed.). Salem Press.

Shanahan, D. (1992). *Toward a genealogy of individualism*. University of Massachusetts Press.

Schilpp, P. A., & Friedman, M. S. (Eds.) (1967). *The philosophy of Martin Buber*. Open Court.

Schubert, F. (1989). *Wintereise* [Song recorded by D. Fischer-Dieskau and G. Moore]. EMI Records.

Steinback, J. (Writer), Johnson, N. (Screenplay & Producer), Ford, J. (Producer), & Zanuck, D. F. (Producer). (2004). Grapes of wrath [DVD]. Twenthieth Century Fox Home Entertainment.

Taylor, C. (1992). *The ethics of authenticity*. Harvard University Press.

Thring, M. (n.d.). *Letter from M. W. Thring to P. J. Harrop*, December 11, 1957.

Tillich, P. (1952). *The courage to be*. Yale University Press.

Tillich, P. (1976). *Love, power, and justice: Ontological analyses and ethical applications*. Oxford University Press.

Turkle, S. (2012). *Alone together: Why we expect more from technology and less from each other*. Basic Books.

Wolin, S. S. (1960). *Politics and vision: Continuity and innovation in western political thought.* Princeton University Press.

Wolin, S. S. (2001). *Tocqueville between two worlds: The making of a political and theoretical life.* Princeton University Press.

Wolin, S. S. (2008). Democracy incorporated: Managed democracy and the specter of inverted totalitarianism. Princeton University Press.

Zweig, P. (1968). *The heresy of self-love: A study of subversive individualism*. Basic Books.

Chapter 12

The Making of a Counterculture Therapist

Shawn Ari Rubin

Seeds & Antecedents

From about the age of eight years old, I began to experience existential night terrors. At the end of my long, activity-filled days—punctuated by experiences of guilt, shame, and humiliation from conflictual parent–child dynamics, as well as often not being understood or empathized with for my own way of being in the world—the immersion into my everyday experiences would drift away. I would tune in to the stored pain and confusion of all that was not understood or languaged in my life and relationships. The overwhelming truth of the inevitability of death and my own impending nothingness overwhelmed me, and I would scream in horror at this reality—and also to dislodge and shake myself out of this terrifying truth. With my heart racing, seemingly in full presence of the reality of death and nothingness, I tried to forget this truth and drift off to sleep.

This was a secret terror that, along with secret shame in response to parent–child conflicts for "bad behaviors" and associated bed-wetting, I kept close with me throughout adolescence. In retrospect, I appreciate how life was bigger, more mysterious, more complex than I could comprehend and beyond my limited capacity to verbalize my experience or begin to give it context and meaning.

In high school psychology classes, I was deeply inspired in my learning about the theories and concepts of Carl Rogers, Abraham Maslow, and humanistic psychology, leading me to consider psychology as a college major and a potential career path. In sophomore year of college, I first read the word "existential" in a theories of personality textbook, and then read about contributions of Rollo May. I was elated to learn that there was a field of study that focused on understanding, therapy, and healing that was grounded in the awesome and terrifying experience and consciousness of death awareness, confrontation, and transcendence. This discovery opened up to me the questions of the meaning of life, purpose, and opportunity for growth and change. This was the beginning of my seeking an all-encompassing psychospiritual paradigm and an answer to the question of the meaning of my life, as well as hoping/believing that an existential-humanistic integration could serve as this organizing framework.

It was an incredible experience to find that not only was I not alone in my secret terror; there was a long and respected tradition in philosophy, the humanities, psychology, and psychotherapy that resonated with my own fears and suffering. I felt known, seen, affirmed, and held by the wise theoreticians, clinicians, and therapists who trod this path long before me.

I was absorbed in a meaning-centered, gravitational pull toward being a practitioner of relational, person-centered, and existential psychotherapy. With my mission established, I applied to PsyD programs that would emphasize the practitioner side of training and clinical experiences. I voraciously explored as many programs as I could, recognizing that existential/humanistic-identified faculty were always a small percentage of every program. A few months later the admissions process was completed and I was accepted into a few APA-accredited PsyD programs. Later, while in a bookstore and browsing a large reference book entitled *Graduate Programs in the Social Sciences*, I discovered the non-APA programs, including a program in Detroit whose primary focus was existential-phenomenology.

I was blown away to see that such a program existed, and after another round of applications, I found a perfect fit and a new home at the Center for Humanistic Studies (CHS). CHS was founded by Clark Moustakas, one of the original founders of the humanistic psychology movement, and Cereta Perry. Clark pioneered existential play therapy, heuristic and phenomenological research methodologies, an existential phenomenological framework for dream analysis, and tirelessly championed equity in the accreditation of diverse programs in training psychology and access to training sites for students in these diverse theoretical programs. Clark, like other radicals and visionaries, stood as a firebrand outside the mainstream. He advocated for a psychology of the heart, which placed ultimate value on the empathic human relationship as essential to learning, growing, and healing. It was grounded in the humanities—the study of cultures, anthropology, history, philosophy, phenomenology, and qualitative approaches—and critiqued the prevailing psychological and clinical theories of his time.

Following the lead of my existential and humanistic mentors, my personal framework of existential-humanistic psychotherapy is an integrative one with contemporary psychoanalytic and psychodynamic therapies and psychoanalytic theories of human development. As Jim Bugental (1981) brilliantly stated,

> The truest existentialism is humanistic and the soundest humanism is existential. The two are not the same, but their overlap is rich in potential for greater understanding of human experience and for greater effectiveness in the effort to enrich that experience. (p. 10)

The second decade of my private practice has grounded my worldview and clinical framework related to diversity and inclusion, social justice, liberation psychology, and advocacy for targeted and oppressed groups in American culture and society.

Finding An (In)Secure Base

Essential to becoming an existential-humanistic therapist is finding a home and community that supports this proud, yet often maligned, approach. I was fortunate to discover the dozen or so alternative graduate programs that nurture and develop those interested in humanistic psychology. These programs are steadily decreasing and have struggled to preserve their own existence and vision in the often-hostile environs of higher education. Some programs have been plagued by their own mismanagement, others taken over by predatory, educational management companies with corporate, for-profit management styles—and a lack of profitability has led to the closing of specialized degrees and certifications.

I believe existential-humanistic training can only survive and thrive in a manner similar to the Psychoanalytic Institute, where theoretical and programmatic autonomy can be ensured. There aren't psychoanalytic university programs that grow the future of psychoanalysts; they have affiliated training institutes where students earn their certifications by meeting the rigorous standards of their tripartite model of personal analysis, class attendance and paper writing, and the clinical supervision of psychoanalytic cases. Fortunately, a few of these have emerged within the EH movement; particularly the Existential–Humanistic Institute and Rocky Mountain Humanistic Counseling and Psychological Association.

The Journey of My Practice

About ten years into my practice, I could recall feeling fortunate and honored to glance at my list of patients for the week and see that, on any given day, I would be: engaging with a child via existential play therapy; consulting with a parent who was concerned about their own trauma influencing their child's development and their relationship; seeing an adolescent negotiating the pain and excitement of romantic attraction and infatuation; young adults embarking on their journey of self-discovery as they moved through high school and college; couples seeking deeper intimacy and connection with one another; and gay men seeking affirmation and acceptance in the world.

I realized that I didn't have a clinical specialization, such as working with a particular diagnostic or clinical population. Rather, my area of focus was the existential-humanistic approach to therapy. The caring, depth-oriented, and person-centered process of treading the paths of suffering, liberation, and healing. I conceived of my daily work as a therapist as "A Day in the Life(span)," a play on the title of a beloved Beatles song. I embodied a sense of awe, bearing witness, and holding a space of caring support and invited and encouraged participation in the emerging processes of self-awareness, curiosity, insight, and growth.

That first decade of training and practice provided a curriculum for observing the simple, yet profound unfolding process of experiential, relationship play therapy. These experiences taught me vital lessons in presence, patience, trusting the process of the other, and validating the groundbreaking theories and approaches of existential and humanistic psychotherapy.

Indeed, beginning existential clinical work with children was a critical foundation for my evolving work with adolescents and then adults from an existential-humanistic perspective. In my second decade of clinical work, my initial mentorship and supervision by LGBTQ experts revealed that the foundational elements of the existential-humanistic approach were the established best practices for gender diverse children, adolescents, and adults. At the time of this writing, my practice is nearly 100% dedicated to supporting gender-diverse people in order to meet their needs as they emerge and integrate in American society: to offer care that is the most informed, accepting, and affirming of this way of being.

Existential-Humanistic Therapy Research & Graduate Schools

To paraphrase Rogers (1961), "Experience is the highest authority;" whatever was brought into therapy by the client was the existential data of life—and the content of therapy and areas to be scientifically researched (p. 26). At the CHS, all the research models were qualitative, and we had the freedom to personally select topics that utilized these immersive models. I completed a master's thesis, doctoral dissertation and served as chair and advisor on dozens of qualitative graduate studies as a CHS faculty member for the next decade.

Existential-humanistic models of therapy were focused on being with the person, creating conditions so they could tell the story of their lives—their pain and triumphs and conflicts: That's where we started. Congruently, psychological research models and topics should explore complex, meaningful experiences and rhythms of our lives, and inform the data collected—that everything about our lives is able to be researched and more fully understood. The "results" of such personal heuristic immersions and phenomenological investigations often yielded meaningful insights, the potential for healing and freedom to grow. In both EH therapy ad research, if we can create the conditions where someone is comfortable enough to trust us, lower their guard, and risk vulnerability, all things are possible to be known, and healed, allowing people to grow and evolve. My colleagues and I marvel at what an incredibly powerful process it is to humbly and sensitively facilitate and bear witness to.

The existential-humanistic model was the foundation of CHS, which sadly does not exist anymore. I don't think a school like that can exist anymore; hence my earlier comments about existential-humanistic survival and expansion through training institutes. But the people who went through those kinds of programs—and I was there as both a student, a faculty member, and program director—were transformed. It was a quasi-therapeutic environment in a lot of ways, and one that had its own challenges and ethical concerns. When I went on to serve as Chair of the School of Clinical Psychology at Saybrook University, it was difficult to preserve existential-humanistic values in a school driven by for-profit motives to education, even if theoretically remaining a non-profit. The profit motive is essentially incompatible with education and academia (along with healthcare and the "justice" system as well), and many of the humanistic programs did not have large endowments, were tuition-based economically, and had unstable financial grounding. The schools became vulnerable to hostile takeovers, rebranding and closings that have occurred throughout the country over the past fifteen years.

Existential–Humanistic Therapy

There also are challenges intrinsic to working with patients who may not have ever had experience with existential-humanistic therapy. Anecdotally, I've heard of a study that mentions how people practicing mainstream therapy approaches seek out depth, relational, and experiential therapists for their own therapy. That's very telling—the idea that it's process-oriented, not chasing symptoms. It's not solution-focused or a quick fix, which is what managed care and mainstream psychotherapy believe and desire it to be. They'd like there to be standardized solutions to diagnoses. But human beings are far more complex. Our lives are not all the same, and our responses to life and its challenges are not the same.

I often have to orient my patients to different possibilities in therapy before we begin our work because even patients have been indoctrinated into mainstream views on what therapy is and what it does/should do. They may say that they want to work on some issue, so I discuss how I would conceptualize and approach it as part of informed consent, and I have a way of explaining without jargon and in the ways that fits with their description of their experience that's right where they're at in their lives. If it resonates and feels promising, they generally agree and are open to trying the relational, experiential, and depth therapy that is existential-humanistic. It can be a successful approach for patients with many different presenting issues and meeting various diagnostic criteria (even if that diagnosis is not utilized). This includes children, adolescents, and adults with a variety of issues.

Whether it's play therapy with children or talk therapy with teens and adults, I endeavor to offer something to patients in every developmental stage. But again, each session they come in and we work to find out where they're at in the moment. It's not "today we do this, today we work on that" style of facilitation. For people who prefer, need, and want that, mainstream approaches work well. However, other patients who do not benefit as deeply, if at all, from mainstream approaches often find value in the existential-humanistic approach. They struggle to find that elsewhere.

It was surprising (although it shouldn't have been) that when I began to focus with a variety of patients—for example, African-American children and teens in foster care who had experienced sexual and physical abuse—the existential-humanistic approach helped them express themselves and open up, bringing up deeper material so they could grow and heal in some small ways from their painful and traumatic experiences.

I found that the existential-humanistic approach also worked for teenagers who were feeling isolated and alienated, and for adult gay men who had been closeted for decades but were now emerging into the world. In the last decade trans and non-binary patients across the gender diversity and neurodiversity spectrums have found a safe and validating space in the existential-humanistic paradigm. It seems to deliver upon that promise from the 1940s and 1950s that Rogers first researched—that if you create the necessary and sufficient conditions for trust, care, openness and connection, people will respond in growthful ways.

Challenges and Growth During COVID-19

The COVID-19 pandemic pushed people from all walks of life to begin living, working, and playing in significantly different ways. Many of the relational aspects of being connected to people in any space were gone, and I, personally, had to find additional ways to feel fully and to stay holistically engaged. I was often feeling under-stimulated, disconnected and on edge. I felt that I needed to find a way to be more wholehearted. But it is difficult to engage your relational embodiment when you are in a room by yourself, viewing each other on a small screen.

In dealing with this world-changing tragedy, I have struggled to engage in the process of growth and evolution—while hoping to deepen humility and gain insight into myself and my existence along the way. I offer this manner of engagement in life to patients, and they have influenced and exposed me to new ideas. This has deeply impacted my own engagement as I work with patients who are activists in the Black Lives Matter, Anti-fascist, and Transgender Rights movements, are playing and discovering the continuum of erotic diversity in interpersonal relationships, and are embarking on psychedelic journeys, research, and therapy.

These experiences affirmed my own curiosities and explorations, including many aspects of activism and being an accomplice for social justice and liberation initiatives, psychedelic consciousness expansion, the areas of kink/BDSM, and the relationship constellations of polyamory, ethical non-monogamy, and other manifestations of relationship anarchy.

For the past decade, I have rediscovered the humanistic and transpersonal researchers who have been investigating expansive and ecstatic states of consciousness and therapeutic growth through psychedelic medicine and therapy. I learned that their work, along with integrating Eastern wisdom traditions and parapsychological concepts, has both remained vital underground and is presently experiencing a renaissance.

Social justice initiatives are seeing a resurgence, as we rediscover those traditions that grew in popularity in the 1960s with strong connections to therapy and research. In many ways, the events of the past few years are helping me to use my power, privilege, and voice to help restore existential-humanistic psychology to its activist roots (and its psychedelic roots) and to grow them—as well as including the sexual dimension, which was looked at as freewheeling and experimental. There has been scant research about the erotic, desire, and sexual pleasure and healing within the existential-humanistic field since the 1960s or 1970s—a curious omission/repression that will no doubt be rectified with younger generations who have access to knowledge regarding the taboos around sexuality, sexual desires, and decriminalized and legalized plant medicines and psychedelic therapies.

During my tenure as editor in chief of the *Journal of Humanistic Psychology*, I was privileged to have the opportunity to help shape the profession by soliciting special issues from experts in our field who are focusing on these topics. My editorial, clinical, academic, and personal efforts call for existential-humanistic to champion the rights and the inclusion of all people, which includes: gender, gender identity, sexual orientation, neurodiversity, ability status, spiritual and religious tradition; facilitating non-ordinary states of consciousness for pleasure, growth, and healing; as well as sexual health and freedom, anti-fascist action, and activism for social justice. It allows for the biggest table—to help make sure that there are as many people as possible being supported and included. These efforts throughout the field will hopefully push us farther into a more equitable future.

How Practicing Existential–Humanistic Therapy Has Changed Me

Thinking more specifically of my personal experience with existential-humanistic therapy, I realize it has helped me to address my feelings of being different and an outsider during my upbringing. Being raised Jewish and living in a lower middle-class socioeconomic neighborhood in Philadelphia presented many experiences of feeling like the "Other." This brought up associated inferiority and over-compensating wishes for superiority. Additionally, I was born with congenital anosmia, which means that I never had a sense of smell; my mother also had the same condition.

I often felt a bit out of step and deficient among others, and maybe that's why I became too focused on relationships with others, loving the intensity of play and connecting with the other kids, and anxious about aggression and rejection. I ended up being/needing to be one of the more popular kids and sought affirmation and care from people outside the home. I needed to feel connected to others when I was often in conflict at home, and those interpersonal dynamics had a powerful, life-shaping impact.

With regard to my Conservative Jewish upbringing in the 1970s and 1980s, it was stressed that we remember the Holocaust, and the survivor rallying cry and defiance of that horrific genocide: "Never Again." As I grew older and recognized genocidal efforts against other targeted and oppressed groups, I applied that same mission as "Never Again for Anyone." I was aware of the hatred being directed most specifically at Black people and gay people, since I had attended racially integrated elementary schools and been taught by Black teachers.

The past 20 years of clinical work as well as growth and learning from existential-humanistic colleagues in the Society for Humanistic Psychology, have broadened and deepened my consciousness of institutional racism throughout American culture, along with patriarchy, misogyny and rape culture, and discrimination against LGBTQ+ people. I became sensitive to other ways of being that resulted in invisible suffering when misdiagnosed or forced into repressive states, or worse, denied. This includes those who experience learning differences, are highly sensitive, and identify as neurodiverse (the Autistic spectrum, ADHD, and other conditions).

Looking to the Future of Existential–Humanistic Therapy

As the above explorations show, throughout my life and career I have found myself drawn to the foundational aspects of existential-humanistic psychology, as well as critical emergent issues that are also beginning to be wrestled with in our profession. Painful childhood experiences of existential angst would later be actively and meaningfully engaged in my energizing investigations of existential-humanistic psychology during my adolescence. My personal and professional identities became deeply ingrained and intertwined in the first two decades of my career, including intensive experiential graduate training in existential-humanistic psychology, and then through my service as a professor, supervisor, therapist, and social justice activist.

Immersing myself in the multidimensional lifeworlds of patients of all ages, graduate students and colleagues opened up my eyes and sensitized me further to the oppression, discrimination, and difficulty experienced on a daily basis by Black people, indigenous people, people of color, women, the gender diverse, the neurodiverse, and the differently abled. Additional stigmatized groups who historically have been less likely to seek support and find competent therapists are those who identify as relationship anarchists, including ethically non-monogamous and polyamorous people, and the spectrum of erotic identities, including Kink and BDSM dynamics. Indeed, as the younger generations have greater access to the most contemporary information about sex, sexuality, gender, gender identity, neurodiversity, and kink and fetishes, they often come to therapy with knowledge and questions about their own connections and experiences with these aspects of being.

For the past decade, I have specialized in my private practice with often under-served transgender and non-binary children, adolescents, adults, and their families. The growing number of individuals disclosing transgender identities underscores the need for competent care for these populations. As I trained to refocus my knowledge, skills, and experiences in this effort, I was delighted to discover that once again, an existential-humanistic, trans-affirming paradigm is the best practice in diagnosis, therapy, and in supporting ongoing, complex clinical needs, and social and medical aspects of emergence, transitioning, authentic development, and integration.

Indeed, my existential-humanistic training and practice has allowed the widest openness, empathy, and desire to act on behalf of the human rights of those who are targeted, oppressed, and harmed in society. I have listened to women speak of their traumatizing experiences of misogyny, toxic masculinity, rape culture, and legislated reproductive injustice; to BIPOC and their emotionally exhausting experiences of daily racism and prejudice; and to the fear of LGBTQIA people regarding daily bullying and the political efforts to remove their rights and wholly legislate them out of existence. As existential-humanistic therapists, our efforts to hold, heal, and transform trauma and pain must be followed by the championing of diversity and social justice to change the social conditions that perpetuate our societal ills. My life mission, and that of my existential-humanistic colleagues, is to restore and affirm the field of psychology to more broadly and effectively realize its foundation of humanitarian ethics and evolve humanistic psychology to a humanitarian psychology (Rubin, et al., 2015).

There is recent precedent for this cultural shift toward social justice across disciplines. Many social, political, and scientific organizations are heeding the voices from targeted and oppressed communities, showing them how they have harmed the very people that they attempted to serve. The American Psychiatric Association has offered an apology to people of color for racist theories and practices, and the division of psychoanalysis of the American Psychological Association has offered an apology to LGBTQ people for harmful theory and practices. Division 32 of the American Psychological Association (Society for Humanistic Psychology) has also presented an action plan to ensure that there are meaningful changes to their organization and practices. The American Psychological Association is working on further apologies and acknowledgment of harm done to various groups.

I recommend that existential-humanistic psychology work with the groups who are assuming a leadership role in pushing for the American

Psychological Association to lobby for reparations and economic justice for BIPOC individuals from the federal government in recognition of the intergenerational trauma perpetuated by the genocide of colonization and centuries of slavery.

Each therapist must educate themselves on the true history of the United States, founded on the genocide of diverse indigenous cultures and the brutality and utter horror and cruel inhumanity of slavery. We must learn about and sensitize ourselves to the complete dominance of white male supremacy, colonialism, and the harm done to women and children through abuse and violence. As existential-humanistic therapists, we must learn how we may have participated in perpetuating the very harms that broader American culture has visited upon historically targeted and oppressed groups—and how our approach to therapy, teaching, and our theories may have reinforced those variables. Existential-humanistic theory and psychology must embrace human rights, humanitarian ethics, economic justice, and access to culturally competent therapies, and further align with the liberation psychology movement.

Finally, existential-humanistic therapy should align with the psychedelic justice movement as these powerful medicines become legalized and looked to as the gold standard for transforming complex posttraumatic stress disorder (PTSD), depression, anxiety, the management of pain and chronic illness, addiction treatment, spiritual and psychological growth efforts, and death with dignity. Many of the founders of the existential-humanistic movement were open and curious, and personally investigated the consciousness-expanding effects of psychedelics. Many of our patients will be experimenting with these medicines, as well. Existential-humanistic therapists should consider becoming competent in preparing and educating people for these journeys, learning about the cultural and historical aspects of these experiences, the risks and the management of adverse experiences, and the ongoing processing of their post-psychedelic experiences as touchstones for their growth and healing endeavors.

Advice for Therapists Looking at the Existential–Humanistic Approach

Like many people who had cyclically conflictual and painful interpersonal upbringings with loved ones, I subsequently learned that there is healing, acceptance, and growth through therapy. Many hurt individuals are instinctively drawn to it. Therapy will continue to draw people to it because it is so galvanizing, affirming, acknowledging, and holding of pain and intends the best for someone's well-being and healing. It unleashes and liberates psychological evolution, which is one of the most profound ways we can grow. This process can be difficult for some people because it confronts the kind of historic pains that we've kept, that we've acquired along the way, and that happen to us—whether it's stress traumas that are experienced daily or the catastrophic abuses and violation that occur.

As people feel safe in the therapeutic space over time, our minds want to integrate and synthesize the past, including the painful past, so the pain reemerges. This process allows us to transform what was a meteoric impact so that over time that impact is transformed. This frees us up to have more energy for other growth and evolutionary needs—psychologically, emotionally, and relationally.

I'm continually in awe of the people that I serve. I'm continually learning and growing alongside them and gaining inspiration from them. The blessing is that you get to live many lives through those of your patients. This is a gift, but not always an easy gift to receive. I have the privilege to experience and come to know many lives. I have now been in this field more than half my life. I'm still finding things to be excited about and contribute to, which is part of what keeps me energized.

Recently, I have had the opportunity to contribute to the establishment of standards for those who will administer and help integrate psychedelic experiences in therapy. It is an honor to work with visionary researchers and therapists, supporting them in their initiatives to make the culture more just, humane, and sustainable. If you enter this field, it is important to be aware of what inspires and energizes you to remain vital in your efforts.

The concepts and conditions of existential-humanistic therapy are foundational underpinnings of many effective therapies. Relational and person-centered therapists are integrated into all effective, insight-oriented growth therapy. The best practices and gold standard of transgender psychological services and therapy is affirming who a person knows themselves to be, a hallmark of existential-humanistic therapy. Because of this, existential-humanistic therapy is amazingly adaptable. It allows you to do a variety of different types of work and to integrate different therapy strategies while maintaining a solid foundation in existential-humanistic therapy. This modality allows one to be expansive, adaptive, and creative while maintaining an essential core. This can be both exhilarating and overwhelming for all involved, both experiencer and witness.

It is important for all therapists to recognize the ethical responsibility and necessity to engage in your own therapy. This may be even more vital for therapists in depth psychology, such as existential-humanistic. Find a therapist who is a good fit for your way of being and your intentions toward healing and growth; then, actively engage in your own existential, humanistic, psychodynamic, or other depth therapy. I personally underwent a traditional, five times per week psychoanalysis for seven and a half years during graduate school and my early career period.

Have your clinical cases supervised by experienced existential-humanistic therapists so they can help to impart the depth and breadth of the framework. This was very helpful for me in my graduate, postgraduate work, and early to mid-career progression. To the extent that what you are learning is not helpful to the groups and populations you are serving necessitates that we have to evolve the model accordingly.

Existential-humanistic therapy emphasizes that growth is a lifelong adventure, not something you do and then you are finished. This does not necessarily mean that you are in therapy consistently for the entirety of your career, although some do find this valuable. Others may return to therapy with different therapists periodically throughout their career. Find what works for you but be sure to find your avenue of continued growth and address your own struggles.

I would share with an aspiring existential-humanistic therapist what a respected peer and beloved colleague said to me when I asked her in graduate school if I should I undergo psychoanalysis. She said with heartfelt enthusiasm, "Oh, Shawn, it's such a wonderful journey." And there it was. That was why I started psychoanalysis as an important integration of personal journey, existential-humanistic graduate study, training, and practice.

It is tremendously rewarding to have enthusiasm and excitement about the process of learning and growing, and to know that it can last your whole life. It is an incredible vocation. It's a calling, and you can grow and evolve each day if you have the opportunity and the privilege to remain vital in the work. To be an existential-humanistic therapist can mean being a bit of a rebel, and it can be lonely. If you decide to take this journey, be sure that you root yourself in a community that will help to sustain you in this environment and help you actualize your potential.

Challenges for Existential–Humanistic Psychology and Therapy

As far as potential existential threats to the existential-humanistic field, I have observed a few that I would like to briefly note: existential-humanistic graduate programs, the American Psychological Association, and internal conflicts. The history of independent graduate institutions in existential-humanistic psychology over the past 40 years has led me to believe that they are not a viable or sustainable aspect of the future of the movement. As mentioned earlier, my contention is that existential-humanistic psychotherapy and psychology will thrive, like psychoanalysis, if it can establish training institutes where courses in therapy, supervision, and research can flourish in a freer context unrestricted by the burdens of accreditation and finance. This requires a context that balances rigor with self-reflection, developing the person of the therapist and experiential learning. Existential-humanistic therapy has been under attack by mainstream forces seeking to manualize therapy. In the American Psychological Association, there is a vested interest in the monopoly of cognitive behavioral therapy and other surface-oriented approaches that target symptoms and are reductionistic. We need the firebrands and rebels who resist and critique this, and those who may repackage what we do under other names to maintain its vibrance in the field.

All social movements and schools of thought within academic and scientific fields experience perennial threats to their cohesion, relevance, and continuity. There is a need to continually seek fresh and diverse individual perspectives to discover and nurture future generations of existential-humanistic therapists who can humanely listen, serve, and heal. The future of existential-humanistic psychology is dependent upon the relational and collegial generativity of the small but dedicated international groups of existential-humanistic therapists, clinical supervisors, professors, scholars, and training institutes. The presence and contributions of new students, graduate students, early career psychologists, allies and like-minded folks energize and invigorate our field and welcome diversity ethnically, racially, and theoretically—including various ways of applying and evolving existential-humanistic approaches.

Upon entering the leadership of humanistic psychology, my friends and colleagues who emerged within the third generation of existential-humanistic psychologists were at times faced with the presence of privileged power, white supremacy and racism, toxic masculinity and misogyny, and the other challenges that plague United States culture. These troubling experiences required many of us in the leadership hierarchy to confront those prejudices and privileges within ourselves, something from which all organizations and individuals ultimately benefit and may more effectively serve. Many of these insidious woes are being reckoned with in an intentional way throughout our culture at this present time. However, in some cases, relationships with mentors, colleagues, and friends were deeply damaged and ruptured and have often taken years to repair. These ruptures are a threat to the movement, but they also have provided an opportunity for healing and growth.

Finally, as a movement already marginalized, it is important that we do not allow internal divisions to threaten the future of existential-humanistic psychology. Generally, existential-humanistic and humanistic psychology has become a close-knit, supportive community. However, at times, internal conflict has caused unnecessary division that has led to some individuals distancing themselves from these affiliations. The conflicts also have thwarted our ability to speak as a united voice on important issues where we could make a difference. While it is important that existential-humanistic therapy remain inclusive of a diversity of perspectives and approaches, it is vital that these differences are appreciated and do not serve as sources of division.

Conclusion

The journey to becoming an existential-humanistic therapist is full of challenges, insights, and inspirations. For me, personally, it began by helping me face and journey into my own angst. Learning that others had taken a similar route gave me the courage to look within myself. On the other side, I found community and personal inspiration that solidified my identity within existential-humanistic psychology and continue to provide a community of fellow sojourners who are committed to making a positive impact on the world. It is a profound and humbling privilege to serve and contribute to our mission of fulfilling the promise an existential-humanistic psychology for all, and for the betterment of humankind, the earth, and all its inhabitants.

References

Bugental, J. F. T. (1981). *The search for authenticity: An existential-analytic approach to psychotherapy.* Irvington.

Rogers, C. (1961). *On becoming a person: A therapist's view of psychotherapy.* Houghton-Mifflin.

Rubin, S., St. John, D., Vallejos, X., & Sebree, D., Jr. (2015). *Humanitarian psychology for the global 21st century.* Paper presented at the 8th Annual Society for Humanistic Psychology Conference. Chicago, IL.

Chapter 13

Concluding Thoughts

Julia Falk
Louis Hoffman

What is the value of a storying approach to an exploration of pathways to becoming an existential-humanistic therapist? We could, after all, have designed and circulated a survey (maybe even a qualitative survey), turning this into a more research-oriented endeavor. If we had, we would have failed to grasp the advantages of inviting narratives that can relay the depth and nuance of our human experiences. People are meaning-making creatures, and the life story is a meaning-creating enterprise. As Josselson and Leiblich (2015) asserted, "experience itself is shaped in story form" (p. 325). If we want to know about a thing in all its complexity, we must nearly always turn toward narrative. Mark Freeman spoke about the importance of hindsight and the value of recalling the past for understanding.

> When I look backward over the course of some portion of my life in order to discern possible connections, I am inevitably engaging in "emplotment," the experiences of times past now being seen as parts of an emerging whole, episodes in an evolving story. (Freeman, 2010, p. 4)

The invitation, then, was for each person to reflect back, tracing and advancing their story and enhancing self-understanding, thereby increasing the potential for readers to perceive and elaborate on the connections laid down in each tale. Freeman also suggested that "hindsight plays an integral role in shaping and deepening moral life" (p. 5) and is the "primary source of the examined life" (p. 8). It seems the perfect vehicle for an examination of the roads to a life with existential-humanistic purpose, an exploration of how we each wish to live our lives in ways that feel right, fulfilling, and responsible

(Schneider & Krug, 2010).

These chapters illustrate many ways in which the transition from "plain person," as Xuefu Wang describes his early self, to existential-humanistic therapist can take place over time. For some, the roots could be discerned in childhood tendencies and concerns, while for others it felt more like a conversion in later life. Regardless, these stories tell of the meanings that each author has assigned to events in their life that led to their present identification or affiliation with existential-humanistic thought and practice. If we receive the authors' meanings from an empathic stance (as we are humanistically inclined to do), the reader will enhance the authors' meanings with their own perceptions. And thus, this community of writers and readers we have created resides in a complex and beautiful web of personal meanings.

A Journey Filled with Meanings

The meanings that we share, each in our own way, reflect the characteristics of life that we recognize as existential givens, those essential poles of experience with which we grapple if we are to grow and flourish. It should be no surprise to find them reflected here in the journey toward professional identity. The great concerns of death, isolation, meaning, freedom, and awe are woven into these narratives, suggesting, as we have often seen before, that they drive our transitions, sometimes explicitly and often well beneath the radar. In this chapter, we (Julia and Louis) review the themes that stood out to us as we read through the narratives. This is not a qualitative or research-based analysis of the stories. The structure of the chapters was kept to a minimum to allow the authors freedom to construct their own narrative in the way that fit their voice and story. This unstructured approach does not lend itself to a formal qualitative analysis; however, there is still value in reflecting collectively upon experiences, ideas, and other themes that commonly emerged in these narratives.

Meeting Death and Life

> Although the physicality of death destroys man, the idea of death saves him. (Yalom, 1980, p. 30)

Woven into the stories here are those encounters with life's finitude that foster a new perspective on living. For some the change came quickly, while for others the transition was slower. When Kathleen

Galvin attended her young brother's funeral, facing her own longer lifespan, she promised she would open her heart to death and, in the meantime, say yes to life. Lisa Xochitl Vallejos chose to embrace life when she was faced with the vulnerability of her young son. She chose to live fully rather than die slowly, facing into her fears and taking each step forward with intention. In the life stories of Ed Mendelowitz and Kirk Schneider, we witness the facing of mortality in one's own life when serious health conditions are encountered and gracefully integrated.

Bugental (1999) spoke of the omnipresence of death. "Death accompanies life day by day, moment by moment.... The very fact of ending can give vitality to that which is, in fact, now and, therefore, in some measure accessible, and it counsels action rather than delay" (p. 256). He goes on to propose that resistance itself represents a client's effort to delay the death of possibilities. Yalom (1980), whose influence is so often cited here, devoted much attention to death anxiety and the many ways in which people defend against it. Our authors' interactions with the great theme of death and its contribution to their valuing of life speak to a significant part of the presence that existential-humanistic therapists bring to the therapeutic relationship. Lisa Xochitl noted: "I learned how to help my clients sit with their discomfort because I was familiar with sitting with my own." These existential-humanistic therapists are able to come to client encounters with their own material digested because they have dared to lean into life's ultimate concern.

Incorporating lessons from facing one's mortality is often discussed in the existential literature. In many of the stories in this volume, it is evident that the authors not only speak to this value but have lived it.

Alone and Together

McAdams (1993), after his many investigations of human storying, identified *communion*, the pull toward love and intimacy, as one of the two major themes in life stories. That same human tendency is prominent in existential and existential-humanistic thought as the polarities of isolation or aloneness versus connection, or Bugental's separate-but-relatedness (Rowan, 2015).

At one side of the pole, several writers described an early sense of not fitting in or being somehow different and apart. Ed Mendelowitz told how "the psychology of not wholly fitting was more or less implicit from the start." Sometimes feeling different arose from the uninvited attributes of birth, such as belonging to a different religious or ethnic group. At other times, it was something inherent or developed in the person. That certainly showed in my own (Julia's) brief portrait, but it was evident, too, in the quality of rebellion that was claimed by Louis Hoffman and Nathaniel Granger. Nathaniel was always prone to hop off the beaten track to the "service road" that held more promise.

Something in this rebel quality that surfaced almost throughout the narratives served to link the aloneness to a call for social justice: standing alone against the crowd while standing up for others. We saw this in Kathleen Galvin's years of service in Hong Kong, in Myrtle Heery's experience of Martin Luther King Jr., in the advocacy for unheard voices of Lisa Xochitl and Shawn Rubin, and in Nathaniel's work to genuinely integrate humanistic psychology itself.

It could also be said that, like Mark Yang stepping off the expected path, these writers (and perhaps many of the readers) have chosen a way of thinking, working, and living that is outside the mainstream of psychology, with its relentless push toward structure and categorization in practice and research. Each of the writers said, "No, there is *more*," and found their way to affiliation with others who valued complexity, subjectivity, and the experiential or phenomenological. Orah Krug believes that "each person constructs a particular world from unique perceptions of the world" and always strives to meet clients and students in the world of their own making. Bringing a European perspective to existential-humanistic therapy's American foundation, Katerina Zymnis allows for the existence of endless possibilities for each individual—and the requisite responsibility that comes with these possibilities—but invites an awareness of interrelationship and interdependence in the world. Even within the band of existential-humanistic psychologists, each of these writers has continued to advocate for *more*, contributing new paradigms (Schneider, Krug, and Zymnis), and new institutions (Heery, Hoffman, and Yang). Perhaps none have been as solitary as Xuefu Wang, who observed and felt the potential relatedness between Western existential and Chinese traditional thought and went on to integrate the two along with many scholars and therapists who espoused them. In ways, existential-humanistic psychology became an opportunity to create community for those often drawn to stand outside traditional forms of community.

On the relationship side of this continuum, it is interesting to note how many agreed that they came to the psychotherapy encounter as "fellow travelers." Not one fails to express the importance of coming to the alliance with unconditional regard for the client, respect for their experience, presence, and authenticity. They have experienced communion in their lives with wise elders, generous mentors, colleagues, and friends, so that, like Xuefu, they can say, "I am not alone." Existential-humanistic therapy deeply values in-depth relationships and, in these narratives, it is evident that these relationships were an important part of the storied journeys.

The Cost of Freedom
Each of the paths to an existential-humanistic profession described here contained many possibilities at nearly every transitional point. As Bugental (1999) has advised, if we reach out toward each experience of "modifying the balance between openness and limitedness" (p. 122), we expand our views of self and change the limits that are imposed on our living and experiencing. We could all have been something else if we had stayed on a path that was prescribed or predicted by the circumstances of our early lives. At some point, though, each of these authors chose differently, and often repeatedly.

> No one, least of all me, would have ever predicted that the little girl with tangled hair and deep emotions would someday be called doctor and would help many people out of their own personal hells…I often need to pause and be reminded that it is my own choices that led me to where I am. (Lisa Xochitl)

This agentic theme surfaced for Mark as he stepped into "Plan B," and for HeeSun Park as she moved away from her early desire to become a Buddhist nun. Bringing awareness to the possibility or freedom to *become* was life-altering for each writer, and it became a value that was operant in their therapeutic practices, as well. Like Katerina, they have all opened to a "responsible and active stance" in their lives, intentionally pointed toward service.

One aspect of this reaching out to grasp freedom and enact it, as it showed up in these stories, bears an orientation toward destiny that is strongly existential. Several writers explicitly represented how they felt *called* to serving the needs of others through existential-humanistic practice. Kathleen Galvin called it a "siren's song," this draw toward a psychology that allows people to be complex, contradictory, alone and together, bodily and spiritual. Along with Nathaniel, Mark, and Louis, she moved from a traditional sense of religious ministry to an expanded view of aiding and caring that served the whole of a person and even a society. One of the meanings that people often draw about the place where they have landed, as they look back over the events of their lives, is that it was somehow meant to be (Falk, 2018; Kray, 2010). For Mark, "my identification as an existential psychologist comes as a calling to me and the agency and will as to what I do can be best described as a mission;" and for Xuefu, "It suited me so well, just as though it were tailored for a person like me!" This was not a passive acceptance of fate, but recognition of what might have been and the choices that led purposefully to a life that was a satisfying fit for one's nature and aspirations. It's in alignment with May's (1981) idea that moving toward what we were meant to become is an experience of authenticity, "a conviction of genuine freedom" (pp. 93–94). This embodies the theme of courage to be who one is—both individually and through one's choices to be part of relationships and communities—which is critical in the writing of Tillich (1952) and May (1981; see also Abzug, 2021).

A Life with Meaning
Constructing a narrative about the events and directions of one's life is inherently a meaning-making enterprise. On one level, the narrator follows a self-reflective process that relates events, influences, and settings to the self through time (Singer & Bluck, 2001). That certainly happened in all these stories. More importantly, the narratives also deal with meaning or purpose in the existential sense. That is more complex: looking for a sense that one's life has meaning or value for oneself, knowing that one contributes to the well-being of others, feeling that one's life is aligned with their beliefs, or perhaps seeking purpose or mission. Mark quotes Victor Frankl in this regard. During a period when the life that his academic efforts seemed to be producing did not feel like it would be satisfying, he sensed an invitation to take responsibility for the active creation of what he desired. Our writers are seekers, examining their own experiences to discern what it is that they really believe and how that connects their past to their present and future.

For several, relationships with mentors were a meaningful component of their development as existential-humanistic therapists. Kirk Schneider and Ed Mendelowitz were fortunate to form mentoring relationships with Rollo May, who has touched so many indirectly through his writing. Orah Krug, Myrtle Heery, and Louis Hoffman found mentoring with James F. T. Bugental, while Orah and Lisa Xochitl learned directly from Irvin Yalom. Each new generation of therapists named existential-humanistic teachers who had actively helped them make a connection with the discipline they would pursue. Louis

Hoffman was mentioned as playing that role for several. Some authors also extended mentoring/teaching relationships to the next generation and experienced that as a meaningful endeavor. Myrtle, Xuefu, Orah, Katerina, Kirk, Mark, and Louis have all devoted their professional energies to the growth and development of the students who will further the existential-humanistic tradition.

Another experience that brought meaning to the lives of the writers was the therapeutic encounter itself. It appears as a critically important value in their stories. Katerina described it eloquently as accompanying a wounded person who is moving toward healing, fully present and authentic: "Being aware of our common humanness while working therapeutically with clients becomes an act of ultimate democracy that requires courage, respect, thorough professional preparation and, mainly, deep *agape* from the practitioner's side toward the human condition." It is remarkable that this same attitude or value emanated from the narratives of fourteen writers who represent very different cultures and life experiences. For each of these individuals, meaning was something that was more than an intellectual exercise; it was something that was embodied and lived.

Opening to Awe
Kirk Schneider (2004) invited people to see the wholeness and complexity of things: "As soon as we fixate, even if we fixate on what appears to be open and multiple, we lose the vitality of our being, the elasticity of our being, and the poignant predicament of our being" (p. xiii). The existential-humanistic psychologists within these pages have moved, and continue to move, through a process of bringing awareness to paradox and intricacy in their lives and allowing—even embracing—it. Sometimes this is explicit, sometimes not. Ed Mendelowitz refers to "those ultimate ambiguities that can never be precisely pinned down;" and, indeed, life's ever-present polarities are present in the contrast between the aesthetics of film and literature that draw him even in times of painful experience. In scary movies, Kirk found both fear and an opening to curiosity and creativity. The idea that existential-humanistic thinkers are even drawn toward disorienting experience is set forth by Kathleen Galvin, who finds it to be an opportunity to question and explore possibilities.

Something akin to awe also surfaces in the way so many of our writers describe their spiritual journeys. Several writers were raised within mainstream religious traditions and followed a path that might have led to the ministry or to lay religious work. In their journey of becoming, they moved from being simply religious to being spiritual, which might also include religious experience. When I (Julia) was asked to develop a personal definition of spirituality in graduate school, I found that I understood it as a *felt* thing, an experience that connects what is deep within me, internal and individual, to what is beyond me, the universal or divine. The experience moves simultaneously up and down, so it is a sharing of myself with the beyond that does not diminish me but enhances me. There is awe in it. Louis, Kathleen, and Mark all encountered a questioning period that summoned them to a more expansive experience that transcended the boundaries they found in the past. Kathleen's faith became "God is love and who abides in God abides in love." Nathaniel experienced amazing acceptedness at a new church where he could engage with the paradox of worshipping the divine while simultaneously celebrating the beauty and diversity of humanity. Moving outside of Western spiritual tradition, Xuefu Wang recalls how the paradox of yin and yang has influenced him. Perhaps awe is present in the Confucian move from smaller self to greater self as he describes it.

In awe, as illustrated in these narratives, there is an acceptance of one's smallness in contrast to the wonderment of the world and universe beyond oneself. This is connected to the recognition or appreciation of a meaning in this mystery that is unknowable beyond oneself. Ernest Becker (1973) said, "Man cannot endure his own littleness unless he can translate it into meaningfulness on the largest possible level" (p. 196). These stories show how that meaningfulness does not necessarily need to be in something definitive, such as God, religion, or an ideology. It can be a meaningfulness embedded in mystery, appreciation, and awe, rooted in the world in which we live.

Othered Threads in the Fabric: Engagement with Culture
Humanistic psychologists have grown increasingly interested in and open to multicultural concerns and influences in recent years, in no small measure due to the work of several writers from this volume. Nathaniel referenced this in his story about inclusivity in the Society for Humanistic Psychology. The editors set the intention of telling a diverse array of stories in the book, but it still stands out that multicultural experience and an openness to human variety has characterized many of these writers throughout their careers. We have already considered the area of social justice for peoples who lack power or access, which is one aspect of caring across racial, gender, socioeconomic, and ethnic

lines. However, many here have also lived or worked in cultures different from their birth culture: Kathleen, Katerina, Myrtle, and HeeSun spring to mind. Others have dedicated a great deal of energy to the admixture of psychological thought between cultures by founding intercultural institutes: Mark, Louis, and Xuefu, for example. Even within the United States, Nathaniel, Lisa Xochitl, Shawn, and others have sought to ease the transition of psychologists and students who come from other backgrounds into the existential-humanistic fold. These voices and the narratives connected with these voices are changing the field of existential-humanistic psychology, including its theory and practice. This illustrates the power of one's story. With many of these contributors, the changes they are helping to bring about are rooted in the personal narratives that inform their lived experience and inform their theory and practice.

Future Stories

These existential-humanistic therapists all clearly see their personal journey as continuing, which points to the fluid and changing understanding of self emphasized by existential-humanistic psychology (Hoffman et al., 2014). The meaning that they derive from using the therapeutic relationship to help others free themselves and pursue their potential seems to reach into the future, supporting others and bringing a richness to their own lives.

Some of the writers have also offered their vision for the future of existential-humanistic therapy. Kathleen Galvin offers a visual scheme for love, power, and justice as a foundation for existential-humanistic psychology. She sees its work as supporting people to "freely and openly engage with others and with communities of people to discover, develop, and express the fullness of their powers" for the welfare of all individuals and communities. This is aligned with Katerina Zymnis's view of existential-humanistic therapy as a haven for connecting hearts wherein people are treated with dignity and respect in their search for what they need.

Ed Mendelowitz hopes for a continued contribution to world literature and conscience, encouraging psychologists to grow their receptivity to the humanities. He sees that the humanities have something to offer to our discourse with science and invites an exploration of how existential-humanistic thought and writing might offer that. Nathaniel Granger, too, advocates for "abounding inquiry and enlarged vision."

Both Orah Krug and Katerina referenced the importance of training and research to the future of existential-humanistic psychotherapy. Both have worked to bring training in personal skills to new therapists who have only known techniques and protocols in their education. Katerina asserts that there is a need to generate research studies that are more broadly accepted so that the application of this valuable approach to healing can be included in national health services around the world. She encourages collaboration with other approaches, such as systems work, that might integrate toward an improved understanding of a client's whole life. Shawn advocates for the support and development of training institutes that are devoted to existential-humanistic psychotherapy in an academic and healthcare environment that mitigates against it.

Your Own Conclusion
Each reader will take away their own sense of these stories. Particular stories will resonate with each one of us in personal and unique ways. Several authors spoke of how organizing and articulating their narratives affected them in a positive way. It may also be worthwhile to speculate on the possible value of this enterprise to our readers.

To read about the journeys of others—especially those we admire—can be stimulating and motivating. These tales prompt us to become more aware of the variety of human experience. There is not just one path to any destination and these stories illustrate that beautifully. Though many could trace the threads of existential wonder even into their childhoods, there was a lot of wandering and experiencing before the precise roadway became clear.

For a student or a prospective student of psychology who doesn't quite "fit the mold" of mainstream psychological or psychotherapy education, these stories might illuminate a new possibility to explore. They could perceive a lot of potential connections through these stories, learning names of practitioners, references, training sites, and institutes. There is also a helpful appendix for those who would like to evaluate more deeply whether they, too, feel called to this path.

A seasoned therapist from a different approach could be inspired by the idea, so evident in these stories, that we are always becoming, deciding it's time to integrate existential-humanistic ideas into their practice. Even a confirmed existential-humanistic practitioner might appreciate the opportunity to think again about their own professional journey and identity, enjoying a little professional life review. There's an appendix for that, too.

Each story within this volume has ended only temporarily on its final page. The writers (and the readers) will all continue to be and, hopefully, to become. The deep, personal sharing of each writer can shape and color the way each of us undertakes the next steps of our own journeys, allowing existential-humanistic thought and practice to inform the way we care for ourselves and others.

References

Abzug, R. H. (2021). *Psyche and soul in America: The spiritual odyssey of Rollo May.* Oxford University Press.

Becker, E. (1973). *The denial of death.* Free Press.

Bugental, J. F. T. (1999). *Psychotherapy isn't what you think: Bringing the psychotherapeutic engagement into the living moment.* Zeig, Tucker & Co.

Falk, J. M. (2018). *A narrative inquiry into the experience of a life story course for adults in transitional life periods.* (Publication No. 10825266) [Doctoral dissertation, Saybrook University]. Proquest Dissertations and Theses Global.

Freeman, M. (2010). *Hindsight.* Oxford University Press.

Hoffman, L., Stewart, S., Warren, D., & Meek, L. (2014). Toward a sustainable myth of self: An existential response to the postmodern condition. In K. J. Schneider, J. F. Pierson, J. F. T. Bugental (Eds.), *The handbook of humanistic psychology: Theory, research, and practice* (2nd ed., pp. 105–133). Sage Publications.

Josselson, R., & Lieblich, A. (2015). Narrative research and humanism. In K. J. Schneider, J. F. Pierson, J. F. T. Bugental (Eds.), *The handbook of humanistic psychology: Theory, research, and practice* (2nd ed., pp. 321–334). Sage Publications.

Kray, L. J., George, L. G., Galinsky, A. D., Liljenquist, K. A., Tetlock, P. E., & Roese, N. J. (2010). From what might have been to what must have been: Counterfactual thinking creates meaning. *Journal of Personality and Social Psychology, 98* (1), 106–118. https://doi.org/10.1037/a0017905

May, R. (1981). *Freedom and destiny.* W. W. Norton.

McAdams, D. P. (1993). *The stories we live by: Personal myths and the making of the self.* Guilford Press.

Rowan, J. (2015). Existential analysis and humanistic psychotherapy. In K. J. Schneider, J. F. Pierson, J. F. T. Bugental (Eds.), *The handbook of humanistic psychology: Theory, research, and practice* (2nd ed., pp. 549–561). Sage Publications.

Schneider, K. J. (2004). *Rediscovery of awe: Splendor, mystery, and the fluid center of life.* Paragon House.

Schneider, K. J., & Krug, O. T. (2010). *Existential-humanistic therapy.* American Psychological Association.

Singer, J. A., & Bluck, S. (2001). New perspectives on autobiographical memory: The integration of narrative processing and autobiographical reasoning. *Review of General Psychology, 5* (2), 91–99. https://doi.org/10.1037//1089-2680.5.2.91

Tillich, P. (1952). *The courage to be.* Yale University Press.

Yalom, I. D. (1980). *Existential psychotherapy.* Basic Books.

Appendix A

Activities for Students Considering Becoming an Existential–Humanistic Therapist

Louis Hoffman & Julia Falk

Many existential-humanistic therapists report that discovering existential-humanistic psychology was more than finding the best theoretical orientation to align with or career trajectory to aspire to. Instead, it has been described as a finding of oneself, an affirmation of one's beliefs, or a discovery that one is not alone in approaching life in this manner. Existential-humanistic psychology is about a way of living and experiencing the world that goes beyond one's career. For most existential-humanistic therapists, this is about how they live. Therapy, of course, is a specific application of this way of being that is different from how one engages in relationships outside of therapy. Yet, the core values—including presence, empathy, compassion, and authenticity among others—are values we bring to our own lives as well as to the therapy room.

In teaching about existential-humanistic therapy for over 20 years, I (Louis) have often heard psychology graduate students note that they were questioning whether counseling or psychotherapy was really the right career choice for them prior to discovering existential-humanistic therapy. Many noted that they were disappointed with the lack of focus on caring and compassion in the field. Others noted that the reductionistic and objective stances of psychology disillusioned them. When they encountered existential-humanistic psychology, it felt like discovering what they thought a career in counseling or psychology was about.

This is not to say that existential-humanistic therapy is superior to other approaches. The mental health professions and consumers of mental health services are better served by having a variety of therapy approaches. No approach to therapy is the right fit for every therapist or client. Finding the right theoretical orientation fit is critical to being an effective therapist. Research has shown that belief in therapy is an important factor in successful outcomes (Constantino et al., 2019; Wampold & Imel, 2015). While this research has focused primarily on the client beliefs in therapy, the client's beliefs are significantly impacted by the therapist's belief that therapy will work. It is difficult for the therapist to foster confidence in a therapy that they do not deeply believe in themselves. For this reason, it can be argued that one of the most important decisions that a therapist makes is aligning with a treatment approach or orientation.

As existential-humanistic therapy is a way of being, aligning with this orientation can be an even bigger decision. In this appendix, we offer some starting points for reflection for those considering embarking upon the journey to becoming an existential-humanistic therapist. For some, this may be about confirming if this is the right approach for them or whether and how to deepen their engagement. For others, it may be about deciding if they will choose this path.

Reflection Questions

In this section, questions are included to help you reflect upon the lessons you learned from the narratives in *Becoming an Existential-Humanistic Therapist* that apply to you personally. Readers are encouraged to write or type out their answers to these questions and return to them repeatedly over time. You may find that your answers change as you grow into your career.

Reflection Question 1
You have completed reading 11 narratives about becoming an existential-humanistic therapist. This first set of questions encourages you to reflect upon what you have taken with you from these stories.

1. As you read through the different stories of becoming an existential-humanistic therapist, what aspects of these stories resonated with you? What does this mean for you?
2. Were there aspects of these stories that elicited fear, anxiety, or hesitation? If so, what meaning do you connect with this?
3. What themes stood out to you in the narratives?
4. In looking at your own decision to become a therapist and, in particular, an existential-humanistic therapist, what are the key moments in your life that have shaped this decision?

Reflection Questions 2
This set of questions is more general, and not directly connected with the narratives of *Becoming an Existential–Humanistic Therapist*. They are designed to further help you reflect upon what it means for you to be an existential-humanistic therapist.

1. What was your own first exposure to existential-humanistic therapy? What was your initial reaction to it?
2. If someone were to ask you why you want to become an existential-humanistic therapist, what would you tell them?
3. How does existential-humanistic therapy fit with your personal and professional values?
4. What are your beliefs about the client-therapist relationship?

Reflection Questions 3
Meaning is central to existential-humanistic therapy. It is important for us to clarify our own sources of meaning in life, which often connect to the values discussed in the previous set of questions. The following set of questions is intended to foster reflection on issues of meaning.

1. What sources of meaning are valued in your family?
2. What sources of meaning are valued in culture(s)?
3. What are your primary sources of meaning in life? Are these sources of meaning evident in the choices you make? Do they differ from the meanings in your family and culture?
4. How does meaning relate to your choice to become a therapist? And, specifically, an existential-humanistic therapist?
5. How do you seek to help clients clarify their own meaning?

Reflection Questions 4
Authenticity is an important value in existential-humanistic psychology; however, the way authenticity is discussed in the psychological literature varies. From an existential perspective, authenticity is connected to facing oneself and one's life directly and honestly. This includes, but is not limited to, being clear and consistent on one's values and how these values guide one's life.

Authenticity is not simple. Often, our values conflict with one another. For example, if one values being direct but also values being empathetic and compassionate, these may, at times, conflict. The values of being empathetic and compassionate may shape the way that a person is direct in their communication. For existential-humanistic therapists, it is important for there to be consistency between one's values in therapy and one's personal life.

1. What do you identify as your core values that guide your decisions in life?
2. How do these values play out in your life outside of therapy? How do these find expression in therapy?
3. In what ways do you seek to help your clients clarify their own values and how these values inform their choices?

Reflection Questions 5

Finitude and death are considered one of the existential givens. These questions are intended to prompt deeper reflections about your beliefs and experiences relevant to death and limitation.

1. What has been your experience with death and mortality? How has it shaped the way that you understand and experience the world? How have these shaped your views on life and death?
2. Now take some time to reflect upon personal limitations that you have to face. How has this impacted your views on life?
3. Imagine working with a client who has lost a loved one or reflect upon your experience with an actual client who has experienced the loss of someone significant. What is/was it like for you to be with this person in the midst of their suffering?
4. Next, imagine working with the client who is facing their own death due to age or an illness, or reflect upon an actual client of yours facing death. What is/was it like to work with this client around these issues?
5. Take some time to journal about how your encounters with death have shaped your beliefs about life and death.

Reflection Questions 6

Many existential therapists have been influenced by philosophy, literature, and the arts. This section includes questions that encourage reflection upon which of these have influenced you.

1. What forms of art have impacted or inspired you? How have these influenced your views of life and meaning? How have these forms of art influenced your view of life and/or therapy?

2. What philosophers or non-fiction authors outside of psychology have impacted you the most? How have these writers shaped your understanding of life and/or therapy?
3. Identify one artist or group of artists (music, visual, dance, poetry, literature/fiction, etc.) that has influenced you. Spend some time reflecting upon why this is important to you. Identify at least one piece of art from this person(s) that has had a particular impact upon you. What is it about this piece of art that impacted you? How is it relevant to your life experience? What have you learned from it that may be applicable to therapy?

Reflection Questions 7

Being relational is in. Many therapists—as well as people outside of the mental health professions—talk about being relational. However, what is meant by being relational can vary drastically. In existential-humanistic therapy, being relational has a particular connotation that is rooted in depth, genuineness, mutuality, and concern. Being relational is recognized as entailing more than being effective in communication or valuing relationships. The questions in this section help you reflect on your understanding of being relational.

1. Think of someone in your life who has deeply impacted you in a positive way. Maybe just being in their presence inspired you to want to be a better person. Describe the qualities of this person that you value. How might this be relevant to the way of being you want to develop as a therapist?
2. What relational qualities—such as genuineness, empathy, compassion, truthfulness, directionless, etc.—do you most value? How do these influence your approach to therapy?
3. How might you work to further develop these relational qualities in yourself?

Presence Exercises

Schneider (2015) advocated that presence is the foundation for the effectiveness of all psychotherapy and, in particular, existential-humanistic psychotherapy. He described presence in existential-humanistic therapy as,

> The Latin root for presence is prae (before) + esse (to be); thus,

> presence means "to be before." Consequently, presence in a therapeutic setting can be understood as the capacity "to be before" or to be with one's being and/or "to be before" or to be with another human being.
>
> Presence involves aspects of awareness, acceptance, availability, and expressiveness in both therapist and client. (Schneider, 2019, p. 252)

Krug (2019) further notes that "presence is both the ground for a genuine encounter and a method for effecting transformative change" (p. 263). Given the central placement of presence in existential-humanistic therapy, it is an important consideration for anyone considering becoming an existential-humanistic therapist. In this section, we discuss two exercises to help you examine your own experience with presence.

Presence Interviews

When teaching courses on existential-humanistic therapy, I (Louis) often assign students a "presence project." This assignment entails interviewing people about what it *feels* like to be with you and then reflecting upon these answers and their personal meaning. This is relevant to the concept of presence, which is foundational to existential-humanistic practice.

This presence exercise is designed to help individuals develop their therapeutic presence. What it feels like to be in one's presence is one aspect of the broader concept of presence. The experience of being with another person is shaped by subjective and intersubjective processes that go beyond the cultivation of therapeutic presence. However, deepening the understanding of what it is like for others to be with you is vital if you are an existential-humanistic therapist, including informing how you cultivate therapeutic presence.

Over the years, as I have engaged in this process myself, I recognized important aspects of what it feels like to be around me in different settings. For example, it is common for students and colleagues to report that I can be intimidating. As I have unpacked this, I have grown in my understanding of why this is. Among the primary factors that influence people experiencing me as intimidating are: 1) my size or physical presence (I am 6'1" and fairly broad-shouldered); 2) I am introverted, which means that I am often slow to speak and can, at times, be withdrawn into my own thoughts and reflections; 3) I am often intense in my listening, including direct eye contact;[1] and 4) there is awareness that I have published a fair amount and have high writing standards.

Obviously, being intimidating is frequently counterproductive in therapy. Therefore, it is important that I remain aware of this possibility. While clients often report a different experience of me (i.e., that I am patient, soft, comforting), I am aware that this intimidation is something that could also emerge in therapy, especially in the first couple of sessions. As I reflect upon the tendency for others to experience me as intimidating, a few things stand out. First, some of this I cannot change. I cannot change my height and can only change my body frame to a limited degree—and I am not likely to do this for therapy. I cannot change that I have published a fair amount, which is something that some clients are aware of and even a reason that some clients seek me out. While I can change aspects of my behavior related to being an introvert and intent listener, these also are things I value in myself. Yet, I do make some changes related to this awareness. For example, in education and training settings, I try to be more intentional about engaging others in ways that are not as natural to me as an introvert. With clients, I am aware than my comfort with silence is not always comfortable for them, especially early in therapy. While I believe silence is important in therapy, I am more patient in cultivating space for silence. Regarding my listening intently, I work to remain aware of when this may be uncomfortable for students, supervisees, and clients and work to look away more frequently.

While this is only a small part of the reflection that I have engaged in pertaining to one aspect of what it feels like for others to be around me, it illustrates several things. First, we cannot change some aspects of what it feels like to be in our presence. Second, there are aspects of what it often feels like to be around an individual that one may not want to change, or at least not fully change; however, it is important to remain aware of these aspects so that one can be cognizant of them when they emerge in therapy. This allows the therapist to work with them more directly and limit negative impacts. Third, what it feels like to be around oneself is different in different settings and with different individuals. Fourth, continuing to gain insights into what it is like to be around us and how that may change over time is something valuable for us to do

---

[1] My eye contact tends to be less in TeleHealth due to the fatigue that can be caused by eye strain from staring at the computer for long hours.

across our career and life. For example, now that my hair is turning gray, this influences the way that I am experienced. As I have learned and refined therapy skills and integrated new skills, this has changed aspects of what it feels like to be in my presence in therapy.

Before introducing the exercise, it is beneficial to consider one other aspect of this assignment. This is an uncomfortable assignment—for the person conducting it and for the people being interviewed. Many people are not comfortable honestly answering questions such as "What does it feel like to be in my presence?" This, itself, can be an important aspect of the project in two ways. First, doing this assignment well requires contemplation about who may be willing and able to provide good feedback.

Second, there is an art to being able to ask these questions and have these conversations in a way that is effective. For example, it is common for people to respond with either praise or appraisals, such as "I think you are a good person," or "You are quite intelligent." While these may feel good to hear, they are not the point of the exercise. Working to establish a relational context where it is clear you are not seeking compliments but are helping to elicit responses that are emotional in nature is a skill relevant to being an effective existential-humanistic therapist. Furthermore, learning to gently redirect the other person toward the responses you are seeking is an important skill. For example, when the interviewee responds with compliments, one might respond, "I appreciate that, and it is meaningful to me. What I am looking for is a bit different, though. I am striving to understand what emotions are often elicited by being in my presence, which is likely a mixture of different emotions."

Here is an overview of the different steps in this assignment:

1. Identify three people you know professionally and three people you know personally that you are going to interview. Be sure to think carefully about who you think will be able to provide the type of answers you are seeking.
2. Develop a plan to explain the exercise to the people you are going to interview, including how you will phrase your primary questions and how you will clarify or redirect if their responses are not what you are seeking.
3. Conduct the interviews. If the participants consent, it is best to record the interviews. If they do not consent to being recorded, take notes.
4. After each interview, journal about your own emotional

reaction to the interview process and the answers you received.
5. After you have completed the interview, review the answers you have received and any consistent themes that emerge.
6. Note any answers that, although not a theme, stood out to you as impactful or meaningful.
7. Add your own reflections on the themes and other meanings you derive from the exercise.
8. Identify: 1) what you appreciate in what you discovered, 2) what you cannot change that is important to keep in your awareness, and 3) what you would like to work to change.
9. Journal about your overall experience with the exercise.

As you finish this exercise, we encourage you to keep this and return to it every couple of years to review the answers and consider how the answers may change.

Mindfulness and Presence

Perhaps one of the things that draws you toward existential-humanistic therapy is the idea that it is not formulaic or fixed in its approach or process. Psychotherapists of this persuasion have brought their own emphases to the therapy encounter (Schneider & Krug, 2017). However, there are some broad areas of agreement: existential-humanistic psychotherapy is an experiential encounter; that experience takes place in a present moment that contains both implicit and explicit material; and it is helpful to cultivate over time an interaction where both client and therapist are fully present.

In each interaction with clients, or even people in everyday life, there is an "I" present, along with the "you" being encountered, and an "us" in the relational space between. The previous exercise invited an exploration of how you might be experienced by another. Now, you might explore the idea of being in your own presence.

Many existential-humanistic psychologists bring an element of embodiment into their work. This means that in addition to cognitive awareness of one's own thoughts and opinions, there is an awareness of sensory experience in the body. Such experience can be very subtle—a sense of tension in the chest or fleeting butterflies in the belly—but it can relate to implicit material that is present in an interaction outside of conscious awareness. Sometimes, when the experience is held in awareness, images, thoughts, or memories may arise that also give a clue to what is present that has not been explicitly invited. Before you can be sure that your own material is not unduly influencing how present you can be for a client or another, it is helpful to build skills in bringing your own "stuff" to awareness. One way to do this is by cultivating a mindfulness practice, but you can also teach this type of awareness to yourself.

In this exercise, you might find a place to sit for a few minutes that is relatively quiet, where you won't be disturbed. Take a few minutes to sit and observe the world around you, noting each thing, saying to yourself, "I'm aware of… (the furniture in the room, the temperature of the air, or whatever comes to your awareness)." Then allow your eyes to close and take your attention inside the body, noting any experience that comes to your awareness. "I'm aware of… (a tingling in my hand, a heavy sensation around my diaphragm, a spacious feeling in my head, or whatever comes to mind)." Simply sit and watch the evolution of your internal experience, as well as thoughts, feelings, and images that arise. Just a few minutes daily of sampling your world in this way will build your capacity to be embodied as you move through life. When you become more sensitive to presence in your own body, you can experiment with holding that awareness during interactions with others.

If you find value in this sort of self-awareness, for yourself and/or in interactions, this may be an aspect of existential-humanistic practice for which you have an affinity.

Conclusion

The journey of becoming an existential-humanistic therapist can be complex, including both challenges and delights. We hope that this Appendix encouraged you to reflect more deeply on this possibility of partaking in this journey. As you go through these exercises, you may find yourself adding your own questions and exercises; if so, this is wonderful!

The decision to pursue this career path should not be taken lightly. It is one that will impact you, your friends and family, and your future clients. If you have read this far in the book, we are thrilled that you are giving such careful consideration to this path.

References

Constantino, M. J., Coyne, A. E., Boswell, J. E., Iles, B. R., & Vîslă, A. (2019). Cultivating positive outcome expectations. In J. C. Norcross & M. J.

Lambert (Eds.), *Psychotherapy relationships that work* (Vol. 1: Evidence-based therapist contributions, 3rd ed., pp. 461–494). Oxford University Press.

Krug, O. T. (2019). Existential-humanistic and existential-integrative therapy: Method and practice. In E. van Duerzen, E. Craig, A. Längle, K. J. Schneider, D. Tantum, & S. du Plock (Eds.), *The Wiley world handbook of existential therapy* (pp. 257–266). Wiley.

Schneider, K. J. (2015). Presence: The core contextual factor of effective psychotherapy. *Existential Analysis, 2,* 304–312.

Schneider, K. J. (2019). Existential-humanistic and existential-integrative therapy: Philosophy and theory. In E. van Duerzen, E. Craig, A. Längle, K. J. Schneider, D. Tantum, & S. du Plock (Eds.), *The Wiley world handbook of existential therapy* (pp. 247–256). Wiley.

Schneider, K. J., & Krug, O. T. (2017). *Existential-humanistic therapy.* APA Books.

Wampold, B. E., & Imel, Z. E. (2015). *The great psychotherapy debate: The evidence for what makes psychotherapy work* (2nd ed.). Routledge.

Appendix B

Guides for Reflection on One's Journey to Becoming an Existential–Humanistic Therapist

Louis Hoffman & Julia Falk

Reflecting on one's journey to becoming an existential-humanistic therapist can deepen connections with associated meanings and help establish or advance one's professional identity. For many existential-humanistic therapists, their choice of theoretical orientation is deeply personal and influences the individual beyond the work they do professionally.

It may be helpful to read through the previous appendix that was designed for students. You may want to begin by answering the questions from that section that are most relevant to you.

The questions in this section are designed to encourage deeper reflection on your own personal and professional narrative as an existential-humanistic therapist.

Reflection Questions 1
This first set of questions for reflection is drawn from the narratives in *Becoming an Existential–Humanistic Therapist*.

1. As you read through the different stories of becoming an existential therapist, what aspects of these stories did you resonate with? What does this mean for you?
2. Are there unique aspects of your journey that were not evident in the narratives in *Becoming an Existential–Humanistic Therapist*?

Reflection Questions 2
The second set of questions for reflection go beyond the narratives appearing in *Becoming an Existential–Humanistic Therapist*.

1. When you first began identifying as an existential-humanistic therapist, what were the primary factors that influenced your decision to align with this therapy orientation?
2. How does identifying as an existential-humanistic therapist influence you *professionally*, including your professional identity? Has this changed over time? If so, how?
3. How does identifying as an existential-humanistic therapist influence you *personally*, including your professional identity? Has this changed over time? If so, how?
4. Where do you find your existential-humanistic community? How has this community impacted your professional identity as an existential-humanistic therapist?
5. How do you see identifying as an existential-humanistic therapist influencing your future career directions?
6. From your journey to becoming an existential-humanistic therapist, what would you share with a student who was considering this path?
7. What do you value most about being an existential-humanistic therapist?

Exercise: Writing Your Own Chapter

Now that you have completed working through these questions, consider writing your own "chapter" on becoming an existential-humanistic therapist. As you do this, consider how your story is similar to the ones you have read. Next, give consideration to how your story is different and unique. Finally, reflect upon what both the similarities and differences mean to you.

Index

Adler, Alfred 79
Adlerian Individual Psychotherapy 78-79
Agency 111, 113, 156, 241
Ah Q
  see *The True Story of Ah Q*
All Quiet on the Western Front 198
American Cinematographer 66
Antisemitism 31
Arendt, Hannah 55
Army 137, 145-149
Arons, Mike 38-39
The Art of the Psychotherapist 79
Art Therapy 1-2
Authenticity xix, 19, 49, 70, 82, 123, 126-127, 178, 181, 187, 192, 198, 207, 213, 239-240, 248, 250
Awakening to Aging 125
Awe ix, 10-11, 23, 26-27, 29, 41-42, 84, 89, 108, 114, 134, 158, 171, 173, 182-183, 222, 231, 237, 242-243
Abzug, Robert v, 241

Bahamas ix
Baker-Fletcher, Karen x
Bargdill, Richard x
Barron, Frank 28
Beatles 222
Becker, Ernest viii, 38, 64, 215, 243
Being and Time 208
Benjamin, Walter 55, 70
Beyond God the Father x
Beyond the Tragic Vision 200
Binswanger, Ludwig 183
Blake, William 205
Bloom, Harold 195

Body and Soul 66
Bormouth, Matthias 69
Boss, Medard 113, 183
Boston Institute of Psychotherapy 65
Breuer, Josef 161
Bricker, Jeff 36
Brown, James 132
Buber, Martin 71, 81, 93, 156, 166
Buddhism xv, 1, 8, 10-12, 19, 191-192, 202, 240
Bugental, Elizabeth 39, 124
Bugental, James F. T. iii, ix, 9-10, 38-39, 48, 51, 79, 83-84, 91, 105, 123-126, 158-161, 163-168, 171, 177, 183, 221, 238, 240-241

Calasso, Roberto 72
Camus, Albert 81, 131, 145, 177
Carlyle, Thomas 195
Charlotte and Karl Bühler Award 184
The Castle 62-63
Center for Growth x
Center for Humanistic Studies 220, 223
Center for Mindfulness at the University of Massachusetts xv-xvi
China xi, 86, 150, 176-180, 185-186, 191-192, 201-202
China Institute of Psychotherapy 183
Chinese Institute of Existential Psychology 86
Choice 93, 190
Christianity vi, 105-106, 133, 135-137, 148, 178, 188, 197, 202
A Christmas Carol 33

Claremont School of Theology x
Claypool, Trent xviii, 2-14, 20-22
Cleveland Museum of Art 33
Color Me Brown 132
Cognitive Behavioral Therapy
  (CBT) vi, vii, 106
Columbia College (Chicago) 137,
  145
Colorado School of Professional
  Psychology x-xi, 149-150
Compassion 248, 250, 252
Confucius 191-192
Concordia College Nebraska vi-vii
Congenital heart defect 46
Conrad, Joseph 195
Consultation 15, 48, 123-124, 158,
  163-166, 168, 170-172
  see also Supervision
Cooper, Mick 85
Coronavirus
  see COVID-19
Courage 188
The Courage to Be 210
The Courage to Create 75
COVID-19 92, 116, 118, 128,
  225-226
Cowan, Emory x, 150
Craig, Erik 86, 183-185
Creativity 12, 28, 30, 70, 86, 93,
  133, 137-138, 144-145, 158, 242
The Cry for Myth 212
Cultural critique x-xii
Cultural Revolution (China) 177,
  191
The Cyclops 30

Dias, Jason xvi
Dallas, Evy 79, 84-85, 90
Daly, Mary x, xi
Dasein 86
Death iii, xiii, 8, 29, 46-49, 73, 90,
  124, 162, 190, 199-200, 251
Demian 36
Democracy Now! 69

Dickens, Charles, 195
Dostoevsky, Fyodor 208
Dreams 36, 63, 66, 73, 85, 156,
  162, 164, 220
Dueck, Al 182, 184
Dreyfus, Amy 123

Elis, Albert 34
Elkins, David 102-103, 182-183
Empathy 19, 122, 168-169, 178,
  182, 229, 248, 252
Encounter 61, 239
Empathy 19, 248, 250, 252
Enyedi, Ildikó 65-66
Erikson, Erik xiv
Esalen 161, 204
Escape from Freedom 155
European Association for
  Psychotherapy 85
*Everyday Creativity and New Views
  of Human Nature* 132-133
Existential-Humanistic Institute
  16, 48, 84, 164-165, 167-168,
  172, 222
Existential-Humanistic Therapy
  167-168
Existence 36, 79, 91
Existential Academy 85
Existential Psychology East-West
  (Volume 2) 184
Existential Psychotherapy viii, 44,
  46, 79
Existential Shattering 47-48

Family systems therapy 106
Fakinos, Michael 79
Falk, Julia xii-xvii, 176, 239, 241,
  243
Faith, see spirituality
Fear and Trembling 208
The Federalist Papers 196
Finitude 70, 81, 89-91, 100, 108,
  126, 237-238, 251
  see also Death

Florida Atlantic University 79
Forest Institute of Professional
   Psychology viii, ix
Frank, Jerome 93
Frankl, Viktor 11, 79, 81, 109-110,
   125, 177, 183, 241
Freeman, Mark 236
Freedom 5, 10, 25, 28-30, 38, 45-
   47, 49, 81-82, 90, 100-101, 111-
   112, 133-134, 136, 146, 148,
   150, 154-157, 190, 192, 200,
   210, 223, 227, 237, 240-241
The French Revolution 195
Freud, Sigmund 58, 144, 177
Friedman, Maurice 36
Fromm, Erich 154-155, 158
Fudan University 86, 184
Fuller Seminary vi-vii, 108-109,
   182

Galvin, Kathleen 195-216, 237-
   240, 242, 244
Gan, Lingling 193
Garrett-Bowser, Brittany viii, x
Gay Science 210-211
Genuineness 15, 58, 252
Georganda, Evgenia 79, 84
Gergen, Ken 80
Gestalt Institute 12
Giganesthia 79, 85-86
The Gift of Therapy 44
Golzmane, Lori 74-75
Gooden, Winston viii, 105-108
Goulet, Victor 166
Granger, Nathaniel 91, 130-152,
   238-240, 243-244
The Grapes of Wrath 202-203
Grateful Dead 39
Greek Society for Adleria
   Psychology 81
Green, Graham 196
Greene, Robert 113
Greening, Tom x, 4, 7, 47-48
Grounded Theory 7-8, 88
Guangdong University of Foreign
   Studies 184
Guignon, Charles 208
Guo, Benyu 183-184
Guo, Xiaosong 193
Gustin, Ann 37

Hamilton, Eleanor 123
*The Handbook of Humansitic
   Psychology* 151
Harisiadis, Alexis 79, 84
Hart, Mickey 39
Hazelton, Debbie 37
The Heart and Soul of Change 79
Heart of Darkness 195
Heery, Myrtle ix, 5-6, 8-10, 16,
   116-128, 239, 241-242, 244
Heidegger, Martin 86, 208
Hellenic Society for Existential
   Analysis
      see Gignesthai
Hennig, Robert vi
Heraclitus 64, 112
Here-and-Now 161, 163
Hesse, Herman 57, 113-114
Hillman, James 111-113, 157
*The History of the Decline and Fall
   of the Roman Empire* 195-196
Hoffman, Heatherlyn ix-x
Hoffman, Louis iv-xii, xvi, xviii, 19,
   86-87, 91, 144, 150, 176, 182-
   183-184, 193, 238-242, 244, 248
Hong Kong University 184
Hope 90-93, 96, 118, 126, 128,
   177, 189, 200, 204, 211
Horror and the Holy 31
Howorth, Charlotte. xvii
Huckleberry Finn 196
Hugo, Victor 177
The Humansitic Psychologist, 6
Humanistic Psychology Citizen
   Diplomacy Project 7
Humanistic Psychology Institute
   39, 161, 199, 203
      see also Saybrook University
Humor 65, 123

Individualism 210, 212-214
Innocents Abroad 196
Integrity 6-7, 16, 33, 57-58, 88
International Conference on Existential Psychology 86, 183-184
International Focusing Institute xvii
International Institute for Humanistic Studies 6, 125
Isolation 116, 237
Israel 31
I-Thou 17, 41-42, 93

James, William 57, 69
Jasper, Karl 68-69, 72
Jewish 28, 31, 55, 67, 162, 227
Jia Xiaoming 184
Jiang, Mingfang 193
Johnson, John viii
Johnson C. Smith University 121
Journal of Humanistic Psychology 4, 6-7, 38, 227
Jung, Carl 58, 177
Jungian Psychology 5, 182

Kabat, Zinn, Jon xv
Kafka, Franz 55, 57, 59-63, 67, 69-72, 75, 177
Kant, Immanuel 70
Kierkegaard, Soren 9, 36, 38, 54, 91, 112, 166, 177-178, 200, 208
Kieslowski, Krzysztof 67-68
King, Martin Luther, Jr. 69, 70, 121-122, 239
Kleiner, Karin 160-161
Korea 1
Kornfield, Jack xv-xvi
Krippner, Stanley 38-39, 64
Krug, Orah 48, 83, 85, 91, 154-173, 239, 241-242, 245, 253

Laing, Ronald D. 34, 39, 57, 183

Lao Tzu 106, 132, 191-192
Lesley University 65
Life Conduct in Modern Times 69
Lincoln, Abraham 196
Lord Jim 195
Love's Executioner 161
Love, Power, and Justice 210
Lucas Ranch 39
Lu Xun 178-179, 185-187
Lying on the Couch 162

Macaulay, Thomas 197
Mahrer, Avlin 87
Mai, Jinli 193-194
Malcom X 70
Malony, H. Newton vii
Man's Search for Meaning 79, 109
Marcel, Gabriel 156
Marquette University xiii
Masek, Bob 37-39
Maslow, Abraham xiv, 28, 39, 57, 192, 219
May, Rollo iii, viii, xvi, 28, 38-39, 41, 47, 55, 57-60, 64, 72-73, 75, 79, 81, 84, 91, 125, 155-156, 162, 166-168, 177, 183-184, 212, 219, 241
May 4th New Culture Movement (China) 179
McAdams, John 238
Meaning v, 2, 6, 8, 14-16, 26, 36, 49, 51, 63, 77, 83, 88, 90-91, 94, 97, 107, 109-110, 112, 117, 125-126, 130, 134-137, 145, 147, 152, 167-169, 190, 197, 209, 212-213, 215-216, 220, 223, 228-229, 236-237, 240-244, 250-253
The Meaning of Anxiety 91
Meditation xv, 4, 18, 72, 122, 192, 198
Melville, Herman 62, 195
Mendelowitz, Ed iii, xix, 6-7, 9, 11-12, 54-75, 183-184, 238,

241-242, 244
Mendelowitz, Khanh 64, 68
Mentors iii, v, viii, ix, xvi, 2, 18-19, 21, 39-40, 60, 68, 84, 91, 102-103, 105, 107-108, 161-162, 165, 170
Merleau-Ponty, Maurice 39, 92
Merrill, Trevor Cribben 68
Microaggressions 151-152
Mindfulness xv-xvii, 3, 17, 23, 256-257
Mindfulness-Based Stress Reduction, see mindfulness
Minuchin, Salvador 79-80
Moby Dick 195
Monitor on Psychology viii
Mortality 73, 206, 238, 251
  see also Death
Moulds, Russell vi, vii
Moustakas, Clark 220
Multiculturalism x, 50
Murney, Robert vii, x
My Twentieth Century 65
Mystery 4, 10-12, 23, 30, 34, 38, 49, 64, 70, 173, 197, 243

Nanjing Normal University 184
Nanjing Population and Management College 183
Nanjing Union Theological Seminary 178, 180
Nanjing University 178-179
Nanjing Xiao Zhuang College 183
New School (London) 85
Nietzsche, Friedrich viii, 9, 36, 59-60, 91, 137, 161, 166, 177-178, 208, 210-211

Ohio University 35
Oistros 87, 89
One Step Beyond 31
Ontological Sensibility 11-13
The Outer Limits 31

Panteion University of Social and Political Sciences 87
Paradox 4, 6, 12, 26, 38, 64, 82, 84, 117, 127, 161, 192, 200, 203, 209-210, 214, 242-243
The Paradoxical Self 38
Park, HeeSun xviii, 1-3, 13-17, 23-24, 240, 244
Parkhurst, Ann Elise viii
Pascal, Blaise 177-178
Peckman, Morse 200, 215
Perls, Laura 12
Perls, Fritz 132
Perry, Cereta 220
Phenomenology 38-39, 168, 208, 210, 220-221, 223, 239
Pink Floyd v
Plato 112
Play therapy 222, 225
Poe, Edgar Allen 31
Poetry 15, 18, 19, 71, 82, 85, 87, 139-144
The Polarized Mind 133
Potok, Chaim 54
Pou sto 124
Powers, Bradley viii
Presence 16-17, 21, 81, 94, 156, 167, 239-240, 248, 252-256
Prince 134
Pritzker, Steve 144
Psychedelics 230
Psychoanalysis/Psychodynamic therapy 106, 222, 232
The Psychology of Existence 39
Psychotherapy Isn't What You Think 79, 125

Qualitative Research, xvii
Quinn, Ralph 101-103, 106, 108, 110

Rank, Otto 71, 73, 213
Rebelliousness vi, 179
Reflections on Sin, Suffering, Hope, and the True Way 72
Religion vi-viii, x, xiii, xv, 28, 57,

63-64, 89-90, 108-109, 112, 133-135, 144-145, 151, 162, 182, 196-197, 202, 209, 212, 227, 238-240, 242-243
see also Spirituality
Remarque, Erich Maria 198
Ren Qiping 184
Renaissance 179
The Republic 112
Rice, Donadrian (Don) 39
Richards, Ruth 132-133, 144
The Rise and Fall of the Third Reich 196
Robbins, Arthur 2, 19
Robbins, Brent Dean x
Rocky Mountain Humanistic Counseling and Psychological Association 222
Rogers, Carl iii, xvi, 6, 28, 34, 79, 89, 122-123, 219, 223
Rollo May Award 126
Rubin, Shawn x, 219-234, 239, 244
Russia 7, 28, 126, 154, 196

Sakkas, Dionysis 79
Saltmman, Sonja 165
Sartre, John Paul 92, 208
Saybrook University x-xi, xv-xvii, 2, 39, 47, 166, 205-206, 224
see also Humanistic Psychology Institute
Schiff, Edwin 29-30, 37
Schneider, Kirk J. iii, ix, xi, 4-5, 8-11, 13, 23, 25-42, 47, 84-85, 91, 133, 166-168, 182-183, 185, 239, 241-244, 252-253
Sculpting the Darkness 70
Sculpting in Time 70
Shabahangi, Nader 48, 165
Shakespeare, William 195, 197
Shen, Heyong 184
Shi, Hu 179
Shirer, William 196

Shu, Xiaoyng 193
The Search for Existential Identity 159
Self-Growth 17-18, 21
Seligman, Martin 88
Serlin, Ilene 5, 10, 12, 183
Shakur, Tupac 53
Sickness Unto Death 208
Siddhartha 113-114
Silence of the Lambs 44
Singer, Beshevis 72-73
Social Justice 31, 50-51, 221, 225-226, 229, 239
Society for Humanistic Psychology x, xi, 64, 73, 151-152, 165, 184, 228, 243
Sofia University 5
The Soul's Code 111, 157
Sperry, Len 79
Spinelli, Ernesto 85
Spirituality vi, ix, xiii, xv, xvii, 5, 7-8, 10-11, 14, 17, 19-21, 34, 39, 69-70, 89, 105, 136, 188, 197-198, 202-203, 206-207, 212, 227, 230, 240, 242-243
see also Religion
Springsteen, Bruce v
Steppenwolf 36
Stalikas, Anastasios 87
Stocks, Mark viii
Students iv, 248-257
Subjectivity 87-88, 116-117, 123-124, 157, 163, 167, 170, 214, 239, 253
Sun, Lizhe
Sun, Ping 193
Sun, Shijin 184
Supervision 91, 96, 108, 123, 171, 222-223, 233
see also consultation
Supervision Essentials for Existential-Humanistic Therapy 167

Tanner, Michael 101
Taoism 11, 86, 103-104, 106, 113
Tarkovsky, Andrei 70
Taylor, Charles 213
Taylor, Eugene 62-64, 69
Theory and Practice of Group Psychotherapy 79
Thessaloniki's Anatolia College 91
The Toilers of the Sea 177
Tillich, Paul 9, 91, 125, 158, 166, 170, 178, 210, 241
To Kill a Mockingbird 33
Tomm, Karl 80
Tonglen Press 125
Torrance E. Paul 28
The True Story Ah Q 179, 186
Trust 70, 82, 88-89, 94, 114, 170, 172, 182, 223, 225
Turkle, Sherry 214
Twain, Mark 196
Twelve Angry Men 33
The Twilight Zone 31

Unearthing the Moment, ix
University of Colorado at Colorado Springs 149-150
University of Massachusetts xv
University of the Rockies 182-183
see also Colorado School of Professional Psychology

Vallejos, Lisa Xochitl 44-53, 238-230, 240-241, 244
Van Deurzen Emmy 85, 183
Vasconcellos, Paul vi
Vassiliou, Vaso 79
Vidal, Gorre 196
Viesturs, Ed 114
Vonnegut, Kurt 196

Wampold, Bruce 168
Wang, Jie 184
Wang, Xuefu xi, xix, 86, 176-193, 237, 239-244
Watts, Alan 39

Weil, Simone 66
West Georgia College 4, 37, 39
see also University of West Georgia
When Nietzsche Wept 161
Whitehead, Alfred North 158, 166
Whitman, Walk 59
Whitmire, A. J. viii
Whole Person Healthcare 5
Wolf, Thomas 196
Wolin, Sheldon 214
World Congress of Existential Psychotherapy 87, 171, 185
The Worlds of Existentialism 36
Wu Wei 192

Xio Yuhan 193
Xiamen University 180

Yalom, Irvin D. viii, 26, 44-45, 48, 79, 84, 91, 93, 107-108, 111, 125, 156, 158-159, 161-165, 167-168, 171, 183, 237-238, 241
Yan, Fengming 183
Yang, Mark iii, xi, 100-114, 176, 182-184, 193, 239-242, 244
Yang, Shaogang 183-184
Ye Bing 193
Yoga xv, 12, 15, 18

Zaoyang Teacher's School 180
Zen 11, 70
Zhang, Xin 193
Zhao, Hongya 193
Zhejiang Normal University 176
Zheng, Richang 184
Zheng, Shiyan 184, 193
Zhengjia, Ren
Zhi mian 86, 89, 183-187, 193
Zhi Mian Institute 183-184, 187, 192-193
Zhuangzi 103-104, 191
Zorba the Greek 33
Zürau Aphorisms 72

Zymnis, Katerina 77-97, 239, 242, 244-245

About the Editors

Julia Falk, PhD, graduated from Saybrook University's doctoral program in humanistic, existential, and transpersonal psychology with a strong interest in the therapeutic aspects of narrative. She lives near Gettysburg, Pennsylvania, where she is active in developing programs that support holistic health and well-being. She has taught Mindfulness-Based Stress Reduction for more than a decade, along with life story courses, mindful movement, and the practice of Focusing. She had a long career in nursing that culminated in her work to support people who live with chronic difficulty. She lives with her husband, Carl, and hand-me-down dog, Trigger. Their children are all grown and away. She is a dedicated and dreadful jogger.

Louis Hoffman, PhD, is a licensed psychologist in private practice and the executive director of the Rocky Mountain Humanistic Counseling and Psychological Association. An avid writer, he has 20 books and over 100 journal articles and book chapters to his credit. He has been recognized as a Fellow of the American Psychological Association and six of its divisions (1, 10, 32, 36, 48, 52) for his contributions to the field of professional psychology. In 2021, he received the Rollo May Award from the Society for Humanistic Psychology. He serves on the editorial boards of the *Journal of Humanistic Psychology* (Senior International Editor), *The Humanistic Psychologist*, the *Journal of Constructivist Psychology*, and *Janus Head*. Most important, Dr. Hoffman is a husband and father. He lives in beautiful Colorado Springs with his wife, three sons, and two dogs.

www.ingramcontent.com/pod-product-compliance
Lightning Source LLC
Chambersburg PA
CBHW050209240426
43671CB00013B/2264